Labour Law in the Mirror

Studies in Employment and Social Policy

VOLUME 58

Editors

Objective

Studies in Employment and Social Policy series seeks to provide a forum for highlighting international and comparative research on contemporary areas of significance for evaluation and regulation of the world of work.

Introduction

Launched in 1997, the Studies in Employment and Social Policy Series now boasts over fifty titles, addressing key policy and development issues in the fields of industrial relations, labour law, social security, and international labour regulation.

Content

With contributions from leading figures in the field, the series brings together key policymakers, academics, and regulators, providing a unique context in which to analyse and evaluate the rapid and dramatic work and social policy developments taking place around the globe.

The titles published in this series are listed at the end of this volume.

Labour Law in the Mirror

Categories, Values, Interlocutors

Edited by

Adalberto Perulli
Tiziano Treu

Wolters Kluwer

Published by:
Kluwer Law International B.V.
PO Box 316
2400 AH Alphen aan den Rijn
The Netherlands
E-mail: lrs-sales@wolterskluwer.com
Website: www.wolterskluwer.com/en/solutions/kluwerlawinternational

Sold and distributed by:
Wolters Kluwer Legal & Regulatory U.S.
920 Links Avenue
Landisville, PA 17538
United States of America
E-mail: customer.service@wolterskluwer.com

ISBN 978-94-035-2798-7

e-Book: ISBN 978-94-035-2808-3
web-PDF: ISBN 978-94-035-2818-2

Editors

Adalberto Perulli is a Full Professor of Labour Law at the Ca' Foscari University of Venice and Visiting Professor at the University of Paris Ouest Nanterre La Défense since 2000. He is the Director of a First Level Master in Global Economics and Social Affairs and Scientific Director of a First Level Master in Labour Law at the Ca' Foscari University of Venice. He did research and studies for the European Commission and for the International Labour Organization (ILO) of Geneva. Prof. Perulli has been rapporteur to the XVIII World Congress of Labour Law on 'Labour Law and productive decentralization' in Paris, in 2006; he is Master EMA Director at EIUC (European Inter-University Centre for Human Rights and Democratisation).

Tiziano Treu is a Professor Emeritus of Labour Law at the Catholic University of Milan, Law School, and former President of CNEL (National Council for Economics and Labour). Previously he has been President of the Italian Association of Labour Law and Social Security and the International Society of Labour and Social Security Law (ISLSSL). During his political experience Prof. Treu has been Minister of Transportation and Minister of Labour and Social Security in the Italian Government, and more recently President of the XI Commission (Labour and Welfare) of the Italian Senate.

Contributors

Marzia Barbera, Full Professor of Labour Law University of Brescia.

Giuseppe Casale, Former Director at ILO and ITCILO, Honorary President ISLSSL.

Massimiliano Delfino, Full Professor of Labour Law, University of Naples Federico II.

Elena Gramano, Assistant Professor of Labour Law Bocconi University Milan.

Brian Langille, University of Toronto.

Julia López López, Pompeu Fabra University.

Antoine Lyon-Caen, Paris Nanterre University.

Mariella Magnani, Emeritus Professor of Labour Law, University of Pavia.

Tonia Novitz, Professor of Labour Law, University of Bristol.

Alberto Pizzoferrato, Professor of Labour Law, Bologna University.

Orsola Razzolini, Professor of Labour Law, University of Milan.

Tatiana Sachs, University of Paris Nanterre.

Valerio Speziale, University of Pescara.

Manfred Weiss, University of Frankfurt.

Anna Zilli, University of Udine.

Summary of Contents

Table of Contents

Introduction

Adalberto Perulli

1 THE MIRROR AS A METAPHOR FOR QUESTIONING THE IDENTITY OF LABOUR LAW

The idea of thinking of labour law as a subject that stands in front of a mirror and reflexively seeks to understand what its identity has become stems from the need to continue to interrogate a subject that is incessantly subjected to the stresses coming from the seismic changes of economic and social reality, in order to understand the reasons for its 'being', and, at the same time, the trajectories of its evolution, its destiny in the history of legal ideas and, more generally, of social regulation in mature capitalist systems.

The mirror is a metaphor; indeed, it is many metaphors.

The first is the metaphor of a presumption: the presumption of defining an image once and for all, of fixing a human identity, which instead is indefinable by definition. The same applies to law, which is a social and human construct, always subject to evolution and change. What we see in the mirror is only a changing image, which invites us to think of labour law in a purely dynamic and evolutionary dimension.

This first metaphor of the mirror invites us to conceive of labour law in a two-way dimension: not only as a normative vector of societal transformation but also as an object that undergoes, due to actual processes, political decisions and interpretative and applicative practices, profound and continuous transformations affecting its structure and function. The image of law in the mirror, in short, does not return a fixed and unchanging face, but an image that changes according to multiple endogenous and exogenous factors, which do not necessarily entail a positive development of labour law, its 'immanent progress', but an emergence of multiple possible determinations and ways of being.

The polytheism of values generates different images of labour law, and none of them can a priori be assumed to correspond to a purported 'essence' of labour law. For example, the idea of labour law as an instrument capable of effectively counterbalancing an asymmetrical contractual relationship has been tarnished. This function, which has long been identified as the true essence of labour law, coexists with functions of a different nature and purpose, so that labour law also shows very ambivalent self-images in terms of the regulation of the labour market and the control of the employer's powers, which in certain legal systems have seen an obvious re-expansion (typical is the case of the power of dismissal in systems such as Italy, France and Spain). The question of the identity of labour law is certainly not new, but it concerns the very origins and foundation of the subject. Labour law is a complex and ambivalent discipline that responds to the needs of worker protection in a social justice and redistributive perspective (this is the emancipatory function of labour law)[1] but at the same time also responds to the needs of the firms (this is the capitalist function of labour law). Under the first profile, there is a common consideration that sees labour law as a countervailing force within a strategy of rebalancing asymmetrical contractual positions in terms of the bargaining power of the parties. Compared to private law, which disregards the substantive inequality of the parties[2] and whose philosophical justification hinges above all on the respect of the moral promise to abide by pacts (*pacta sunt servanda*),[3] labour law therefore follows a different moral justification, directly linked to the idea of social justice and its values of freedom and equality, and for this reason deviates from the scheme of contract law.[4]

Mandatory rules to protect the worker, the recognition of the rights of association and collective bargaining as a collective countervailing power, the establishment of forms of industrial democracy and worker participation in the workplace are all aspects of labour law that are justified in this social justice perspective. This strategy has solid constitutional and rule of law foundations, as well as human rights protection, insofar as it concerns the protection of the worker as a person and the associated values of freedom, dignity, solidarity and equality. However, the success and effectiveness of labour protection strategies are increasingly weakened by the growing importance of the reasons connected to the second function of labour law, namely its function of rationalising the use of the labour factor to make it useful to the production process, to the creation of surplus value. In fact, labour law is also the law that 'organises' the exchange of the labour factor in the labour market and its employment in the

1. *See* H. Collins, *What Sen's Capability Approach Can Offer to Labour Law*, in B. Langille (ed.), p. 34, according to whom 'labour law was born out of the demands for distributive justice during the battles between capital and labour in early industrial society ... it would be a mistake to deny that the battle is still going on'.
2. This is the traditional view, which should, however, be corrected in the light of the evolution of private law in the area of power inequalities between parties, with reference, for example, to consumer law and business-to-business relations: *see* the chapter of M. Magnani in this book.
3. *See* G. Klass, G. Letsas & P. Saprai (eds), *Philosophical Foundation of Contract Law*, Oxford, Oxford University Press, 2014; J. Gardner, *The Contractualisation of Labour Law*, in H. Collins, G. Lester & V. Mantouvalou (eds), *Philosophical Foundation of Labour Law*, Oxford, Oxford University Press, 2018, p. 37, according to which '*Pacta sunt servanda* is a conceptual truth that no pactum, and no legal system, can counter.'
4. *See* H. Collins, G. Lester & V. Mantouvalou, *Introduction: Does Labour Law Need Philosophical Foundations?*, in H. Collins, G. Lester & V. Mantouvalou (eds), *Philosophical Foundations of Labour Law*, Oxford, Oxford University Press, 2018; H. Collins, *Justice at Work*, LSE Law, Society and Economy Working Papers 18/2019.

enterprise, legalising the enterprise as a hierarchical structure and justifying the subjection of the worker to the private powers of management (directive, control and disciplinary power).

In other words, labour law, in addition to performing an essential function of protecting the worker, is also the law that sanctions the worker's subordinate and dependent status. In the traditional perspective, these two 'souls' of labour law prove to be complementary: the worker is protected insofar as he is subordinate (employee), the qualification of the employment relationship in terms of subordination being the 'keys to access' the protections of labour law (keys that are in fact not handed over, in principle, to the self-employed worker, on the very questionable assumption that this worker is not restricted in his freedom, he is precisely self-employed). The organisational function of labour law in the sphere of production – which some authors openly describe as the 'capitalist' function of labour law – thus competes with the typical protective function: the balance between these two different souls of labour law, expressing two different forms of freedom (the employer's economic freedom and the worker's 'social' freedom) is historically variable due to a number of factors, including the power relations between capital and labour, the ability of trade unions to effectively play a collective countervailing power role, the political orientations of governments in social matters, etc.

This changing and unstable dimension of labour law is thus, primarily, the profound fruit of its being a crossroads of different and conflicting values: many distinct value spheres claim our attention and commitment, and different political philosophies are invoked to justify this or that image of labour law, without it being possible to define a priori which of these philosophies is the 'right' one.

A second metaphor concerns the reflection and thus the reflexivity of the mirror. The mirror reflects and includes in this reflection the observer. The beholder can now look at himself. This means that in the reflection of labour law, we must include ourselves, our scholarly work, and our commitment as scholars, interpreters, and critical thinkers. We are not external observers; we are part of the observed image, we define its contours and contents, and we trace its values. But in addition to the scholars, there are the actors who act as instruments of labour law and its social function: legislators, judges, trade unions, business organisations, associations and movements expressing civil society, all striving to make labour law a reflexive law, capable, through its many articulations, of producing regulation and stabilising latent social conflicts. During the COVID-19 pandemic, we saw the reflexivity of labour law at work in many significant examples of reflexive and decentralised regulation, such as in the case of the preparation of health protocols negotiated between the social partners in order to contain the spread of the virus, or in the actions to counter the loss of income due to the closure or suspension of production activities, through the intervention of social shock absorbers or new forms of remote work. Reflexive labour law thus expresses the capacity to innovate through actors ready to devise and implement solutions based on reflexive evaluations produced by an emergency that has upset the normal parameters of judgment and the normal models of balancing values.

A third metaphor is that of the double, of the dual. The mirror is a symbol of duality and otherness: in the famous Book X of Plato's Republic, the gap between the world of ideas and sensible reality is understood from the knowledge that there is a reflected image, which, however, does not express true reality. And so the mirror helps us to understand and distinguish the true and the false, the just and the unjust, the reasonable and the irrational. In labour law, too, as in every area of law, these distinctions and this need to conceive of a law that has its own 'truth' (not the platonic or naturalistic truth, but a truth historically determined by the legal system and its values), the expression of a universalistic 'social justice', apply. A labour law that sees in the mirror the image of a regulatory system that has become a mere receptacle of impulses coming from the market or, more generally, from the economic system should understand critically that somehow a wrong path has been taken, one that does not reflect its raison d'être, its intimate justification. With this, I do not intend to contradict what has been said above about the polytheism of values, and I do not intend to assert an alleged ontological preference for a labour law unidirectionally aimed at protecting labour rather than responding to the needs of the production system. Rather, I intend to assert that, on the basis of this axiological pluralism, it is necessary to use the mirror as a metaphor for the verification of a possible 'disproportion' of the changes that have taken place in labour law, in its aims, and in its capacity to hold together economic and social rights, making economic freedom and social progress coexist. This disproportion occurs whenever the balancing of values is not carried out correctly, with reasonableness and fairness, with the consequence that labour law, instead of performing its essential function of 'synthesis' of antagonistic values, ends up serving only one value (usually the economic one), failing in its ability to ensure sustainable progress and development and becoming itself the cause of certain social pathologies.[5]

Last metaphor: the mirror can shatter and shatter into a thousand pieces. The shattering of the mirror is, in turn, a metaphor for an identity that fragments, breaks down, loses identity and falls into the vertigo of nothingness. This is what the myths of Dionysus and Narcissus, Perseus and Medusa, the great metaphors of mirroring, still tell us. These metaphors testify to our elusive identity and our ambivalent nature. A labour law that holds itself up to the mirror therefore accepts not only the risk of its own critical reflection but also of its dissolution as a given system, as a 'dogmatic' system, in favour of a new paradigm, perhaps still to be defined, perhaps never completed, but more in keeping with the values that are assumed to justify the matter: libido virtutis.[6]

Now, what do we see in the mirror of labour law? In this book, we propose three major macro-themes that are unified in the idea of 'identity' and, at the same time, deconstruction of the identity of labour law.

5. Significantly, the Italian Constitutional Court, in Judgment No. 194/2018 concerning the constitutional legitimacy of the law reforming dismissals (Law No. 23/2015, so-called Jobs Act) recognised that the legislator had not correctly balanced the values of labour protection with those related to the interest of the company. *See* A. Perulli, *Il 'trittico' della Corte costituzionale sulla disciplina del licenziamento: Dalla Law&Economics ai principi di tutela del lavoro*, in Lavoro Diritti Europa, 3, 2021.
6. *See* T.C. Kohler, *Disintegration of Labor Law: Some Notes for a Comparative Study of Legal Transformation*, 73 Notre Dame L. Rev. 1311, 1998.

The first area is that of *categories*. Labour law is founded on certain basic categories. Categories are instruments of knowledge, but at the same time, they are conditions for the very existence of law. What would labour law be without the categories of 'subordination' (or, to remain faithful to the common law approach, of 'employee'), or without the category of collective interest, or without the category of contract? However, it is necessary to question these founding categories of labour law in order to understand whether they are still relevant and whether they are adequate to structure labour law in the climate of change.

The second area is that of *values*. Every normative system is rooted in a system of values that founds the axiological substratum of norms, orienting their meaning and providing them with moral content. Although legal positivism tends to expunge – sometimes clearly and radically, sometimes more subtly – the value system from the sphere of law and its understanding, labour law, as a normative system oriented to constitutional values of labour protection, is proof that it is not possible to discern norms from their axiological premises. As we have said, however, there are many values and they are in conflict with each other; there are many gods and they all demand to be worshipped. Labour law, precisely because of its inherent axiological dimension, has been able to produce 'syntheses' of values. However, it certainly cannot be denied that in labour law, there is a tendency to make 'tyrants' out of certain values: the tyranny of economic values, for example, is perhaps the most obvious result of neo-liberal globalisation, which has contaminated the normative fabric of labour law, even creating the preconditions for its transformation into labour market law.

The third sphere is that of *actors and interlocutors* at the same time: the economy, the market, the state, international organisations, etc. All these interlocutors are actors in labour law and operate in conditions of necessary interrelation: none of them can think of being sheltered from the moves of the others. Here again, the evolution of labour law is literally 'embedded' in the evolution of the actors and depends on the ability of these actors to maintain their function despite rapidly changing economic and social contexts.

None of the interlocutors/actors of labour law sleeps soundly. The state, first of all, from being an authority capable of regulating the market and guaranteeing social rights, has become an actor much more interested in attracting investment and playing the role of a competitive state in the great scenario of globalisation. At the same time, however, it is precisely the state that maintains its irreplaceable function as a regulator of social processes, as we have seen, in particular, in the period of the pandemic, in which, in the absence of a true supranational government, each state had to be responsible and adopt measures – even controversial ones – to protect public health, even in contrast with economic initiative and the right to work itself.

2 CATEGORIES

Let us start with the categories. First of all, the 'dogmatic' categories, whose strenuous defence is offered here in Elena Gramano's chapter.

Aristotle and then Kant taught us that categories are important intellectual tools that enable us to know reality. We cannot know without categories with which to interpret reality, whether natural or ideal-normative. This is why the 'genius' of legal construction has rationally constructed the categories of law, placing its actions under the domain of abstractions. Indeed, legal categories make it possible to conceptualise the normative ideas (which in civil law systems we call in Italian 'fattispecie', from latin *facti species*, and in German '*Tatbestand*') that express the ought-to-be of the norm, and underlie the processes of interpretation and application of law.

Categories are therefore essential both for a 'science' of labour law, aimed at the knowledge of what labour law is, i.e., of its identity and 'qualities' with respect to other areas of legal experience, and for the interpretation and application of labour law norms. But categories are not only necessary tools for knowledge of normative reality (and for the interpretation and application of law) but also powerful technical means of constructing the object of legal science. Categories are the bricks of the edifice and, at the same time, the architectural blueprint necessary for its construction.

A first categorical question concerns the relationship between labour law and private law, i.e., the system that in civil law systems has forged the dogmatic categories starting with Roman law, passing through Pandettistica and the great nineteenth-century codifications. It is evident that labour law, in the course of its historical evolution, has moved away from civil law categories and elaborated its own categories, which have served to give this new regulatory subsystem its own peculiar physiognomy. At the same time, labour law cannot do without civil law categories, which are, however, adapted and undergo changes of their own. Often, these categorical mutations are closely linked to the social function of labour law and its purpose of rebalancing extremely asymmetrical relationships in terms of contractual (as well as economic) power.

Let us consider the category of contract. In civil law, the rules of contract are generally available, i.e., they are at the disposal of the parties who, with their private autonomy, can forge rules suited to the set-up of interests shared between them. This principle of private contractual autonomy is modified in the area of labour law to the extent that the rules of labour law are mandatory and cannot be superseded by a different will of the parties. As Mariella Magnani explained well in her chapter, labour law is the realm of mandatory rules, both in form of leases and collective agreements, which, in principle, are also mandatory. However, if today's labour law looks in the mirror, it will see that this perfect non-derogation has come to an end and that the system is much more subject to the derogatory solicitations, both in the individual and collective sphere, coming from the economic imperative of flexibility. The monolithic character of the non-derogation of labour law has broken down, giving rise to much more flexible and adaptive systems: at the level of the individual employment relationship, one need only think of the various techniques by which, by agreement, one can derogate from imperative rules, such as those of dismissal. Exemplary is the French case of the conventional break,[7] with which labour law, after a long journey

7. *See* P. Bouaziz & N. Collet-Thiry, *La rupture conventionnelle du contrat de travail à durée indéterminée: mode d'emploi*, in Le Droit Ouvrier, 739, 2010, p. 65.

away from the rule introduced by the Napoleonic Code, has rejoined the general categories of the Civil Code (Article 1134 du Code civil) which expressly permits it.[8] But many other examples could testify to this tendency, such as in the Italian case of agreements in a protected venue (before an administrative commission or in a trade union forum) whereby the parties can derogate in a pejorative sense from many mandatory rules (on duties, professional grading, etc.). One might, from a certain point of view, welcome this approximation of labour law to the categories of private contract law as an expression of a 'regulatory subjectivation' that enhances the worker's autonomy in the search for a more adequate arrangement of interests (think of the case of the employee who, with an exception agreement, renounces the responsibilities of the superior job and opts for a lower classification for the sake of reconciling work and private life). However, it must be acknowledged that regulatory subjectivisation runs the risk of returning the worker, who is the weaker party in the contractual relationship, to a sort of 'state of nature' in which the interests of the strongest prevail: the reduction of protections is always just around the corner when the rule loses its mandatory nature. The same path of regulatory flexibility applies to collective bargaining, which in many European systems has undergone a process of decentralisation in which collective bargaining has become a vector for the derogation of labour law norms (e.g., in wage regulation)[9] also of legal nature (exemplary is the Italian case of proximity bargaining introduced with Article 8 of Law 148/2011, or the French case of the so-called performance collective agreements with which less favourable conditions can be established on working hours, minimum wage and professional mobility).

A second categorical issue concerns the specific categories that have been forged by labour law and that represent the cornerstones for the regulation of individual labour relations and collective bargaining. These categories are often unknown to contract law: think of the category of subordination, which is both a contractual type (the subordinate employment contract), a subjective figure (the employee), and the raison d'être of employment protection legislation.

It is only thanks to the 'category' of subordinate labour and the value (or dis-value) assigned to it by the legal system that labour law has been able to construct its own normative subsystem within the general legal system, freeing itself from private law.

The same applies to the category of collective interest, which, in the world of modern legal experience, is centred on an individualistic and proprietary philosophy typical of the ruling class, which was born and substantially established as a legal category thanks to labour law. The origin of the category is in this case largely linked to the actual phenomena of coalition and union representation of workers' interests, and it was only thanks to a legal formalisation that the category of the collective interest operated as a vector for the construction of other related categories typical of labour

8. '*Les conventions légalement formées tiennent lieu de loi à ceux qui les ont faites. Elles ne peuvent être révoquées que de leur consentement mutuel, ou pour les causes que la loi autorise.*'
9. For the specific issue of decentralisation of wage bargaining from the (inter)sectoral level to the company level through the use of derogation clauses, *see* M. Keune, *Derogation Clauses on Wages in Sectoral Collective Agreements in Seven European Countries*, European Foundation for the Improvement of Living and Working Conditions, 2010.

law, such as that of the collective agreement. From its doctrinal origins, the 'tariff agreement' (*Tarifverträge*) appeared as a socio-political and economic phenomenon that required a new scientific treatment, a work of 'adaptation' of civil law categories, e.g., the rule that a collective agreement cannot be derogated from by an individual contract, clearly departed from general contract law, and the thesis of the invalidity of the derogatory contract with respect to the conditions established by the tariff agreement, put forward by Philip Lotmar in his seminal study of 1900 on the basis of the belief that the clauses of the collective agreement were incorporated into the individual contract, was opposed by the industrial courts.[10]

As Manfred Weiss brilliantly points out in his chapter, the two categories are closely related: the individual could not have become a category if the collective had not been there to support it. However, the latter category is in steady decline in all systems, both because of the social transformations of the enterprise (increasingly dematerialised, less and less a physical place for the aggregation of labour interests) and because of the difficulty of trade unions in correctly reflecting labour's now too diverse social interests. As a result, what was once a social experience of virtuous support for the values of labour protection has been tarnished and is fatally declining, opening a void of meaning and regulation at the very heart of labour law.

But the categories are also nexus shirts, which immobilise the normative dynamic, which do not allow one to leave their invisible but solid walls, the walls of legal dogmatics, of the 'categorisation' of reality through legal concepts on which the functioning of the system depends. This happens especially when categories are set in opposition to each other, so that one is an alternative to the other. And since the categories of dogmatics are also, and essentially, instruments for conveying the values of the legal system, the rigidity of the categories amounts to a denial of the axiological circulation of values in the overall system (or subsystem).

This is why a labour law capable of being 'critical' (in the Kantian sense) must have the ability to recognise the limits of its own historical categories and to deconstruct them. A law is critical when it programmatically questions the foundation of the knowledge of its being and reflects on the limits and validity of its own constituent categories.

Let us again take the category of subordination as an example. The category of subordination, understood as a cognitive category of the world of work and of the systems of protections that must be guaranteed to the worker *qualified as subordinate* (employee), prevents labour law from looking beyond its historical scope of application to respond to the need to protect self-employment, economically dependent work, or simply what is now emerging as 'personal work'.[11] Today, labour law focuses and

10. P. Lotmar, *Die Tarifverträge zwischen Arbeitgebern und Arbeitnehmern, in Archiv für soziale Gesetzgebung und Statistik*, XV, 1900, p. 1.
11. On the category of personal work *See* N. Countouris & V. De Stefano, *New Trade Union Strategies for New Forms of Employment*, ETUC, Brussels, 2019, p. 65; N. Countouris, *Defining and Regulating Work Relations for the Future of Work*, ILO, 2019, p. 15; ma già M. Freedland & N. Kountouris, *The Legal Construction of Personal Work Relations*, cit.; the first version of this thesis is due to M. Freedland, *The Personal Employment Contract*, Oxford University Press, Oxford, 2003; M. Freedland, *From the Contract of Employment to the Personal Work Nexus*, in

concentrates on the category of subordination which is, in some ways, anachronistic and inadequate to the demands for social justice coming from the world of work. As Brian Langille writes, labour law, rather than 'hunting' for subordination in order to apply protections to the worker who has been labelled as subordinate, should, on the contrary, be the law that applies protections to the worker who needs them, without the need for labels and categorical classifications.[12] For this reason, the regulatory logic of 'principles' takes on renewed importance, which, unlike categories, on the one hand, makes it possible to incorporate the values that are introduced and circulate in the regulatory system (thanks to the cognitive openness of legal systems), and on the other hand to respond more effectively to the demands for justice-equity that emerge from practical 'cases', which are not always subsumed within the given categories.

This deconstructive path of the traditional normative logic centred on subordination has been expressed by Brian Langille in his chapter in these terms: the notions or categories of 'qualified' work (subordinate worker, self-employed worker, worker, other 'intermediate' categories) do not exist in nature, they are the result of normative rationalisations (real 'fictions of the legal imagination') that are not reflected in reality. The protections of labour law do not apply to a concrete case (in Italian, '*fattispecie*') insofar as it is a case subsumed under the abstract category of legally subordinate work; on the contrary, it is the latter category that is qualified as such because labour law applies to it.

In this radical view – according to which it is not a concrete fact qualified by law according to arbitrary and time-honoured tests that are subsumed under an abstract norm, but it is the application of the norm to the concrete fact according to a purposive rationality that determines its legal qualification – the application of labour law no longer follows the logic of the correlation between a contractual 'type' and the effects that the legal system attaches to that type, but a new regulatory rationality, that of the values and principles aimed at protecting work 'in all its forms and applications' (as expressed in Article 35 of the Italian Constitution).[13]

In this perspective, the deconstruction of the category of subordination allows the legal system to transform itself into a system that is broader than that referring only to subordinate labour: a system in which what matters is not so much the subjective qualification of subordinate worker or employer, but the existence in concrete terms (in factual reality) of 'workers and firms', understood as concrete 'facts' that must be concerned in the light of normative (constitutional) principles of labour protection (in the perspective of Langille: rule of law, legality, ideal of equality, human freedom, human capability). The rationality of this system must be understood no longer starting

Industrial Law Journal, 2006, p. 1 ss.; M. Freedland, *Application of Labour and Employment Law Beyond the Contract of Employment*, in *International Labour Review*, 2007, Nos 1-2, p. 3; A. Perulli, *A New Category Within European Union Law: Personal Work*, 15(1) European Labour Law Journal 2024, pp. 184 ff., https://doi.org/10.1177/20319525231221225.

12. B. Langille & B. Mayer-Goodman, *Hunting for Employees, Employers, Independent Contractors, Dependent Contractors and Other Figments of the Legal Imagination*, 48:1 Dal LJ 2025 (forthcoming).
13. *See* A. Perulli & T. Treu, *In tutte le sue forme e applicazioni. Per un nuovo statuto del lavoro*, Giappichelli, Torino, 2022.

from the oppositional 'categories' to which human labour is artificially brought back (according to what, in a civil law system, we call the 'logic of the case') but by reason of the specific purposes (of the 'teleology') of the system itself, in its value articulation and modular diversification.

This 'Copernican revolution', which reverses the qualification process by making it depend not on presumed qualities of the 'fact' to which to link certain legal effects but directly on the protective function of the law, allows us to rethink the idea of a 'system' of labour law, currently lacking and indeed decisively supplanted by an asystematic trend in the ordering/selection of labour protections, still mainly centred on the category of subordination. In this perspective, it appears fundamental to draw from the immanent sphere of primary values, constitutional rank, the teleology of the system, and thus the stabilising function of normative expectations expressed as needs for protections and capabilities from the social sphere, contributing decisively to the stabilisation of the overall social system. Labour law can thus become – to use the words that Philip Lotmar employed more than a century ago – a 'right of the person to a condition such that he can develop his own nature and thus live'.[14]

The categorical opposition concerns not only the field of subordination/ autonomy dualism but also other fundamental fields of labour law. The category of the 'collective' interest, for example, if understood as a rigid and dogmatic category of labour law, does not allow room for the category of the 'individual', and this is to the extent that the tendency of labour law towards the 'colonisation of the individual', which is one of the historical characteristics of labour law, causes the category of the collective to become a hegemonic category and exclude its negative (the individual). But the 'rediscovery of the individual', to recall a still fundamental essay by Spiros Simitis, teaches us that the individual dimension must also have its place in the regulatory sphere of labour law, as the level and scope of a subjectivised regulation, to give space to the subjective pluralism expressed by the world of work;[15] a subjective pluralism that the collective, due to its structural limits, often cannot recognise and finds it difficult to represent and therefore also to discipline.

With this, I certainly do not intend to deny the continuing importance of the category of the collective representation of workers, nor do I intend to reduce the relevance of the collective interest in current labour law. Without the category of the collective interest as a supra-individual interest, labour law would reflux into private law, i.e., it would lose its main characteristic that is the result of a history of struggles and collective conquests. However, it is undeniable that the historical categories of the collective in labour law (collective representation, collective bargaining, participation) are suffering and need profound rethinking. For example, in terms of the individual

14. P. Lotmar, *Der Arbeitsvertrag nach dem Privatrecht des deutschen Reiches*, I, 1902, Duncker& Humbolt, Leipzig.
15. S. Simitis, *Il diritto del lavoro e la riscoperta dell'individuo*, in *DLRI*, 1990, p. 83.

    As his great friend Manfred Weiss recalls, Simitis advocated the rediscovery of the individual, i.e., a regulatory framework that provides a realistic possibility for everyone to live a self-determined life. For him, the promotion of legal protection and protection through collectivisation were prerequisites for this self-determination; *see* M. Weiss, *Spiros Simitis: In memoriam*, 11(3) E-Journal of International and Comparative Labour Studies 2022.

employment relationship, the need for greater regulatory attention to the values expressed by the worker as a subject does not seem to be taken up by the category of the collective: the trade union has proved quite incapable of facing the 'challenge of differences' that has invested the world of work,[16] fragmenting it and making it increasingly difficult to act on the assumption of a homogeneous collective interest. Consequently, collective bargaining, with its assumption of 'homogenising' workers into homogeneous categories, has itself undergone a process of change in function of a more accentuated demand to regulate specific and differentiated work contexts at the level of the individual company. In this reading key, the phenomenon of decentralisation of industrial relations systems (especially those traditionally centralised) does not only simply take on the sense of a crisis of collective bargaining to the advantage of the economic logic of the enterprise but also a positive value of adaptation of collective autonomy to the different conditions in which work is structured in the enterprise due to differentiated economic and social needs.

Public/private are other oppositional categories that must be analysed in their dogmatic complexity. On the one hand, this dichotomy refers to a historical difference in regulation between the employment relationship of public employees and that of private employees. This distinction is based on the different nature of the employer: the public employer is a public body, which may be the state or an articulation of it, and from this diversity in the legal nature of the employer derive very significant consequences in terms of the 'sources' of regulation of the employment relationship. For example, in many industrial relations systems, collective bargaining in the public sector will have to respect budgetary constraints that do not exist in the private sector and may have a more centralised structure than in the private sector. Moreover, in collective bargaining in the public administration sectors, there will be more heteronomous regulatory intervention (laws, administrative acts), whereas the individual employment relationship, although it is a contractual-based relationship, may have not only a more 'authoritarian' character but also more guarantees for the public employee (think of the issue of dismissal). This distinction has undergone an important evolution over time. As Tiziano Treu reminds us in his chapter, the last thirty years have seen a long process of 'privatisation' or 'contractualisation' of public employment, which has been very controversial and problematic, leading to a tendentially unitary discipline. But important differences still remain and the two categories continue to reflect different regulatory statuses.

On the other hand, the public/private distinction concerns the sources of law production in general and the dynamics between these sources. To simplify a discourse that would be much more complex, we can say that the category of 'public' is equivalent to 'law', the category of 'private' to the dimension of private autonomy and hence 'contract'. Labour law is based on a mix, varying from system to system,

16. I am not referring to a culture of individualism in the workplace, nor to the individualising practices typical of human resources management. Instead, I am referring to the major changes that a non-hierarchical work organisation and a workforce that is no longer homogeneous as in the Fordist period may entail in terms of workers' subjective preferences and aptitudes, in a perspective in which recognising different capabilities due to different subjective propensities should be one of the objectives of a renewed labour law.

between law and contract as sources of production of labour law. In systems such as Italy, France and Spain, labour law is strongly rooted in the law, i.e., in the public sphere. In other systems, such as the United Kingdom, it is rather the other way round: think of the famous image of contracting developing in the shadow of the law or in a sphere characterised by the 'abstention of the law'. The weight of the law is undoubtedly greater in civil law systems than in common law systems, where written law (statute law) takes on a secondary character with respect to the system of sources.

However, we can say that in recent years, this relationship has been progressively reversed, even in the more statute-based systems. We have witnessed a general withdrawal of the public sphere to the benefit of the private one. Privatisation is a direct consequence of the attribution to private operators of missions previously ensured by the state. We have therefore witnessed and continue to witness privatisation in so many essential sectors of our societies, from labour to health, from transport to welfare. The justice system is also affected by this process of privatisation: just think of the importance that arbitration has assumed even in systems that did not have this kind of tradition in dispute settlement.

The consequences of this inversion of the public/private categories are well known and produce very problematic effects for the legal systems of labour and the welfare state. This privatisation current has at its base a theoretical elaboration of a neo-liberal matrix that wants to reduce the looming and oppressive role of the state, freeing private energies. More profoundly, on closer inspection, the dissolution of the public-private couple in favour of the latter expresses a precise choice of value, a choice of deregulation of protection and reduction of labour law to a reversible, derogable, flexible discipline.

More generally, it is the idea of categorical opposition between public and private that, again, seems to have entered a crisis. Rather than oppositional categories, it is now a matter of categories in continuous regulatory osmosis. On the one hand, osmosis concerns the regulation of public employment relations, which are increasingly regulated according to the logic and powers of the private employer; on the other hand, osmosis concerns public and private regulatory instruments and the sources themselves, which are increasingly interrelated and follow either a logic of 'integration' (as when the legal source refers to collective bargaining in a derogatory function), or a logic of 'exclusion' or 'substitution' (as in the case where private regulatory instruments, such as codes of conduct for businesses, take the place of heteronomous norms). For the other pairs of categories, such as labour law/civil law, the categorical pairs linked to 'geographical' and spatial dimensions (e.g., the categories of global and local, sometimes merged into 'glocal' or national/supranational), similar considerations apply, although, in this case, they are mostly heuristic categories rather than normative and dogmatic ones. Even in these cases, however, oppositional pairs perform a 'constructive', or cognitive, function, but at the same time, because of the changes taking place, they may end up weakening or rendering inadequate the overall categorical apparatus of labour law. The relationship with private law is very clear of this ambivalence. On the one hand, oppositional categories allow labour law to provide an identity; on the other, they take away its strength. Suffice it to think of the labour law 'categories' of damages for wrongful dismissal and compare them with the private law categories of damages for breach of contract: the civil law categories are much more generous because they allow full compensation for the damage suffered, while in systems such as France, Italy, Spain, Germany, and the Scandinavian countries themselves, compensation in the event of unlawful dismissal now has a maximum limit (so much so that the European Committee for Social Rights has repeatedly reiterated – most recently with reference to the Macron reforms – that Article 24 of the European Social Charter does not allow a ceiling on compensation for invalid dismissal). Rather than reasoning about oppositional categories in this case too, it would be more appropriate from a scientific point of view to look at these categories as broad reference points, which in turn intersect with each other and give rise to hybrid forms of legal rationality, irreducible to pre-established schemes, dogmatically non-communicating. Global and local, national and supranational: these are perhaps the most problematic categories at a time when the advent of globalisation has now settled in and produced a series of distortions and social pathologies that have directly affected labour law and its ability to respond to the changes in a world of work that is increasingly in need of social justice but, at the same time, increasingly overwhelmed by the distorting effects of competition between legal and social systems.

The history of these categories reminds us of the ancient spatial origin of every legal discipline, of every *nomos*, which in its etymology means at the same time to graze, locate and enclose.[17] Labour law, too, is a local law, which is born localised and deals mainly with economic and social phenomena circumscribed to what used to be called 'national economies'. However, for some time now, this localised character of labour law has become increasingly problematic and inadequate to deal with phenomena and problems that inevitably take on global dimensions: not only the economy, finance, the market but also social and environmental justice, under the mantle of the category (or paradigm) of Sustainability.

This globality of the world of production challenges our internal categories: how can labour law, which is local and national, be able to regulate global phenomena? These categories then become inadequate, if not obsolete, if they are conceived as alternative categories. As Antoine Lyon-Caen explains in his chapter, the process of globalisation coexists with re-nationalisation tendencies, and new virtuous combinations of local and global scale regulation demonstrate a strong ambivalence of governance, with a prevalence of the local in the creation of obligations and a subsequent extension on a global scale (as in the case of the recent European Union (EU) 'due diligence' Directive).

Labour law needs to think about its possible transformation in a transnational sense, about its possible extraterritorial projection, and this by all possible means, as Harry Arthurs taught us, by building global networks of regulation that correspond to the challenges launched by the global networks of value production.[18] One example

17. C. Schmitt, *Der Nomos der Erde im Völkerrecht des Jus Publicum Europaeum*, Duncker & Humblot Gmbh, 2012.
18. H.W. Arthurs, *Extraterritoriality by Other Means: How Labor Law Sneaks Across Borders, Conquers Minds, and Controls Workplaces Abroad*, Stanford Law & Policy Review, Forthcoming, Osgoode CLPE Research Paper No. 25, 19 July 2010. Available at SSRN: https://ssrn.com/abstract=1645248.

above all: the European directive on 'corporate sustainability due diligence', which not by chance finds its normative referent in the law of a State (French) and seeks to extend its regulatory mechanisms of corporate behaviour along the entire value chain, becomes the emblem of the overcoming (at least on a functional level) of the national/global categories, to the extent that national, and now supranational (the duty of vigilance) regulatory instruments oblige EU-domiciled companies to implement due diligence with a combination of territorial and extraterritorial effects. This occurs by virtue of two elements that were introduced by the directive: on the one hand, the obligations imposed on European companies extend to cover the activities of subsidiaries and partners, even if they operate outside the national and European territory; on the other hand, because the companies subject to the obligation are not only medium-sized companies that have their registered office in a Member State but also those established outside the EU and active, above a certain turnover threshold, on the European market. The relationship with supranational law would deserve an in-depth examination that I cannot make here. I can only state that the national/supranational pair has always been very problematic for labour law, even though, after all, it is the most 'institutionalised' pair, given that, with accession to the EU, a legal system is automatically integrated into European law, with all that this entails in terms of hierarchies of sources, multilevel protections, etc. The question to be asked here concerns the extent of the Europeanisation of labour law in matters subject to European regulation. This question tells us how much weight the European category has in the dynamics of a system. We have historically found different levels of Europeanisation, sometimes satisfactory, other times totally inadequate. And another question may be: how far can the European social model be considered a useful level of regulation for advancing national labour law systems, given that Europe, before being social, is an economic reality? Again, on the one hand, we have a European economic law that has in fact rewarded economic freedoms over social rights (think of the well-known cases of the Court of Justice in Viking, Laval, Luxembourg);[19] on the other hand, we have positive experiences, in which Europe has served as a model for disciplines that states are not always able to produce on their own, and that it is right to have a supranational discipline. The topic is approached from a particular perspective in the chapter by Orsola Razzolini, who compares the relationship between antitrust law and labour law in the United States (US) and Europe, emphasising the positive aspects of European policies in combating inequality. But there are also other positive novelties in this attempt to relaunch the European social model: think, for instance, of the recent EU Directive on platform work, which, on the one hand, extended the discipline of algorithmic management to all persons working via a platform, and on the other introduced a relative presumption of subordination, albeit with a very problematic technique that risks not achieving its objective.

It is certain that even in this case, rather than categorical contrasts, one must detect intertwining and contamination between categories in a complex mirroring of these different levels of regulation.

19. *See* S. Giubboni, *The Rise and Fall of EU Labour Law*, 24 Eur Law J. 2018, pp. 7-20 https://doi.org/10.1111/eulj.12239.

3 VALUES

Regarding the values and political philosophies that affect labour law, the discourse is even more complex than that concerning the categories. Even the term 'values', when referring to the legal sphere, is very problematic. Do these values, which we often refer to, really exist when we mean the basic regulatory principles of labour law? Are they legal or moral values? Are they part of the legal system, or are they external to it, belonging to the sphere of ethics? Freedom, democracy, social justice, solidarity, equality and non-discrimination, and human dignity are the values we normally refer to – and invoke – when we think of the function of labour law: well, are they really values that underpin the normative system of labour law, or are they entities external to it? A positivist *civil law* jurist would probably argue that when we speak of values, we are talking about something pre-legal, outside the sphere of positive law, and which, moreover, belongs to the irrational sphere of subjective preferences: this is the traditional position of Kelsenian normativism, which still today appears prevalent in the general theory of law, and which is accompanied in moral philosophy by the non-cognitivist positions that deny the objectivity and rational knowability of values. But legal formalism, by evacuating values from the normative system, expresses a strong scepticism and axiological relativism, which is ill-suited to a law inspired by the idea of social justice and the values of equality, solidarity, freedom and dignity of the person. It is a road that leads to relativism of values and, at the end of this path, to legal nihilism, which sees law as a merely formal structure, ready to accept any content and thus justify any arrangement of interests, even the most socially unjust.

Yet, labour law, due to its natural porosity towards values and principles, has much to say on this point and can be regarded as the emblem of an anti-formalist law, which is not based on the mere formal-procedural recognition of what is law (the positive norm), but bases the law on a material (non-formal) axiological system and aims to achieve substantial results in the protection of the person. Labour law is a matter that arises from below, from the material needs of working people who are exploited by a capitalist system that, from its origins, treats labour as a commodity. In the face of the 'great transformation' described by Karl Polanyi as a process of fictitious reduction of the factors of production to commodities, the states that signed the Philadelphia Declaration felt the need to affirm that, on the contrary, labour is not a commodity; the spirit of Philadelphia hovers over the system of international labour law that has made the International Labour Organization (ILO) *Core Labour Standard* Conventions mandatory for all Member States even irrespective of their ratification, precisely in order to avoid the commodification of labour. Thus, labour law actually translates values into its normative fabric in a material, not a formal sense. That is why it cannot be said that in labour law, values do not exist, that they are subjective preferences, irrational desires, because those values are 'objectivized' and positivised by the system. Often, these values coincide with human rights: if a person is entitled to receive a *fair wage* in exchange for work done, there is in this demand for social justice the appeal to a value in the material sense, not the formal sense, which translates into a universal right. In labour law, it is not just a matter of affirming the equivalence or equality of the parties in the sense of private contract law; instead, there is an instance of (distributive) justice that has an ethical rather than logical, moral rather than juridical-positive foundation; something that makes labour law an inalienable instance of human dignity and freedom.

Another example is offered by the value of solidarity: what would labour law be without the many solidarities that bind people, create a collective fabric and fuse different interests into a common instance not only at a local level (the community, the enterprise) but also at a national and transnational level? Julia Lopez's analysis of the prospects for a cosmopolitan solidarity shows how the fight against the demercification of labour passes through the affirmation of democratic values and fundamental rights in a complex interplay of sources and normative levels in which solidarity is 'inscribed' in the forms of regulation. Other examples of new, emerging values germinated by the general value of solidarity are offered by *intergenerational solidarity*, which underpins the paradigm of sustainable development, and by *ecological solidarity* between man and his living environment, which underpins a new relationship of labour law with Nature. In short, there is a world of human and humanistic values pulsating at the heart of labour law. Scholars like Hugh Collins and Virginia Mantovalou invite us to think of labour law in terms of human rights. In civil law systems, this reference to labour rights as human rights is rather expressed in the form of 'fundamental rights'. This theme is taken up by Tonia Novitz in her chapter, where the emergence of labour-relevant international labour standards goes hand in hand with the consolidation of a sustainability paradigm; consequently, the challenge is to align Sustainability and human rights in order to enhance, also on the jurisprudential front, the universality and significance of labour rights.

This is undoubtedly a correct view. Human rights are, of course, very high in the legal sphere, but they can be ineffective in their practical application, especially if the level of regulation shifts to the international. It is therefore necessary to insist and commit oneself to promoting a multilevel experiment in human rights that also involves civil society. Hanna Arendt wrote that there is only one human right that counts, and that is the 'right to have rights'. Arendt was not only referring to people who had lost all capacity to have rights in concentration and extermination camps but also to stateless people. Let us think, then, about how important the idea of the 'right to have rights' is in today's historical condition, when faced with millions of people, economic migrants, refugees fleeing wars and famine, who are deprived of basic rights in internment camps or simply prosecuted as illegal immigrants by the states that should welcome them and instead treat them as criminals. We think of what Virginia Mantouvalou has defined as 'state-mediated structures of injustice', systems apparently based on legitimate laws when considered in isolation, but which, however, when considered at the system level, produce an increase in social vulnerability and the exploitation of entire groups of disadvantaged people (migrant workers, prison workers, agency workers, etc.).[20] In this situation, reference to the values expressed by human rights can play a positive role in addressing social injustices and hold governments accountable for this increase in labour exploitation, as well as, more

20. V. Mantouvalou, *Structural Injustice and Workers' Rights*, Oxford university Press, Oxford, 2023.

generally, provide a useful and powerful tool for transformation at the legal and cultural level in order to bring about structural change.[21] If labour law is a system of values, it is clear that these values are not conceivable as expressions of subjective preferences (as relativists would have it) but must have their own 'objectivity' and be located within a framework of philosophical reference, moral philosophy or practical philosophy.

Consequently, labour law, looking in the mirror, seeks to understand what sustains it in its being 'of value', what gives it a meta-positive ethical force rooted in its basic values. A scholar firmly rooted in positions of positive law might respond that any reference to philosophy is a useless ideological superstructure and that what counts, at the end of the day, are the *policies* and the decisions of the political sphere, which do not need philosophies on which to base themselves because politics is the sphere of sovereign decision. In my opinion, this answer would be wrong. With all due respect for policies, which are also fundamental in creating law, labour law, without a solid philosophical basis of reference, loses legitimacy and justification and is reduced to a mere act of will, ready to receive any content. This is precisely the positivist view of law as an act of sovereign will that follows codified procedures of production and finds its legitimacy (or rather, its 'legality') in these legislative procedures. But the theses that have openly opposed labour law in recent years, reducing its regulatory authority, were not simply acts of will, mere 'political' acts; they had a very clear, albeit not very sophisticated, theoretical structure upstream. We need only think of the economic analysis of law, which had the task of putting law at the service of mainstream economics, focused exclusively on the efficiency of the system and paying little attention to social and environmental aspects.[22] Focused solely on the rational relationship between means and ends and indifferent to the content of the ends themselves, the economic analysis of law has acted as a battering ram to delegitimise the social function of labour law, contributing to the creation of false beliefs (e.g., about the negative effects that overly strict dismissal regulations would have on the general economy). One cannot agree with the thesis that law and economics are not only an anti-regulation theory:[23] one only has to think of the well-known thesis of the efficient breach of contract and its application in labour law (the att-will rule) to realise that it is, on the contrary, a theory that looks favourably on strengthening the self-regulating mechanisms of the economic system, denying rationality to heteronomous norms. In the same way, one cannot share the assumption – truly surprising, considering that it is a labour law scholar who formulates it – that a rule such as the one conditioning the validity of dismissal to a just cause means that incompetent or ill-qualified workers could not be dismissed.[24] Such theses, completely unconfirmed empirically and thus

21. Mantouvalou, *supra* n. 20, p. 167.
22. *See* M.C. Nussbaum, *Flawed Foundations: The Philosophical Critiquew of (a Particular Type of) Economics*, 41(4) The University of Chicago Law Review, Autumn 1997, p. 1197 https://doi.org/10.2307/1600214.
23. *See* S.J. Schwab, *Law-and-Economics Approaches to Labour and Employment Law*, 33 International Journal of Comparative Labour Law and Industrial relations, 2017 https://doi.org/10.54648/ijcl2017006.
24. Schwab, *supra* n. 23, p. 115.

clearly ideological, demonstrate how corrosive law and economics can be to the basic values of labour law. Neo-liberalism, which has affected labour law so much in recent decades, producing, in some systems, a veritable 'destruction' of social norms, draws on philosophical-political conceptions that go from classical economic liberalism to the theory of the minimal state, from Hayek's ordo-liberalism to ethical relativism and non-cognitivism. Why, then, should labour law not propose a different political philosophy, one that is adequate to the theoretical challenges of the idea of social justice and capable of providing a plausible justification for its being a normative system aimed primarily at labour protection?In reality, not one but several currents of contemporary philosophical-political thought affect labour law. There are different models and different philosophical perspectives that can usefully serve as a philosophical-political compass for labour law. The *capabilities* approach is one of them.[25] Neo-republicanism is another. The neo-Hegelian doctrine of social freedom based on mutual recognition (*Anerkennung*)[26] is another rich perspective for labour law in search of a confirmation of its values or a fresher justification of its social aims.[27] These are philosophical reflections that enrich labour law and, at the same time, point the way forward for policy-makers. They are not alternative theories to each other; on the contrary, there may be ample room for an eclectic philosophy of labour law, linking the approaches of authors such as Sen, Nussbaum, Honneth and Pettit.[28]

While being different, such philosophical doctrines bear significant axiological syncretism because, according to both, the individual self-determination of the subject is not conceived in a liberal sense (as mere non-interference)[29] but is ascribed to its

25. The *capabilities* approach is expressly referred to by P. Pettit, *A Brief History of Liberty And Its Lessons*, Journal of Human Development and Capabilities, 2015, p. 12 https://doi.org/10.1080/19452829.2015.1127502. The capabilities approach in fact closely linked to an idea of 'positive' and 'social' freedom. A. Sen expressly conceives the human being as a 'social person' whose value is 'understanding and a commitment to ethical norms': *see* A. Sen, *Individual freedom as a social commitment*, Laterza, Bari-Roma, 2007, p. 41.
26. *See* T.L. Brownlee, *Recognition and the Self in Hegel's Phenomenology of Spirit*, Cambridge, Cambridge University Press, 2022.
27. *See* A. Honneth, *The Idea of Socialism: Towards a Renewal*, Polity, 2017.
28. On the connections between the republican theory and recognition, *see* F. Schupper, *Freedom, Recognition and Non-Domination*, Dordrecht Heidelberg New York London, Springer, 2013; J. Bohman, *Is Hegel a Republican? Pippin, Recognition, and Domination in the Philosophy of Right*, 53(5) Inquiry: An Interdisciplinary Journal of Philosophy, pp. 435 ff. https://doi.org/10.1080/0020174x.2010.516676; F. Neuhouser, *Actualizing Freedom: Foundations of Hegel's Social Theory*, Cambridge, MA: Harvard University Press, 2000.
29. By freedom in the sense of 'liberalism' I refer here to the kind of freedom that a liberal thinker like Isaiah Berlin defines as 'negative freedom' to distinguish it from 'positive freedom': I. Berlin, *'Two Concepts of Liberty,' Four Essays on Liberty*, Oxford, Oxford University Press, 1969 (on Berlin's philosophical thought, qualified as an expression of an unorthodox liberalism, *see* W.A. Galston, *Moral Pluralism and Liberal Democracy: Isaiah Berlin's Heterodox Liberalism*, 71(1) The Review of Politics, Cambridge University Press, 2009, pp. 85 ff.). H. Collins places this 'negative' '(freedom from interference by the state)' at the centre of 'liberal values'; while M. Biasi, *An Essay on Liberty, Freedom and (Decent) Work*, p. 364, on the basis of H. Arendt's thought, *On Revolution*, London, Penguin, 2006 (orig. 1963) – which distinguishes between the concepts of liberty and freedom – approaches negative liberty as the notion of 'liberty' referred to the absence of unjustified restraints, while the notion of 'freedom' as positive liberty 'requires the social recognition of a collectivity of peers'.

intersubjective and social root, thus becoming a 'positive freedom'.[30] In fact, both within the neo-republican and neo-Hegelian perspective, individual freedom may not be exercised subjectively but only inter-subjectively, that is, in the social and institutional dynamics of recognition and to the extent that subjects enjoy protection and resources available to exercise their functions, as also suggested by the capabilities approach.[31] In this perspective, the different approaches of political philosophy are combined by emphasising what they have in common, first and foremost, the reference to freedom, conceived in a very different way from freedom-liberal freedom (understood as negative freedom, as 'non-interference', or as freedom 'from'), but understood in a social sense, as positive freedom, freedom 'of', as a capacity that is based on recognition and creates the conditions for non-domination. Social freedom – a key value of the French Revolution, aimed at achieving social freedom in the economic sphere[32] – is not just an abstract ideal of social rationality but a normative design that plays a founding role in the legal system. It is precisely recognition in the perspective of *political, economic and social solidarity* – together with the absolute value of dignity, placed by Kant at the basis of self-respect by all reasonable creatures in the world[33] – that represents not only the founding value of the entire legal system but also a normative criterion to be *applied directly in interprivate relations.*[34] Thus, the employment relationship acquires substantial importance as a normative structure that

30. I refer here to a notion of freedom as positive freedom advocated by many orientations of moral philosophy: from the capabilities approach to neo-republicanism to the theory of social freedom based on recognition, about which we shall now speak. With regard to the capabilities approach, a careful reading of Sen's work clarifies that capabilities are 'positive' freedoms conceived as real opportunities: in this sense that one has all the required means necessary to achieve that doing and being if one wishes to. That is, it is not merely the formal freedom to do or be something, but the substantial opportunity to achieve it (Robeyns, Ingrid & Morten Fibieger Byskov, 'The Capability Approach', *The Stanford Encyclopaedia of Philosophy* (Summer 2023 Edition), Edward N. Zalta & Uri Nodelman (eds), https://plato.stanford.edu/archives/sum2023/entries/capability-approach/.) This interpretation is confirmed by what A. Sen writes about 'positive freedom to live without premature mortality', poverty as a 'lack of positive freedom' and in general to the full consideration of the freedom of the individual as a commitment of society to increase people's capabilities; in any case, for Sen 'social commitment to individual freedom must concern both freedoms, positive and negative, together with their extended mutual relations' (A. Sen, *Individual Freedom as Social Commitment*, Editori Laterza, Roma-Bari, 2007). Emphasises the relevance of the capability approach in promoting positive freedom '(a freedom to)', with particular reference to 'valuing and promoting the worker's knowledge and skill' R. Del Punta, *Is the Capability Theory an Adequate Normative Theory for Labour Law?* in B. Langille (ed.), *The Capability Approach to Labour Law*, Oxford, Oxford University Press, 2019, pp. 98 f., according to whom 'the capability theory appears to have a comparative advantage, in that it potentially covers the most dynamic area of labour law which presides over the discovery of the worker's subjectivity'.
31. *See* F. Schuppert, *Freedom, Recognition and Non-domination. A Republican Theory of (Global) Justice*, Springer, Heidelberg New York London, 2014; in neo-republican terms the liberal vision constitutes a paradox on the assumption, dating back to the scholastic political philosophy, that the human animal is natural social et politicum so that freedom can only be a social freedom: *see* Q. Skinner *The Paradoxes of Political Liberty*, in S. McMurrin (ed.), *The Tanner Lectures on Human Value*, Vol. VII, Salt Lake City, University of Utah Press, 1986, p. 232.
32. *See* A. Honneth, *The Idea of Socialism: Towards a Renewal*, Polity, 2017.
33. I. Kant, *The Metaphysics of Customs*, Rome-Bari, Laterza, 1983, p. 294.
34. *See* Art. 2 of the Constitution of the Italian Republic: 'The Republic recognises and guarantees the inviolable rights of the person, both as an individual and in the social formations where the

reflects the priority of the moral commands of reason over selfish interests, leading to the realisation of the ideal of equal rights in social freedom[35] within the environment in which people create the forms, institutions and social structures that are an expression of freedom.[36]

Labour law has had the merit of demonstrating that the scheme of the 'free and autonomous' subject of the modern liberal tradition is totally inadequate: the starting point of social relations is not the abstract subject, but, on the contrary, the subject as the product of *social and institutional relations*. Institutions, in Hegelian terms, constitute the normative vectors of recognition and, hence, of social freedom. Just as in neo-republican theory, the freedom of subjects is guaranteed by institutional processes of domination reduction; so, too, in the recognition perspective, the role of institutions is crucial in guaranteeing social freedom. Moreover, just as in workplace republicanism, freedom as non-domination is projected from the public sphere towards economic institutions in general and business in particular; in the neo-Hegelian perspective, democracy will only be realised if it facilitates and strengthens aspirations for social freedom both within the state dimension and in the other two spheres of social interaction, i.e., in personal relationships and the market.If it is true – as Axel Honneth argues – that modernity presents an intrinsic 'social normativity' of the economic sphere capable of reuniting the idea of freedom with that of justice, and if, however, freedom and social justice are conceived neo-republicanistically as conditions for non-domination in an intersubjective relationship of a private nature, a space can be opened to revisit the theory of the employment relationship as a relationship of subordination, in connection with the conceptions of the enterprise and its *governance* advocated by the theorists of industrial democracy and, today, by *workplace republicanism*.

In short, a space can be opened up to look in the mirror at the employment relationship from a different perspective than the one described at the dawn of the modern era, in terms of full and total subjection of the worker to the employer's domination; a new horizon, in order to rethink both the field of economic domination

human personality takes place. *The Republic expects the fulfilment of the fundamental duties of political, economic and social solidarity*'. The Constitutional Court has recognised the direct application of the principle of social solidarity laid down in Art. 2 to interprivate relations (Art. 2) to interprivate relations (No. 248/2013 and No. 77/2014); in doctrine *see* S. Rodotà, *Solidarietà*, Laterza, Bari, 2016, pp. 45 ff. who provides an indication of the solidaristic method also in relations between private parties, especially to cope with 'arbitrary amputations of the constitutional order' in the parts deemed incompatible with economic conditions. Considering the applications of the solidarity principle in the context of interprivate relations, it would be interesting to discuss the thesis of H. Collins, *Interpersonal Justice as Partial Justice*, 2022, which clearly separates 'interindividual' contractual justice from 'social' justice.

35. Even in the past, the struggles of the labour movement for equality and redistribution were part of a deeper motivational and ethical horizon than purely 'material' claims (e.g., wages), characterised by the workers' aspiration for a different life, linked to that egalitarian ideal in which freedom is not individualised and referred to the individual person, but is realised in the community of solidarity: *see* A. Honneth, *La libertà negli altri. Saggi di filosofia sociale*, Il Mulino, Bologna, 2017, and in particular the essay *Tre e non due concetti di libertà*, ivi, pp. 273 ff.
36. A. Honneth, *The Right to Freedom: The Social Foundations of Democratic Life*, Columbia University Press, 2015.

(in its institutional aspects of the market and the enterprise) and to call for a reactivation of the moral and solidaristic prerequisites of economic activity, as well as the institutional structure of the labour market, and, finally, the strategic role of labour in the enterprise in creating a common world (and the suggestions, here, range from the enterprise as a common good to approaches of the enterprise as a 'political actor'[37] with a view to workers' participation in the governance of the enterprise).[38]

4 INTERLOCUTORS

Third mirror image: the actors and interlocutors of labour law, who are part of its dynamics and identity. These interlocutors are sometimes internal to the labour law system, sometimes external to it. Again, these interlocutors may have institutional features, such as the state, or social functions, such as the trade union, or they may be impersonal entities, spheres or 'fields' with which labour law is confronted, interacts or is integrated (as in the case of the economy and the market, or as is now the case of the environment and its increasingly inescapable demands). And it is precisely with the latter that the dialogue of labour law is as important as it is delicate and difficult, even almost 'impossible' considering the divarication of interests that interact and fight each other in the Weberian struggle between values.

Dialogue with the economy, first of all. A close and particularly difficult dialogue, which has called into question the entire axiology of labour law in favour of values of an economic matrix, the values of market efficiency and the enterprise as an economic activity generating 'value'. Again, the dogmatic construction was based on an opposition, that between the universalism of economic rights and the particularity of social rights. But this opposition has nothing scientific or natural about it: it is only an ideological construction that must be uncovered in its assumptions and fought as a false conscience that creates in society and in public debate the idea that labour law is an anti-economic, anti-market right. How much more false! Valerio Speizle, in his chapter on the relationship between labour law and the economic sphere, quite rightly emphasises on the intrinsic economic nature of the labour contract and criticises the predominant economic approach to labour law, even going so far as to identify a 'genetic shift' in the last 25 years, marked by the colonisation of labour law by mainstream economic thought. In fact, the economic DNA of labour law goes back to its very origins. Labour law has always been a market law, a component of economic regulation law. Gerard Lyon-Caen has even written that it actually came into being as

37. For the conception of the enterprise as a political system a little republic, according to William Blackstone's statement: 'Corporations are little republics' (J.B. Lippincot, *Commentaries on the Laws of England in Four Books*, Philadelphia, 1893, p. 468), *see*, in the more recent philosophical-political literature, I. González-Ricoy, *Little Republics: Authority and Political Nature of the Firm*, in Philosophy and Public Affairs, Vol. 50, 2022, pp. 90 ff.; I. Ferreras, *Firms as Political Entities*, Cambridge, Cambridge University Press, 2017; D. Ciepley, *Beyond Public and Private: Toward a Political Theory of the Corporation*, 111 American Political Science Review, 2017, pp. 418 ff.; H. Landermore & I. Ferreras, *In Defense of Workplace Democracy: Towards a Justification of the Firm-State Analogy*, 44 Political Theory, 2016, pp. 53 ff.

38. *See* A. Perulli, *Workers' Participation in the Firm: Between Social Freedom and Non-Domination*, WP C.S.D.L.E. 'Massimo D'Antona' .INT-149/2019.

part of competition law and that labour protections are only a consequence, an epiphenomenon of this regulatory function of the market: just think of the initial functionalist view on which the first bricks of the European edifice were laid, which only later identified social values as an autonomous field of regulation. One may or may not agree with this assertion, which closely links the protective function of labour law to that of market regulation, but it is evident that a deep root of labour law links this regulatory system to the instances of rationalisation of market and enterprise dynamics. However, it is equally clear that labour law cannot be reduced to this alone, to being the *instrumentum regni* of an economic universe: one cannot pretend – as has sometimes happened – to transform labour law into labour market law. Nor can one think – as has happened, with some excesses, even in European systems, such as France and Italy – of reducing labour law to a law governed by mere economic calculation, according to the axioms of *Law & Economics*, which is by definition based on a quantitative rationality guided by the criterion of cost: the reduction of law to a superstructure ancillary to economic rationality is the result of a short-sighted view of what law is in its vital complexity, of what 'having to be' expresses in its inexhaustible dialectic with the world of life. This difficult coexistence of labour law with the economy must therefore find new syntheses, as for example happens (in theory) thanks to the emerging paradigm of Sustainable Development; provided, however, that Sustainability is conceived as a real moderating mechanism of the economic sphere, in an equi-ordered relationship with the social and environmental pillars of that paradigm. In short, the way forward is to make labour law a 'sustainability' law rather than a 'sustainable' labour law.[39] But this possibility depends to a large extent on the relationship that labour law has with its interlocutors, such as the company and its collective representation, the state and international organisations; all these relationships are, after all, decisively oriented by the law's main confrontation with the economy.[40] Another interlocutor with whom labour law has begun a new dialogue is the environment.[41] The topic is extensively addressed in the chapter written by Tatiana Sachs, who analyses the evolution of a growth-based paradigm in which the environment is a factor external to labour law. But things are changing, as shown by the French case and the position taken by the EU, which gives hope for an 'endongenisation' of environmental consideration into labour law. For some time now, labour law and industrial relations studies have been turning to the topic of Sustainability and, more specifically, to the environmental aspect of labour relations in order to ascertain whether, how and to what extent labour law and industrial relations are involved in the challenge of Sustainability, i.e., the fight against climate change and the realisation of a ' *just* transition' – i.e., socially fair, in accordance with the EU recommendation of 7 June 2022, which indicates a fair transition (from now until 2050) that leaves no-one behind. This transition should lead us from an industrial system based on the uncontrolled exploitation of Nature and its resources – a system therefore indifferent to

39. *See* V. Cagnin, *Labour Law and Sustainable Development*, Kluwer Law Intl, 2020.
40. *See* A. Jeammaud, *Le droit du travail dans le capitalism, question de fonctions et de fonctionnement*, in WP C.S.D.L.E. 'Massimo D'Antona'. INT-41/2005.
41. *See* A. Lyon-Caen, A. Perulli, *Vers un droit du travail écologique*, in *RDT*, 2022, p. 429.

the ecological externalities of production – to a climate-neutral and environmentally sustainable economic system that respects Nature and is capable of reducing negative externalities in both environmental and social terms. The results of these studies, which are still at an early stage, are problematic and certainly not definitive. First of all, it is clear that the issue of Sustainability is very delicate and not immediately feasible for labour law insofar as this discipline is part of the legal system that accompanies economic development with rules that are compatible with the dignity of the person involved in production processes. The subject is delicate because labour law is not traditionally an ecological law; it does not contain rules regulating the environment outside the workplace: the environment that is taken into consideration by the rules of labour law is circumscribed to the working environment; it does not extend beyond it. But there is more: environment and work, in certain cases, come into conflict because they are values that do not immediately coincide nor can be reconciled. Let us think of an exemplary case that of ILVA, in which – in addition to economic and production interests – two conflicting interests or values are at stake: on the one hand, the interest in the preservation of jobs (which presupposes the continuation of production activity) and, on the other, the opposing interest in the suspension or cessation of polluting production activities to protect the health of the workers themselves but, more generally, of the population of Taranto. There is therefore a problem of balancing conflicting interests, but even this balancing is not always achieved, and it is no coincidence that the Italian State has twice been condemned by the ECHR for its inability to find a synthesis capable of protecting people's lives. There is then another, even more general aspect that I would like to emphasise, which concerns the environmental interest with respect to the other two pillars of Sustainability; while economic and social interests are human interests, referable to man, the interest of the environment is a non-human interest, it concerns an external entity – Nature, the physical world, understood as the ecosystem in which man lives and dwells. Man therefore has only an indirect interest in protecting the environment and is not necessarily the best interpreter, the best representative of Nature and its 'demands'. This is reflected in the functioning of the legal system, which always requires the presence of a disinterested and impartial third party (typically the judge): in this case, we do not have an impartial third party because the judge is still a man, who participates in human nature and not in environmental nature. We do not think that these are abstract and not very concrete considerations because they have an enormous relevance to the issue we are dealing with in the sense that the lack of an impartial third party changes the axiological perspective of the ethical-legal responsibility of the economic actor in interpreting a regulatory role in this matter, bringing in a new value, the environmental one, which is not immediately ascribable to the reference values of the company.

Having said this, let us take a concrete look at the regulatory and contractual framework starting from the impulses of the *European legislator*. The first element to be emphasised concerns the strictly employment side. Not only the European institutions (but also the ILO) have urged Member States to modernise the education and vocational training system to facilitate the transition to new green and high-tech jobs, minimising the risks of unemployment that mainly affect the most obsolete jobs and creating new green jobs. For this reason, vocational training has been included in the financing assets of European funds with various programmes and should also be placed at the centre of industrial relations at the various bargaining levels. The European institutions have also started a legislative process on the duty of vigilance on the part of European companies that have led to the formulation of a proposal for a directive to protect human and environmental rights in global value chains. A sort of codification of corporate social responsibility that should stimulate precisely that ethical-legal responsibility I mentioned earlier. Finally – and this is the point that is most interesting to emphasise here – a clear input is coming from Europe towards the use of social dialogue and collective bargaining for the development of production and labour parameters that make it possible to internalise environmental issues and make both actors, companies and communities of workers, orient their behaviour towards greater environmental responsibility. In a recommendation to the European parliament, the commission calls on states to help the social partners to adapt their activities to the digital age and to explore new activities adapted to the future of work to the green and demographic transition and new labour market conditions. The strengthening of social dialogue is called for, and the culture of informing and consulting workers on environmental issues is proposed in another communication.

There are also virtuous examples of European systems, such as that of France, which have stimulated collective bargaining on these issues. I refer to the 2019 law on soft mobility, which introduced compulsory bargaining for companies with at least 50 employees on mobility, which has produced – according to data from the search engine *legifrance* – as many as 1195 company agreements and 17 category agreements relating to more sustainable modes of movement. There is also a provision in the labour code that provides for collective agreements on ecological and energy transition issues, which has produced 34 industry agreements and 294 company agreements on ecological transition. The Climate Act of 22 August 2021 was followed by the national interconfederal agreement of 11 April 2023 on ecological transition and social dialogue, which encourages social actors to address environmental issues at all levels of bargaining.

If the relationship between law and economics really found a new balance capable of recognising social and environmental demands, it is clear that a new space would also open up a new regulatory role of the State in the market and the economy. But which is the State that labour law needs as an interlocutor? The State, which still in modernity pretended to place itself on the plane of supreme values to protect every member of society from injustice or oppression, has become a *state* – which etymologically means *condition of stability* – functional to the homeostasis of power relations at risk of decomposition, a mere producer of the security that the unlimited dynamic of economic freedom continually demands. *Auctoritas* without transcendence, freed from any *Veritas*, state law is decisive for the fate of labour law, which has in itself a strong component of autonomy from the state sphere (just think of the system of collective bargaining, especially in common law systems) but, at the same time, depends on it (especially in systems where trade union law is more institutionalised and governed by heteronomous norms).

The perspective of the State as the privileged interlocutor of labour law is, however, one-sided; indeed, it risks being marginalised in an era of globalisation.[42] The destabilising effect of the values of social justice caused by globalisation through its main vectors of development – international trade and the geographical mobility of the multinational enterprise – has highlighted both the legal limits of the norms of domestic law and those of international labour law: lacking *erga omnes* efficacy, they risk representing a normative *self-service* in which each legal system remains free to choose which ILO conventions to ratify and apply in its own territory, in order to attract foreign direct investment.

The reflection of labour law is therefore necessary within the framework of a law with an international vocation, albeit weak in its foundations. The topic is addressed in the chapter written by Giuseppe Casale, who traced the relationship between the ILO and other international organisations (in particular, the World Trade Organization (WTO) and World Bank) and highlighted well the different tendencies that coexist (one more liberalist, the other more social) and the challenges of a more cooperative approach.

Since the post-World War II period, labour law has been present in the debate on global economic governance. But with the failure of the Havana Charter, which was intended to recognise and institutionalise the functional link between trade liberalisation and respect for fair labour standards, and after the exclusion of social clauses from the regulation of the World Trade Organisation, the dialectic between economic freedoms and social rights developed mainly within regional and bilateral trade integration spaces, to expand later with the so-called international mega-treaty on trade and Sustainability.[43] It later expanded with the so-called intercontinental mega-treaty, together with a new awareness of states and international organisations of the need to place economic development and its global trade mechanisms within coordinates of social and environmental 'sustainability'. As the unlimited spaces of economic globalisation open up, the demands for social justice remain unsatisfied to the extent that – as Simone Weil teaches us – law is reduced to something commercial, pertaining to the notions of 'sharing, exchange, quantity'.

But in what, then, can this increasingly insistent call for the *Sustainability of* a right thrown into the unlimited and encroaching dimension of the Economic consist? Evidently, it does not consist in the unlimited faith of the market as the self-regulator of society, nor in simply relying on *moral suasion* actions (such as that of the International Labour Organisation or other humanitarian, governmental and non-governmental organisations) for companies to become sustainable.

Rather, when looking at Sustainability, it is necessary to focus once again on *law* or mechanisms assimilated to it, avoiding what Carl Schmitt already described as the nihilistic inflation of innumerable mutually contradictory pacts, which banish global

42. *See* A. Perulli, *Social Justice and Reform of Capitalism,* in Brian Langille et Anne Trebilcock (Dir.), *Social Justice and the World of Work: Possible Global Futures, Essays in Honour of Francis Maupain,* Hart editions, 2023.
43. A. Perulli, *The Perspective of Social Clauses in International Trade,* WP C.S.D.L.E. 'Massimo D'Antona' .INT-147/2018, and in Bulletin of Comparative Labour Relations, Kluwer Law International, Vol. 105.

political-economic issues from the sphere of law and thus of scientific self-understanding. To fulfil this task and become the guarantor of a new *nomos* of the earth, labour law must promote, in place of globalisation, a new sustainable *mondialisation,*[44] a word that comes from *mundus*, the circular pit dug in the centre of the city to allow the souls of the dead to ascend to the earth, and at the same time the whole of the cosmos ('sky, earth, sea and air' says Festus); which is opposed to *immundus*, that which is morally vile, but also that which is 'outlawed'. Not referring to man (who should live in universal acceptance of the other and respect the juridical bond of solidarity), *immundus* refers here to the asphyxiating rationality of the global economy, with its *koinós* of exploitation of people and Nature, driven by the uprooting force of money and technology.

In the face of this unclean globalisation stands the inexhaustible quest for justice in the a-future, for the social and democratic values of equality and the redemption of the last. Can the legitimacy of sustainability law be founded, then, on the techniques of inter-normative regulation of global phenomena, which exploit the ever-present links between international trade and fundamental social rights, between trade liberalisation and compliance with defined social and environmental standards by Member States and companies? It is precisely in the inter-normative links that the *legality of* international agreements (which, as such, could transpose any covenant content) and their *legitimacy* guaranteed by non-formalistic institutional devices are welded together but which are characterised in terms of content by links with sustainability values (such as environmental protection, respect for fundamental human and social rights) that act as legally binding conditionality to the free unfolding of mercantile logic.

In this inalienable search for *global justice*, Simone Weil's last words in *La personne et le sacré*, known in English as *Human Personality*, still resonate, where she speaks of institutions destined to protect law - because law also needs to be *protected* - by people and democratic freedoms, above which (in a supranational perspective) it is necessary to invent *others*, indispensable, 'destined to discern and abolish all that in contemporary life crushes souls under injustice, lies and ugliness'. And the private interlocutor? The company is the main actor in an incessant interlocution between labour law and its 'environment'. But it is at the same time the weakest link in the labour-law dialectic both at the domestic level (except in cases where there is a precise qualified interest and/or convenience of the enterprise to develop the dialogue: think of the case of corporate welfare, or the development of proximity contractual dynamics) and at the international level, where the thesis attributing a certain international legal personality to the enterprise under international law has remained a minority. Consequently, even if states or international organisations encourage enterprises to voluntarily submit to codes of conduct or voluntary standards, this does not lead to the emergence of a rule of customary international law attributing legal subjectivity.

But if the company is not really conditioned by the state or international organisations as a subject of law, how can it really - not in words, but in deeds -

44. *See* A. Supiot, *Aux origines des États: la souveraineté de la limite. La geste gaullienne à la lumière de l'histoire des institutions*, in *Revue Défense Nationale*, Février 2022, No. 847, p. 30.

embrace the sustainability paradigm and really become a socially responsible company?

If Sustainability really became a driver of our societies, and was 'internalised' by corporate governance, even the relationship between labour law and business would take on a different valence from the current one, and the latter could really be perceived as a factor of socially responsible growth. It seems clear to me, however, that beyond much rhetoric, we are still far from achieving this goal and that the contradictions of the capitalist system of production are there for all to see and are *mirrored* in the dynamics of labour law. This is why I believe that the future of labour law is uncertain, and it is the task of the doctrine to support it in all public arenas and to nourish it with our reflections and research efforts.

This book is intended to be a contribution in this direction.

PART I Do the ‘Categories’ of Labour Law Still Exist?

CHAPTER 1

End of Transformation of Legal Categories?*

Tiziano Treu

1 THE IMPACT OF CHANGE ON LEGAL CATEGORIES

The increasing complexity of the digital society has put under stress not only many legal provisions received from the past but also the legal categories used to frame the law.

This is particularly true for the norms and the categories of labour law which are exposed more directly than other legal sectors to the changing modes of production and the impact of technologies on the forms of employment.

The implications of the new digital economy on the categories of labour law have been discussed in a comparative perspective during the international seminar held in Venice on 29-31 May 2023, where have been asked to analyse in particular one of the categories commonly used in labour law, namely the category of public and private.

But after presenting my specific contribution, I want to expose some remarks which have been suggested to me by the general discussion of the seminar, aimed at comparing the different evolution of three categories analysed there: not only public versus private but also subordination versus autonomy, and collective versus individual interests.

2 THE CHANGING RELATIONS BETWEEN PUBLIC AND PRIVATE SPHERES

Labour law has always been confronted with both public and private categories in different degrees of intensity and directions according to time periods and the major

* The text reproduces with integrations the presentation and debate at the seminar Labor Law and climate changing, Venice, 29-30 may 2023.

areas of our discipline. The borders between public and private law and their categories have been variable and often uncertain, like their reciprocal influences.

There have been frequent intersections among these categories, whereby legal institutions and regulations of public law can be found in the domain of private law and vice versa.

Moreover, the areas and contents pertaining to the two domains do not follow clear distinctive criteria due to the changing nature of labour law and the difference in its major components: the law of individual employment relations, collective labour law and social security.

An accurate analysis of the changing relations between the two categories would require an in-depth research which goes beyond the scope of this paper.

But I can submit some tentative remarks. On the one hand, labour law rules have some time contributed to shaping public institutions, as in the case of negotiated regulations, of the contractualisation of public employment and social participation in some public institutions.

On the other hand, public law principles have influenced the shaping of many imperative labour law rules aimed at protecting basic employees' rights, limiting the powers of the employers, and in general, the diffusion of anti-discrimination law.

Similar principles have inspired the attribution of public authoritative power to Labour Unions, which still maintain a private law status.

This interaction between public and private spheres is not neutral because it brings about an adaptation or even an alteration of the institutions affected by its impact. In some cases, the exchange of principles and institutions has contributed to bringing the two dimensions, public and private, close together.

I will try to test this hypothesis by analysing two specific areas of labour law where public and private rules have interacted with reciprocal influence.

The first area of analysis will concern the process of privatisation (better contractualisation) of the Italian public employment and the impact of collective agreements in the organisation and functioning of public administrations.

A second area will analyse the evolution of Italian social security and their institutions following the development of private forms of welfare complementary to public institutions of social protection.

The historical regulation of public services, not only in Italy, has excluded any influence of private principles.

The Italian State Council a few years ago (1992) declared that the privatisation of public employment was objectively impossible because the regulation of public employees is linked to the public nature of the interests involved in the service and of the connected powers of the public employer.

Consequently, a contractual regulation of the employment relationship was to be considered incompatible with any activity representing the public administration. The public nature of their activities required 'ontologically' that employment relations be regulated by law and by administrative acts (according to Article 97 of the Italian constitution).

Starting from these premises, a long process of privatisation and contractualisation of public employment has begun, initiated first by Act 93/1983, continued with Act

29/1993, which first challenged the separate status of public employees, and then by Act 125/1998 which has (almost) completed the normative integration between public and private employment.

The process of inclusion of public employment relations in the realm of private law has been controversial and frequently interrupted until the present.

The reasons for these difficulties are many, some common to other reform processes in Italy: namely the different political orientations of the governments which have succeeded in the last 30 years, the resistance of public bureaucracies, of the administrative magistratures and of part of the public law culture, still linked to the ontological separation between public and private, which considered any contact between these two worlds an 'act against nature'.

The pressure for a rapprochement or integration between the two conceptions of public employment was, however, supported by structural elements which were to become clearer in the course of time to most legal scholars and to the Constitutional Court.

Already in 1996, the Court indicated the necessity of this rapprochement, arguing that public law principles did not allow the normative and organisational flexibility needed for implementing the tasks required to the public administrations in providing new services to the citizens and in guaranteeing adequate results to the local communities.

Massimo D' Antona, a major inspirer of the 1998 reform, argued that the necessity to overcome the traditional public law regulation of public employment was due to the need to finalise the activities of public administrations to the attainment of measurable results and not simply to respect of formal procedures; an argument well sustained but difficult to implement in practice as proved by following events.

The Act of 1998 on Public Employment was accompanied by other administrative reforms which entrusted to local governments many powers originally pertaining to the central State, thereby contributing to strengthening the pressure for change in the public bureaucracies

But the distinction made by the Act of 1998 between the private law dimension attributed to management of human resources and the general organisation of the administrative structures, which was to remain under public law, proved to be uncertain and repeatedly challenged until now.

Contrary to some opinions which envisaged a simple relocation of public employment from public to private law, the rapproachement between private and public law principles in the regulation of public employment was to alter many aspects of its original status and the very traits of the private institutions operating in the new context.

The exercise of the contractual autonomy of the social parties in the regulation of public employment could not be absolute, since it found limits in the necessity not to prejudice the efficiency and effectiveness of the public administrations but to respect the pursuance of the public interests attributed to them.

Moreover, the management of human resources in the public sector, subject to private law rules, could not be completely separated from the decisions concerning the organisation of the basic administrative structures which remained under public influence.

In fact, the very distinction between the management of human resources and the organisation of administrative structures proved to be uncertain, even apart from the frequent overlapping caused by the opposite pressures of the bureaucracy and of the labour unions.

Similarly, the proposed flexible regulation of employment met with quite a few obstacles in the traditional administrative practices, often not challenged by the influence of collective agreements.

However, public managers were not entrusted with the same powers available to their private colleagues and were often limited in their decisions by opposite or convergent pressures coming from the trade unions and from the political authorities.

Not to speak of the limits to the autonomy of both parties of collective agreements deriving from the constraints of the public finances, which were variable according to the different political and economic contexts but which responded to factors different from those present in the private markets.

All these factors confirm that employment relations in the public sector, even when privatised, maintain a specific connotation since they are to be finalised to the institutional objectives of public interest pursued by the administrations.

One can say that, when operating in the environment of public administrations, the contract itself is no longer simply an act of autonomy but assumes some kind of 'functionalisation'.

This character is emphasised in the case of collective agreements because not only the unions but also many legal experts have attributed to them a major, if not decisive, role in the reform of public administrations.

It is true that collective bargaining, liberated from (many) public constraints by the 1998 reform, has assumed the nature common to private collective agreements of voluntary expression of the interests of the employees represented.

But beyond this common character, the regulation of these agreements, particularly by Act 396/1997, has been different in many decisive aspects from the correspondent institution known to private industrial relations systems.

While the latter in post-war Italy has developed outside any legal framework concerning its major aspects, in the public sector the actors, the procedures and the effects of collective bargaining have been tightly regulated by law.

The reasons for this difference depend precisely on the specificity of bargaining with the public administrations.

Here, the collective agreement is not an act completely voluntary based on power relations between the parties as in the private sector because it interacts with public administrations which are bound to respect financial targets and objectives of general interest.

Precisely, this specificity has prevented other countries from following the same route of 'privatisation' adopted in Italy and has implied a series of relevant and controversial consequences.

One side, it has allowed to tackle some problems which have remained unresolved in the private sector, namely the definition of the criteria of representativeness of the unions and the general binding efficacy of national collective agreements.

On the other hand, these stringent legal rules have not been sufficient to guarantee stability and to govern the dynamics of labour management relations, beginning with the regular renewal of the agreements, which have been repeatedly frustrated by financial constraints, to the control of decentralised bargaining which is exposed to centrifugal pressures and even to the respect of the criteria of unions representativeness.

The repeated attempts (more than ten in the years) to adapt the legal rules have not produced the expected results, in particular, in assuring the capacity of the public administrations to respond to the increased expectation of services by citizens.

The reasons for this insufficient performance cannot be fully analysed here. But it is possible to remark that, here as in other areas, the innovation of legal techniques, even though well designed, has not been sufficient to produce the expected results, since they have not been accompanied by parallel innovation in the organisation of the public structures, in the skills, and the culture of the people working in the administrations.

Some improvements with respect to the previous conditions have remained limited and not sufficient to activate virtuous imitations and a general modernisation of the Italian public sector.

Public sector collective agreements, even though more protected and sustained than those operating in private markets, have been similarly weakened by the impact of liberalisation policies and the recurrent economic and international crisis of the last few years.

These external constraints have greatly reduced the capacity of collective bargaining to play a role in the reforms and modernisation of the public sector which was envisaged by the acts of the 1990s.

On the other hand, this role has not been supported by the various forms of employee participation existing in many public administrations, which often have been inclined to corporatist or sectoral arrangements instead of operating as a collaborative force in order to pursue the common public interest.

In consequence, the trust in collective bargaining and employee participation has been reduced to the point of favouring attempts to reopen the scope of legal regulations of public employment to the detriment of collective bargaining.

In conclusion, the Italian experience of the regulation of public employment has invalidated the traditional idea that the two worlds, private and private, cannot communicate, but it has shown that the application of private law techniques and instruments in the public sector has required quite a few adaptation and changes in their functioning.

This experience confirms a conclusion, which can be reached in other areas of law, that the context in which legal institutions are located is not neutral, but it can imply more or less profound modifications in their use and possibly in their effects; indeed, that of the legal environment may be decisive in determining the quality of the institutions and even the impact of the normative sources regulating them.

In our case, the functioning and the effectiveness of the privatisation of public employment have been limited by the reactions of the bureaucratic environment and by the behaviour of the parties involved: namely, the ambiguity of the unions' strategies vis a vis the reform, the weakness of both the collective bargaining process and the public management.

Social security, in its different components, is a second area where the public and private dimensions have variously interacted in the course of time.

The original measures of social protection handled by private mutualism have been followed by the expansion of public welfare instituted and regulated by the State, which has performed almost completely the functions of protecting the citizens from their needs and risks.

The two dimensions, public and private, of social protection have been for a long time not only separated but opposed in the evaluation of policymakers and of the social parties.

The Italian constitution (Article 38) has confirmed that the measures of social protection are of general public interest since they are finalised to promote substantive equality (Article 3.2), but at the same time, it adopts a pluralistic approach by stating that the functions of social protection can be performed not only by the State but also by others public institutions, in particular the Regions, and by private organisations which pursue social objectives, including various kinds of welfare and social assistance.

This pluralistic approach has been interpreted in different ways and has received various and often contrasting normative applications.

The relationship between the public and the private dimension of welfare has been particularly controversial following the development of many complementary forms of social protection: first, private pensions, then supplementary health care and personal assistance, and lately, various kinds of welfare benefits applied at the firm level.

In Italy, the growth of private supplements to the public welfare, not only individual but also collective, has been strongly opposed both for ideological and practical reasons: due to the fear that this private welfare might divert resources from the public budget, that private management might be removed from public control, and in any event, might favour a disproportionate distribution of resource contrary to the objectives indicated by the Constitution.

Only in recent times have the major organisations representative of the social parties overcome their diffidence, recognising the importance in particular of private pension funds as an important component of the welfare system (2018 framework agreements for the industrial sector).

Indeed, even before this (late) acknowledgement, the Constitutional Court, with Decision No. 393 of 2000 stated that public and private forms of social insurance were functionally connected given their common finalisation to pursue general interests recognised by the Constitution. This decision is important because it has refuted the idea of a structural separation between the private and private dimensions of social protection.

The consequence derived by the Court was that the legislator (national and regional) was legitimised to regulate and limit the forms of this private welfare.

This acknowledgement of the complementary forms of private welfare as a fundamental part of the Italian social protection system has been confirmed by the constitutional reform of 2001. The reform has established the principle of subsidiarity, whereby the Italian republic is committed to favour the autonomous initiative of citizens, individual and organised, aimed at performing activities of general interest.

The principle fixed by the 2001 reform has been implemented by following legislation in many areas of social security.

This legislation has given different answers to the relations between public and private welfare.

The Italian law has regulated in great detail the supplementary pensions in all major aspects: the forms of the constitution of pension funds and their functioning, the requisites for receiving the pension, the fiscal incentives, and the controls on fund's management which have been entrusted to a specialised public agency (COVIP).

The supplementary health care, and the funds in charge of it, despite following similar structural schemes, have received a rather thin regulation, which has been indeed deemed inadequate to the importance of the interests at stake and to the great dimensions acquired by this form of welfare. At present, more than 15 million beneficiaries receive private health care, not only complementary but often in lieu of that provided by the national health service.

A more recent development has seen the growth of various kinds of benefits, provided by unilateral decisions of many (mainly large) firms or following agreements with the plant union representatives and, subsequently, by national collective bargaining. The diffusion of these benefits has created a further important segment of the private welfare system.

The legislator has decided that this kind of benefit deserves to be fiscally supported because it enriches the content of employment relations with elements other than wages, which are an expression of companies' social responsibility useful for the improvement of both the enterprise productivity and the wellbeing of the employees and their families.

The fiscal incentives for these benefits are granted on condition that they are attributed not individually but to broad categories of employees and that they respect objectives and contents indicated, indeed rather loosely, by the law (Act No. 285/2015 and following).

The lack of precise conditions for supporting these benefits with fiscal incentives has been criticised because it contradicts the more stringent conditions required for other kinds of welfare and may favour a dispersion of resources in measures deprived of real social value.

Some proposals have been advanced with the aim of promoting a more selective and equitable approach to the fiscal treatment of these benefits: finalised to favour low-paid and low-skilled employees or to promote the extension of the benefits to small firms where these benefits are scarcely adopted.

Similar forms of integration between private and public institutions have also developed to provide monetary support to employees in case of economic crisis.

Here, the integration between private and public measures is particularly complex and has been regulated by a system of bilateral funds instituted and managed by employers and union representatives.

The so-called autonomous funds regulated by collective agreements represent a 'symbiotic' integration between public and private, exempted from any public control.

A second type of fund is more institutionalised and regulated by law; consequently, the collective chances are generally binding and apply to sectors where public support for employees' income is not available.

A third type of fund is obligatory and strictly regulated by law, and it performs a public function in substitution for public interventions.

These bilateral funds are quite diffused and perform important functions in supporting employees' income in case of economic needs, sometimes complementing and often substituting the intervention of the State: their integration with the public is accompanied by more or less strict legal regulation.

In conclusion, the original separation between the private and public dimensions in the area of welfare has left room gradually and with some difficulties for different forms of integration which are in line with the institutional pluralism envisaged by the Italian Constitution and confirmed by the constitutional endorsement of the principle of subsidiarity.

This integration has been implemented with different degrees of links between the elements characterising the two dimensions, namely autonomy and heteronomy of the regulation and organisation.

Like in other fields, this cross-contamination has caused some adaptation and even distortion of the categories and techniques typical of each dimension.

It has brought about not only limits to the parties' autonomy but also a functional orientation of the contracts, individual and collective. Moreover, it has developed new instruments like the bilateral bodies instituted by agreements in charge of managing sectors of social security, health care and measures of income support.

In the public sphere, the adaptations are different but equally important. The State and public institutions have withdrawn from or shared some welfare activities while maintaining functions of regulation and control on the private institutions.

One can say that the direction and the intensity of these public functions are not always in line with the social importance of the matters involved.

Public intervention has hardly been directed to finalise these private activities to redistributive objectives and to expand them in order to reach disadvantaged areas.

This first appraisal seems to confirm that the relations between the two fields, public and private, remain uncertain both in their contents and coverage.

Some factors seem to push the private welfare to occupy further room, integrating the public or to its detriment: scarcity of public budgets and the tendencies towards an increased personalisation of social needs which are better met by private actors than by public institutions.

But the growth of this trend will depend not only on the general economic prospects and on the kind of public policies but also on the characters of the different sectors of social protection, e.g., the expansion seems likely in the forms of private health care and company welfare benefits, while this is not the case for pension funds which are stagnating.

The complexity of the matter and the evolutions analysed so far seem to suggest that public and private are not legal categories in the sense used when referring to autonomy versus subordination and collective versus individual. More appropriately, they indicate fields of rules, activities and institutions having common characteristics, even though they themselves are variable.

The cases analysed here confirm that in the frequent interactions between the two fields, they exchange objectives and techniques with two main consequences. One: the techniques may adapt to the change of field where they are used, often with unforeseen variation; two: the borders and the very identity of the fields may become blurred.

3 DIFFERENT IMPACT ON THE CATEGORIES: CRISIS, TRANSFORMATION, OSMOSIS

None of the categories discussed in the Venice seminar has resisted the impact of the great social and economic transformations of recent years, even though each one of them has reacted differently and undergone more or less profound modifications.

The category subordination, which in Italy is explicitly defined and endorsed by the law, has been most directly affected by change; probably for this very reason, its central role in determining the regulation of work has been progressively reduced by the multiplication of forms of employment different from the industrial worker on which our discipline has been built in the last century, and often characterised by mixed traits of subordination and autonomy. The very conceptual borders between the two areas and, consequently, the substance of the category subordination have been blurred. The crisis of this category has been endorsed by the Italian legislator which has repeatedly extended some of the legal rights and protections originally granted to subordinate workers to these hybrid forms of employment and often also to self-employed persons, beginning with those economically dependent or in a weak position in the labour market.

Interestingly enough, this extension of protections has not followed categorial schemes, as has been the case in other legislations, which have created new categories, such as 'worker', 'parasubordinate employee', 'TRADE', etc.[1]

Instead, the Italian legislator has decided on a case-by-case basis to respond to the different needs of protection for the new types of personal work, following a sort of remedial approach. Italian courts, which are institutionally bound to respect the legal scheme of subordination, have reacted by interpreting loosely the definition of the

1. L. Menegatti, *The Evolving Concept of Worker in EU Law*, Labor Law Journal, vol. 12, 2019; L. Menegatti, *Taking EU Law Beyond Employment Contract: The Role Played by the ECJ*, E.L.L. Journal, 2020, pp. 26 ff. https://doi.org/10.1177/2031952519884713; A. Perulli, *The Legal and Jurisprudential Evolution of the Notion of Employee*, Eur. Labor Law Journal, 2020, pp. 117 ff. https://doi.org/10.1177/2031952520905145; European Parliament Study, *Social Protection Rights of Economically Dependent Self-Employed Workers*, 2013.

category so as to include within its borders quite a few of the hybrid types of work and consequently to apply to them the protections of subordinate employment. The trend to extend some legal rights and protections beyond the borders of subordination is likely to continue, in line with the needs of many types of personal work, more or less autonomous, emerging in the digital forms of production. This trend has been supported not only by the international sources of the ILO (*Declaration for the future of work*, Geneve, 21 June 2019; *World employment and social outlook*, 2021; *The role of digital labor platforms in transforming the world of work*, 2021) and by the *European Pillar of social rights* (2017) but also by recent social directives of the European Union (EU) *Proposal for a directive of the EU Parliament and Council* on improving *working conditions in platform work*, Brussels, 7 December 2022, (COM 2021/752 final) and by several decisions of the European Court of Justice which is less bound than the Italian courts by a rigidly defined category of subordination.

The social and economic transformations which have challenged the category of subordination have a direct impact not only on the contents of the individual employment contracts but also on the dynamic of collective bargaining and labour relations. The Italians, like other European legislators, differently from the case mentioned above, have not reduced the area of these relations. On the contrary, they have mostly supported them by recognising a series of rights to the labour unions vis a vis the employers.

The category of collective interests, again different from that of subordination, is not legally defined but is a creation of the Italian doctrine.

It was shaped mainly with the aim of providing conceptual and legal support to the system of industrial relations which followed the fall of the corporatist regime. Beginning in the first post-war years, when a direct intervention of the Italian legislator in labour relations was seen with diffidence by the unions, this doctrinal category has been used to provide legal foundations for the effects of collective agreements on the individual contracts of employment; and this use has continued for years, also due to the persistent abstention of the legislator in regulating these agreements.

But here, too, the new social and economic conditions brought about by digital technology were to change the very basis on which the category had been built.

The varied morphology of productions and employment emerging in place of the Fordist industrial system and the once homogeneous working class has not only weakened the representative strength of the labour unions but also altered the very sense of collective interests.

It has deprived them of the original meaning attributed by the doctrine and, indeed, somehow corresponding to reality, of being the expression of substantive interests common to the working class or to homogeneous groups of workers, which for this reason deserved to be supported by the legislator. The fragmentation of working conditions, not corrected by legislative measures nor by the weakened initiative of the unions, has reduced the capacity of this category to represent the new reality and dynamic of labour relations.

The recent trend toward the individualisation of social relations, which has also affected the world of work, has introduced a further variable that is unprecedented and exogenous to the traditional conceptions of our discipline.

It is difficult to foresee the long-term implications of this trend, but it certainly will require discontinuity in the regulation of most aspects of employment relations, first and foremost in the traditional balance between individual and collective interests and values.

The unions will be challenged to respond to the new demands of recognition and participation, particularly of the workers present in the digital economy, often more educated and self-conscious than their predecessors.

Moreover, in this search for workers' allegiance, traditional organisations have to compete with the initiatives of HR management which too needs to be more attractive to young knowledge workers. Innovative management practices in technologically advanced enterprises are experimenting with more personalised and flexible forms of employment regulations, which aim at better reconciling the reasons for firm efficiency with the personal needs and expectations of the employees and their families. Collective agreements are also challenged to experiment with new forms of regulations that are less uniform than in the past, which set loose guidelines open to different choices of individual employees. The opportunity to experiment with forms of personalised regulations and participation is favoured by the new flexible types of work organisation and by the diffusion of remote working often endorsed by the legislator. The most promising of these experiments are those which promote personalised regimes of working time, new forms of work-life balance, and innovative negotiated welfare.

The labour unions and the organisations of civil society should not be indifferent to these requests for more personalised work rules because the lack of response may favour forms of extreme individualism contrary to the solidaristic values of our Constitution.

The specific analysis presented above confirms that the transformations of the context, not only socio-economic but here also political, have greatly altered the traditional relations between the domain of private and public institutions and regulations.

Similarly, they have rendered variable and uncertain borders between the two areas, causing quite a few overlapping of institutions, but in this case, the interactions between these institutions and their regulatory contents have not been reduced.

On the contrary, the exchange of practices and rules between the two areas has increased, not only in the field of labour law. Suffice it to mention the use of contractual instruments in many public initiatives, beginning with public procurements, which are widely adopted by public administrations in order to externalise their activities.

Equally significant is the diffusion of so-called social clauses in these procurements, which are aimed at conditioning their implementation to the pursuance of goals of social sustainability. Further relevant examples come from the various forms of public-private participation in implementing activities of general public interest and from the involvement of private organisations in public activities based on the principle of horizontal subsidiarity.

The two cases analysed in detail, public employment and social welfare, confirm that the traditional opposition between the goal and instruments of the public and private areas has been overcome and has left room for different forms of osmosis.

The private regulation via collective agreements has been entrusted by the legislators to make more flexible and productive the functioning of public employment.

This legislative endorsement has allowed and even promoted a wide contamination between public and private institutions, with quite a few reciprocal adaptations.

These adaptations and also some limitations of the exchanges confirm the resistance of public structures and cultures to fully absorb the techniques and the forms of private negotiations.

In the area of welfare, the reciprocal influence of the public system and private actions has been more limited than in the field of public employment, mainly due to the different natures and origins of financing.

The functional connection between the two forms of welfare recognised by the Constitutional Court has allowed, indeed requested, common rules concerning the conditions of access and of the use of welfare benefits, but not of the contributions and the possibility to use these.

The difference in benefits before the fixed age and the lack of common rules are the prevailing characteristics of flexible benefits adopted at the firm level. Only partially common are the rules concerning the functioning of bilateral institutions of welfare which have private origins but perform public functions.

In conclusion also, in the area of welfare, the initial opposition between public and private initiatives has left room for various degrees of integration corresponding to the pluralistic system sanctioned by the constitutional principle of subsidiarity.

Any forecast of possible future trends is challenged by a variety of determining factors. The identities of the traditional categories are certainly being transformed by these factors, but the directions and the implications of change are uncertain.

The borders between subordinate and autonomous work tend to become evanescent due to the expansion of fundamental rights and protections. But it remains to be seen which rules will still be reserved for the (possibly enlarged) category of subordination and those which will be applied to the proteiform category of self-employment.

The decision may still come from legislative measures approved in response to the changing characters of work and to the new expectations of working people; the relations between collective and individual interests will also be influenced by structural and political factors, but these relations might be even more fluid due to the impact of cultural and anthropological variables.

The impulses towards personal autonomy (also) in the performance of work will be conditioned by the unknown evolutions of digital technologies and by the cognitive and communications structures framed by artificial intelligence.

Finally, the borders between public and private institutions and activities will probably remain a contested ground with different combinations of autonomy and authority in the regulation of social and economic relations, but they might also be a testing area of contamination and overlapping of institutions.

CHAPTER 2

The Inseparable Connection Between Individual and Collective Labour Law

Manfred Weiss

1 THE BASICS

The shift from status to contract, from the master/servant relationship to a contractual relationship, was originally meant to liberate the working population.[1] The experiences made in the period of industrialisation, however, demonstrated that this is a naive assumption. It ignores the asymmetric power relationship between employer and employee as well as the fact that competition between individuals in the labour market may turn out to be a destructive competition. The possibility of acting collectively, getting organised in labour unions and concluding collective agreements with the employers' side is not merely an option; it is a necessity and a precondition for a functioning labour market system. As long as workers merely act as individuals competing with each other in the labour market, exposed to the mechanism of supply and demand, the danger of a race to the bottom is always present. In case the offer is lower than the demand for labour, impoverishment might be the result of individual competition between workers.[2] Therefore, the restriction of competition between individual workers should not be forbidden but allowed and encouraged. Only if workers are able to join forces can they prevent the race to the bottom by negotiating and, if necessary, fighting via collective action for adequate working conditions contained in collective agreements. And the collective organisation also is a lobby to promote State intervention, mainly via protective legislation.

1. For this important change of paradigm *see* the comprehensive analysis by B. Veneziani, *The Evolution of the Contract of Employment*, in B. Hepple (ed.), *The Making of Labour Law in Europe. A Comparative Study of Nine Countries up to 1945*, London/New York 1986, 31-72.
2. For this assessment *see* K. Marx, *Das Kapital*, in K. Marx & F. Engels, *Werke*, Bd. 23, Stuttgart 1968, 557-564 (first published 1877).

There were, however, many obstacles in history for employees to be allowed to join forces in collective organisations and to become active therein. The development went from repression via tolerance to recognition.[3] Since attempts at collectivisation tended to be linked to unrest and strikes, collectivisation was forbidden by specific laws. Sometimes, this even happened in order to preserve a wrongly understood individual's freedom, as shown by the famous Loi Le Chapelier[4] in France. These repressive laws were strictly executed. The bans on trade unions, however, were repealed in the course of the nineteenth century. But significant restrictions were kept. The real turning point towards full trade union recognition in Europe was the First World War. The Weimar Constitution in Germany, for the first time, contained constitutional rights for trade unions. Today, freedom of association, including the right to collective bargaining and collective action, is one of the basic pillars of labour law contained in the International Labour Organization (ILO) Conventions 87 and 98 and, in particular, in the Declaration on Core Labour Standards of 1998.

Freedom of association also includes the guarantee of free collective bargaining which – as already indicated – implies that trade unions and employers or employers' associations in concluding collective agreements are to be exempted from competition law. This was already very early well expressed in the Clayton Antitrust Act of the United States of 1914. Its section 6 reads as follows: 'Nothing contained in the antitrust laws shall be construed to forbid the existence and operation of labour organizations, ... or to forbid or restrain individual members of such organisations from lawfully carrying out the legitimate objects thereof; nor shall such organizations, or the members thereof, to be held or construed to be illegal combinations or conspiracies in restraint of trade, under the antitrust law.' The same approach is reflected in the famous Albany judgment of the Court of Justice of the European Union (CJEU).[5]

2 CRISIS AND PROBLEMS

2.1 The Terminological Divide

For the founding fathers of modern labour law, it was taken for granted that labour law had to be an inseparable entity of individual and collective labour law. The quality of workers' individual rights cannot be understood without the law on collective bargaining, the law on strike or the law on workers' participation. The close interaction is evident. Collective and individual labour law are two sides of the same coin.

However, the understanding that individual and collective labour law inseparably belong together is by no means uncontested. The plea for a divide is even reflected

3. For a comprehensive description of this development in Europe *see* A. Jacobs, *Collective Self-Regulation*, in Hepple, *supra* n. 1, 193-241.
4. This French law of 1791was named after the person who took the initiative: the lawyer Isaak René Guy Le Chapelier, member of the 'assemblé nationale'.
5. CJEU judgment Albany International BV of 21 September 1999, Case C-67/96.

in the terminology.[6] In Anglo-American countries, labour law is conceived as merely referring to collective labour relations and individual labour law is renamed employment law, thereby indicating that it is a separate entity on its own. This misunderstanding also leads to a strict divide in academic teaching and it is further promoted by the new academic discipline 'human resources'.

2.2 The Attack on the Right to Strike

For a long time, it was taken for granted that the right to strike was implied by the ILO Convention 87 on Freedom of Association. This, however, has changed after the fall of the Iron Curtain and the disappearance of the communist countries in Eastern Europe. The employers' group at the ILO has more and more questioned this implication and, since 2012, has openly refused to accept that the right to strike is implicitly contained in Convention 87. Many attempts to resolve the conflict with the trade unions group failed. In early November, the Governing Body of the ILO referred the case to the International Court of Justice (ICJ) in the Hague. The Governing Body decided that after receiving the advisory opinion of the ICJ, it would consider appropriate follow-up action. It is totally uncertain what the outcome will look like. And it may well be doubted whether the ILO might succeed in passing a new Convention on the right to strike if the ICJ denies that the right to strike is implied in Convention 87.

2.3 The Problem of Individualisation and Isolation

If individuals and collectives are not perceived as inseparable parts of one entity, it is impossible to understand how much the quality of the individual position of workers depends on collective strength. And it is exactly this collective strength which is in danger. As we all know, labour law is a product of industrialisation. It has been developed in view of a social and economic reality which is no longer the reality of today. The point of reference for the development of labour law was the Fordist model.[7] The workplace was embedded in a factory of manufacturing industry, a more or less large unit, where employees - mainly blue-collar and only to a small extent white-collar - did not work in splendid isolation but as a collective entity. The workforce - at least in principle - was relatively homogeneous, as were the employees' interests. Continuity and stability were a characteristic feature of employment. Homogeneous interests of the workforce as well as the experience of being part of the collective were ideal preconditions for collectivisation.

In today's post-industrial era, practically everything in this scenario has disappeared. The factory as a location where employees cooperate with each other is eroding to an increasing extent. Outsourcing, networking, sub-contracting and similar dislocating strategies are on the agenda. The enterprise is often turned into a merely virtual

6. *See also* M. Weiss, *Re-inventing Labour Law*, in G. Davidov & B. Langille (eds), *The Idea of Labour Law*, New York 2011, 43-56 (43).
7. For an explanation *see* D. Watson, *Fordism: A Review*, Labor History 2019, 144-159.

entity. Manufacturing is becoming an ever smaller part of the economy, and the service sector is increasing. Due to technological changes, work organisation has changed dramatically. The workforce is no longer homogeneous; it is fragmented and segmented into core groups and marginal groups, with less traditional employment and more and more new forms of work. The number of part-time jobs, fixed-term contracts and temporary agency workers is significantly increasing. There are growing numbers of economically dependent self-employed, so-called solo self-employed. This trend has dramatically increased the digitalisation of work. The example of the platform workers shows that there is no more link between the acting individuals; they – at least in principle – don't know each other and work in isolation. In short, even if the need for collectivisation is as urgent as ever, the conditions for collectivisation and the consciousness of being part of a collective are rapidly declining.

It is a universal trend that trade union membership is declining everywhere.[8] The big question, however, is whether and how individualisation can be overcome by patterns of collectivisation, whether such collectivisation can be embedded in existing structures of industrial relations, in particular collective bargaining, or whether new specific structures are to be developed, as for example new trade unions or alternative associations exclusively for platform workers or for groups of other new forms of work to promote their interests. There are attempts in both directions.[9] The question is whether alternative associations will be powerful enough to form an efficient counterweight against the platforms which, in many cases, are powerful oligopolies. This might, of course, be different for high-skilled platform workers who cannot easily be substituted than for low-skilled whose substitution is not a problem. And it also might depend on the possibility of how traditional forms of industrial action can be substituted or even strengthened by using digital tools.

An additional challenge is the fact that the workforce, again particularly in the context of crowd-working, is transnational. This leads to the question of whether efficient international collectives can be organised. This would need worldwide transnational regulation which is not easy to be developed. This problem, of course, is not new; it has been a challenge for workers' collectivisation along with the existence of transnational companies, but it has been intensified by digitalisation. In short, to make the point: as far as the chances of overcoming the individualisation and isolation are concerned, there are mainly open questions.

For those who are self-employed, there is an additional problem. According to the CJEU, they cannot be included in collective agreements because of the competition rules contained in the Treaty of the Functioning of the European Union (TFEU).[10] This archaic and narrow-minded view of competition law which is based on a reality of the

8. Interesting in this context is an analysis on the impact of austerity politics for trade unions in N. Bruun, K. Lörche & I. Schoemann (eds), *The Economic and Financial Crisis and Collective Labour Law in Europe*, Oxford/Portland, Oregon 2014.
9. *See* the comprehensive overview in A. Aloisi, *Negotl.iating the Digital Transformation of Work: Non-standards Workers' Voice, Collective Rights and Mobilization Practices in the Platform Economy*, European University Institute (EUI), Max Weber Program Working Paper (MWP) 2019, 1-41 (11-20).
10. CJEU judgment FNV Kunsten of 4 December 2014, Case 413/13.

past has to be overcome. At least the Commission of the European Union (EU) has understood the problem. It has developed guidelines[11] on how to reasonably cope with the problem. There is hope. Unfortunately, the EU cannot pass a directive on this question since it does not have the power to legislate collective bargaining.

2.4 The Informal Economy in the Global South

For a long time, it has been overlooked that the biggest problem is located in the Global South. In Africa, Latin America and Southeast Asia, the majority of people work in the informal economy. There is a lack of collective patterns; they exist only in a very rudimentary space. The international community and, in particular, the ILO is well aware of the problem. But the ILO is faced with the problem that rules developed for the formal economy cannot simply be transferred to the informal economy.[12] An attempt in this direction, the Convention on Domestic Workers, does not resolve the deficiency on the collective dimension. Instead of formalisation of the informal economy, a problematic slogan developed by the ILO, new alternative patterns have to be developed. The very diverse and promising attempts in this direction and the possibilities for the way ahead are well presented in a recent study published by the ILO.[13]

2.5 The Horizontal Dimension

So far, I have only discussed the need for collectivity as an instrument to defend and promote workers' interests against the employers' side. This vertical dimension, however, is only one part of the problem. There is also the horizontal dimension which has become more important as the workers' conditions have become more heterogeneous. The interests of full-timers might be totally different from those of part-timers, the interests of single parents might be significantly different from those of fathers or mothers of traditional families, or the interests of those who have to care for relatives may be very different from those who do not have such obligations. These few examples simply may give an idea of the enormous tensions within the workforce in modern societies. This has far-reaching implications: The internal structure of the collective has to be organised in a way which allows each group to have a voice and be represented. This task of integrating the different interests is very ambitious and requires internal democracy in each collectivity, be it a trade union or a representative body in the context of workers' participation.[14]

11. Guidelines on the application of Union competition law to collective agreements regarding the working conditions of solo self-employed persons 2022/C 374/02.
12. For this problem *see* A. Blackett, *Learning from the Past for the Future of International Law*, in B. Langille & A. Trebilcock, *Social Justice and the World of Work*, Oxford/London/New York/New Delhi/Sydney 2023, 35-42.
13. V. Schmidt et al., *Negotiatings by Workers in the Informal Economy*, ILO Working Paper 86, Geneva 2023.
14. For a very good presentation of this complex problem, *see* E. Kocher, *Individual Rights as a Critique of Labour Law Collectivity: Looking at Labour Law from the Perspective of Its Outsiders*,

3 CONCLUSION

My very brief and sketchy remarks may be sufficient to show that not only is the understanding of an inseparable link between individual and collective labour law no longer taken for granted, but that collectivisation as such is confronted with many challenges. To a great extent, this is due to the dramatic change in the reality of working life. The strike issue reminds us that power manifestations, as they were characteristic of the era of repression, are by no means over. And the indicated problems of the Global South may remind us that a Eurocentric perspective is not helpful in resolving problems in a globalised world. In short, to make the point: The collective dimension of labour law is coping with many problems. They are to be resolved in order to strengthen the efficiency of labour law as a whole.

in E. von Adamovich & M. Zernikow (eds), *Philosophical and Sociological Reflections on Labour Law in Times of Crisis*, Cambridge 2022, 115-128.

CHAPTER 3

Categories Mistake

Brian Langille

1 CATEGORY VERSUS CATEGORIES MISTAKES

Suppose I said to you, 'The number two is blue.' (In case you think there is an English-to-Italian translation problem here, suppose I said to you, in Italian, 'Il numero due e blu.') Or, suppose I said to you, 'The theory of relativity is eating breakfast.'

In 1949, the Oxford philosopher Gilbert Ryle coined the term 'category mistake' to capture the problem on display.[1] Something is obviously wrong with these expressions – but pinning down what exactly is going on behind such mistakes presents a complex philosophical problem.[2]

So, you will be relieved to learn that this paper is not about the exact philosophical nature of Category Mistakes in general, fascinating as that inquiry may be. It is, rather, about the very idea of legal categories as deployed by labour lawyers. The question is whether categories are what we need, do have, and can have in our labour law. Most critically, what sort of work can they do for us when 'the scope' of the law of work is in question? Some of the all-too-familiar categories deployed in this exercise are: 'employee,' 'self-employed,' 'independent contractor,' 'dependent contractor,' 'employer,' and so on.

My rather large question can be put this way: is the very idea of categories a mistake? That is the question I am asking. Hence, the title: 'Categories Mistake', not Category Mistake. I come to this inquiry by the route Adalberto has set out for our seminar here in Venice. He asks us to directly confront and consider the basic,

1. Gilbert Ryle, *The Concept of Mind* (Routledge 2009) 6 (Ryle's famous example was of a visitor to Oxford who, having been shown 'a number of colleges, libraries, playing fields, museums, scientific departments, and administrative offices' then asks, 'but where is the University?').
2. For an introduction, *see* Ofra Magidor, 'Category Mistakes', *The Stanford Encyclopedia of Philosophy* (5 July 2019), http://plato.stanford.edu/archives/fall2022/entries/category-mistakes (accessed 14 November 2023).

inescapable questions when we look at ourselves in the labour law mirror. We must ask: Do the 'categories' of labour law still exist? Should they? Can they?

Categories or dichotomies, such as individual versus collective, subordinate versus self-employed, public versus private, local versus global, labour law versus civil law and national versus European, are not only familiar but also fundamental to those who toil in the field of labour law. To ask whether they still exist is quite brave. There are, however, several ways to understand just how brave these questions are.

First, one might reasonably take the view that these familiar structures of our thinking are now, in 2023, not so clearly defined as they once were because changes in our world have now blurred them. On this view, in earlier halcyon days, labour law reality was easier to deal with because everyone was in their appropriate place, and thus, it was easier to be categorized along various lines. But globalization, financialization, fissuring, the gig economy, pandemics, and all the rest have 're-booted' our labour law reality and blurred the old lines. I think this is a sensible line of thought. It leads, as many commentators have pointed out, to the conclusion that the world, as we now find it, has confused us to such an extent that we are misapplying our categories and consequently making mistaken decisions. For example, we are labelling folks as contractors who are really employees, or we are missing the 'real employer.' It really is harder to know what an employer or employee might look like these days. As a result, we are making category mistakes – putting people in the wrong categories.

Second, one might go further and say that the world has changed so much that new dichotomies, classifications, and categories are necessary to fit our new reality. Such is a very common idea and has received a lot of attention. This line of thinking led, in Canada, for example, to the creation of the legal category of 'dependent contractor.'[3] You will no doubt recognize examples of this approach in your respective legal regimes.

But I wonder if these two important lines of inquiry, interesting and well-developed as they may be, take us as far as we need to go. In fact, I think they do not. The two understandings are about category mistakes in the sense of either: (1) having the wrong categories, or (2) misapplying the right ones.

I think Adalberto's questions require a deeper appreciation and suggest a deeper answer. Hence, the idea of Categories mistake: Our problem is not with applying our existing categories or inventing new ones. It is with our very understanding of our categories that this is not an easy problem; It is difficult.

Am I suggesting that we should not have categories? Perhaps not having categories is one way of seeing the fruits of my line of thinking. But, I think another, perhaps easier-to-digest way of understanding is: My view asks how legal categorization really operates. It asks how categories work, what makes them possible, how they

3. Why that label, rather than 'independent employee,' remains a mystery. But in any event – this act of legal creation was unnecessary, unhelpful, and testimony to the problems this essay tries to expose. *See* Brian A. Langille & Ben Mayer-Goodman, 'Hunting for Employees, Employers, Independent Contractors, Dependent Contractors and Other Figments of the Legal Imagination' (2025), 48 Dalhousie Law Journal (forthcoming) ('Hunting') and 'Don't Mess with Mr. In-Between' (2025), 48 Dalhousie Law Journal (forthcoming) ('Mr. In-Between').

figure in legal decisions, and how they are able, or unable, to deal with the challenges we face.

That is, my point is not that categories should not exist but that we have radically misunderstood them and how they work. This misunderstanding has been detrimental to our labour law. Finally, I say – perhaps this is the most surprising aspect – this is all rather unnecessary.

2 TWO APPROACHES TO CATEGORIES

There are two approaches to distinguish subordinate work from independent work – or employees from independent contractors. One familiar and the other less so. I am here on behalf of the less familiar – the underdog – in this fight.

2.1 The Familiar Approach

Labour law cases typically proceed as follows. Labour law holds (as most do) that it applies to 'employees' and 'employers.' An objection, most often by the alleged employer, takes the following form: 'This person who claims from me the benefits of the law in question cannot have them, and/or I do not have to provide them, because that person is not my employee and/or I am not their employer.'[4] To address that objection, the court or labour tribunal all too often proceeds with the following assumption. Employees and employers (and independent contractors, dependent contractors, or whatever other categorical terms are at play) are treated as real creatures inhabiting the real world. They can be found in this world just like species of animals (in the way we have lions and zebras) because they are real creatures, making a living out there in the world. The task of our courts and tribunals is thus to simply look for them in the field. To tell these creatures apart, we use well-known differentiating features. The features are, over time, gathered into a judicial 'field guide'. This is the legal test, almost always a 'multifactorial' one. Judges and other labour adjudicators, with field guide/legal test in hand, then go on safari and spot and identify the lions and zebras that are out there.

We can note, right off the bat, some downsides of this approach. For example, employers are incentivized to, and will start, dressing up zebras as lions. Or they may make zebras sign a contract saying, 'I am not a zebra, I am a lion.' And so on. All are rather unedifying, and all are made possible by this standard way of proceeding.

But those points are, for now, a distraction, back to the main point about hunting for employees and independent contractors.

There are many versions of these guidebooks in various jurisdictions. They all seem to have some very common boxes to be ticked for spotting different 'creatures.' For our purposes today, it does not matter which version of the test is set out in our field

4. Variations of this objection are not important for current purposes. Sometime employers claim the person claiming employee status is not an employee at all. Sometimes the claim is, 'well, they may be an employee, but I am not their employer.'

guide. The problem lies with the very concept of 'field guide,' not the particularities of any specific test or field guide. Our problem is rather large and may be described as 'methodological.' It is a problem not with the details but with this whole way of proceeding.

2.2 The Alternative Approach

Here is the problem with the familiar approach: Employees and independent contractors (and all the others in our cast of characters in the standard labour law drama) do not exist in the real world. They must be invented, imagined, and called into legal beings. As a result, we cannot go out hunting for them. They cannot be 'spotted.' They cannot be 'tested for.' Therefore, no list of factors can characterize their way of life and mark them off into separate species. Simply put, the problem is the very idea of a field guide.[5]

On this idea, we attempt to identify non-entities. We are looking for the man on the stairs who is not there. This way of putting it comes from a poem called Antigonish, in which we find:

> As I was going up the stair
> I met a man who wasn't there!
> He wasn't there again to-day!
> I wish, I *wish* he'd go away! [6]

But our law has developed in just this flawed way. Being an employee is, on the familiar approach, the 'reason' for applying our labour law to that person. This is wrong. 'Being an employee' is not, and cannot be, a reason to apply our labour law. This is so because such creatures do not exist in the real world. The main problem of the familiar approach is that it comes at the important legal issues at stake from the wrong direction. Being an employee is not the reason for applying our labour law to a person. It is, rather, a conclusion that labour law applies to that person.

In short, labour laws do not apply to certain persons because they are employees; They are employees because labour law applies to them. For too long, courts and tribunals have confused the direction of the legal causal arrow.

Many important consequences flow from this basic point. By mistaking the direction of the causal arrow, the currently dominant approach presupposes the existence of 'employees' and the other categories at play. For example, there are many cases in which decision-makers ask, 'Is this worker an employee or independent

---

5. The way we go about looking is well described by the hunters' methodology in Lewis Carroll, *The Hunting of the Snark* (The Porcupine's Quill 2019) 53:

> They sought it with thimbles, they sought it with care;
> They pursued it with forks and hope;
> They threatened its life with a railway-share;
> They charmed it with smiles and soap.

6. William Hughes Mearns, 'Antigonish', in Martin Gardner (ed.), *Best Remembered Poems* (Dover Publications 1992) 107.

contractor?' without any reference to the statutory or other legal issue in play.[7] Yet, the only light which can guide the interpretive arrow is the light of our labour law's purposes. A hunting or spotting 'test', no matter how multifactorial, is worse than useless unless this point is grasped. This is so because we cannot possibly identify which factors are relevant before we understand the purpose of our whole undertaking. In other words, no 'test' can tell us why certain factors are 'The Factors' without first identifying the test's fundamental purpose. As a close analysis reveals,[8] most of our cases - even the ones which come to sensible results - involve a bunch of factors wandering in a fog of faux legality uninformed by any rational purposive inquiry. The factors have slipped the moorings of rational thought and have taken on a life of their own - autonomous descriptions of a non-existent empirical world, apt for inclusion in a field guide.

But, once we discover and discard our flawed assumptions, we reveal something radical: Purpose is all we need and all there can be. It sheds light and is doing all the work. In applying labour law, we can work through rationally, why it is that this person falls within its scope and thus is an employee (or employer) for these purposes. The purpose of the law identifies the scope of the law. Accordingly, its legal scope cannot be declared through some list of factors for which we cannot provide an answer to the question, 'Why those factors? - what is that animates them?' In contrast, once we proceed rationally in light of our purposes, we have a rational yet simple way of identifying the truly relevant consideration: How do we best advance this purpose? Factors do not work.

Here is a short example. Suppose we have an anti-harassment provision in our labour law. We can say that law seeks to ensure a harassment-free working environment. This is its purpose. The provision is said as usual to apply to employees and employers. On the standard view, we would begin by hunting for employers and employees. We deploy our test and our guidebook to spot them. Having spotted or failed to spot them, we then declare whether complainants have remedies and whether respondents must provide remedies. End of story.

But the law exists for a reason; It is not the barking of an unhinged and arbitrary authority.[9] On the rational view, we do not start by hunting for imaginary creatures in the real world. We start with the question: 'What are we trying to do?'[10] We work from our law to the world, not the other way around.

7. *See*, for example, the cases discussed in Langille and Mayer-Goodman 'Hunting', *supra* n. 3.
8. Langille & Mayer-Goodman, *supra* n. 3.
9. For a very useful account, *see* T.R.S Allan, *Constitutional Justice: A Liberal Theory of the Rule of Law* (OUP 2001). *See also* Brian Langille, 'Speaking Rationality to Power', forthcoming in Vanessa MacDonnell, Gerald Chan & Stephen Bindman (eds), *Justice Rosalie Silberman Abella: A Life of Firsts* (University of Toronto Press 2025).
10. Recall Fuller and Perdue's paraphrasing of Nietzsche's observation, '[t]he most common sort of stupidity is to forget what it is one is trying to do' (Lon L. Fuller & William R. Perdue Jr, 'Reliance Interest in Contract Damages: 1' (1936) 46:1 Yale L J 52, 52) https://doi.org/10.2307/791632.

    Nietzsche's exact words are, 'During the journey we commonly forget its goal. Almost every profession is chosen and commenced as a means to an end but continued as an end in itself. Forgetting our objects is the most frequent of all acts of stupidity' (Friedrich Wilhelm Nietzsche, *Human, All-Too-Human* (RJ Hollingdale tr, 2nd edn, Cambridge University Press 1996) 360).

How can this methodology be put into practice? In our example, our goal is, simply put, to ensure a harassment-free working environment. Thus, in determining to whom this law extends protection, we do not need to make distinctions between employees and independent contractors. We do not hunt for them. Those creatures, and the distinction between them, do not exist for our purposes: 'Both' are protected. Whether an employer is harassing an 'employee' or an 'independent contractor' (if we insist on seeing these species) cuts no ice. There is no rational reason to think otherwise, given what we are trying to do. They are all 'employees,' if that is the word the law uses to describe those whom a given law protects. Think of it this way – if we are establishing wildlife sanctuaries free from human predation – we do not ask – is this only for the lions or the zebras?

Similarly, in determining who an 'employer' is, we ask – who can best advance our purpose? Who is in the best position to prevent harassment in the first place and remedy the situation when it does occur? That is your 'employer' – if we are stuck with that legal term.

This rational approach – based on purposes and pragmatism in achieving them – has other knock-on or collateral benefits, mentioned briefly above. Failure to use this rational method and sticking to the field-guide approach incentivize businesses to use their 'bargaining power' (and 'lawyering power') to construct working relationships that, at least on the surface, do not contain the identifying factors in the guide of labour laws. Such manipulations result in an elaborate set of imaginative but often sham arrangements attempting to fit the description of one field guide entry, e.g., independent contractor, but not another, e.g., employee. Alternatively, employers can respond to these incentives and go further than merely fiddling with the structure and terms of a contract and adopt the more radical strategy of avoiding contracting with their workers altogether. This process of 'decontractualization'[11] is at the core of what is now commonly called the 'fissuring' of work. This too is a load of nonsense from the purposive point of view. But, through its insistence on a form of legal nonsense and its continued re-publishing of its field guide, labour law has created the conditions for just this sort of 'goings on' and, as a result, contributed to its own demise: No legal purpose can ever be fully achieved if the underlying assumptions and methodology used to apply a law to the world functionally undermine, and incentivize the undermining of, the achievement of the law's own purposes.

Here is another way of making my basic point. At common law, the most common historical test or factor in the field guide for spotting an employer/employee is 'control.'[12] Classically stated, a person hired by another to perform work is an employee of the hirer, i.e., the employer if the hirer can dictate not only the result of the work but also dictate (control) how the result is brought about.

---

11. *See* Brian Langille, 'The Political Economy of Decency', in *ILO 100: Law for Social Justice* (ILO 2019) 503; Seth D. Harris & Alan B. Krueger, 'Proposal for Modernizing Labor Laws for Twenty-First-Century Work: The "Independent Worker"' (The Hamilton Project, 7 December 2015), www.hamiltonproject.org/publication/policy-proposal/a-proposal-for-modernizing-labor-laws-for-twenty-first-century-work-the-independent-worker (accessed 14 November 2023).
12. Which still and often rears it unhelpful head.

To reiterate, the correct question is not, 'Who can control another person in the real world.' Instead, the questions are: What is our purpose? And will including this person within the legal scope fulfil that purpose? This is how we find our employees. Similarly, the answer to 'who is the employer of this employee?' is also driven by the law's purposes. We ask: who is in the best position to advance that purpose by ensuring its fulfilment in the first place and remedying circumstances when there has been a failure in that regard? This is how we find our 'employer'. In a nutshell, we ask not who can control another person but who can control a particular purpose. We are not hunting in the real world with a guidebook in hand. We are making up and creating them. We are using the light of our legal purpose to rationally determine to whom the law applies. We are, thus, rationally willing to be a legal reality (or fiction, if you prefer). This is not spotting; it is creating.

2.3 So, If That Is Correct, Where Are We?

Where does all this lead us in our discussions about categories? In an important sense, we have turned the idea of categorization on its head. The standard and still prevalent idea is a legal decision declaring your 'membership' in a category ('employee'), i.e., the reason our labour laws apply to you. We now see that membership in a category ('employee'), to the contrary, is the statement of a conclusion that our labour law (better, that this part of our labour law) applies to you. The reason it does so lies in the law's purpose.

Categories are not doing the work. To say that Joe Smith is an employee is really like saying 'The number two is blue,' or 'The theory of relativity is eating breakfast.' Human beings are not employees. They can only be employees for specific purposes[13] Like 'the number 2 is blue' - can be meaningful in a certain context - for example, saying, while in Venice, 'the number 6 is blue' (meaning Vaporetto line 6 is the blue line on the Venice Vaporetto (Water Bus) map).

Here is the surprising bit. We have had, at least in the common law world, a door wide open to the alternative approach for a long time. Not only a door open to the alternative approach but a door which simultaneously and effectively closed the door to the familiar approach. Walking through that door should have altered the direction of the causal arrow. But we have not, at least not often, walked through that door. On those occasions in which we have, explicit reasoning and comments are very rare.[14] No one seems to have taken seriously the impact on the old pattern of thought.

The basic idea is that for many decades now, common law judges have been doing several remarkable things - without most of us quite grasping the importance of their wisdom.

13. *See* Ludwig Wittgenstein, *Philosophical Investigations* (G.E.M. Anscombe, P.M.S. Hacker & Joachim Schulte trs, 4th edn, Wiley-Blackwell 2009) at 33e-34e; Brian A. Langille & Guy Davidov, 'Beyond Employees and Independent Contractors: A View from Canada' (1999) 21:1 Comp Lab L & Pol'y J 7, 14.
14. E.g., *Robichaud v. Canada (Treasury Board)*, [1987] 2 SCR 84, 40 DLR (4th) 577.

First, they have, at least sometimes, glimpsed and deployed the central insight of the non-hunting, i.e., purposive approach – that there are no employees or employer out there (or on the stairs), the guidebook is useless, and a laser-sharp focus on purpose is and should be doing all the work. There are some remarkable examples[15] of this.

Moreover, in some cases, they have specifically spelt out the mode of thinking required to achieve sensible results. Here is one particularly useful case from Canada. In 1936, the Ontario Court of Appeal decided on *Carter v. Bell & Sons (Canada) Ltd.*[16] In that case, a firm in England appointed Mr Bell as 'superintendent of agencies' to lead their expansion into the prairie provinces of Canada by selecting and training agents to sell the firm's products, being paid on commission for his own sales and 5% 'cut' of the commissions earned by the agents. To do this job, Mr Bell had to move, along with his wife and children, to western Canada. The issue was whether Mr Bell was, in these circumstances, entitled to reasonable notice of termination. The Court reasoned as follows:

> The fact that the plaintiff was entering a new territory as representative of the defendant and was endeavouring to create a market for the defendant's products and that to their knowledge he was taking his wife and children with him to the West indicate a relationship that could not be terminated at will by either party. The test often applied in cases in which it is sought to make a master liable for the acts of the servant is not applicable here. *The question is not the same.* In the one case the inquiry is as to the liability of the master for the servant's acts. In the other the inquiry is as to the existence of an implied contract to terminate the relationship only upon reasonable notice. Here there was no such contract as would make the employer liable for the agent's acts, but I think this is by no means conclusive as against the plaintiff. The contract was one which I think could only be terminated upon reasonable notice.[17]

'The question is not the same.' Those are words for the ages. They alone are enough. Once we see what is going on in *Carter*, the jig is up for the hunting/field guide/spotting approach. The question is not whether there is a 'Mr. Bell the employee' out there. There are just different labour law purposes: Some of which bring Mr Bell within their ambit (reasonable notice); others do not (vicarious liability). This is what we have. This is all that we need. This is all that is possible. What more do we want?

15. One of my favourites is *Denham v. Employers' Mutual Assurance Ltd*, [1955] 2 QB 437, [1955] 2 All ER 561. That case is an old decision by the English Court of Appeal – with a very familiar (triangular, two employers – one employee) structure. Mr Clegg died at the brickworks where he worked and assisted a drilling company that had come on site to do some drilling. There were two issues – which firm, brickworks or drilling – was liable? The drilling company is in charge of the fatal operations. With control comes responsibility. For that purpose, the drilling company was the employer and Mr Clegg was the drilling company's employee, although the brickworks was his long-time employer).

    When it came to the second question – under which insurance policy, employer, or public liability, was payment for that liability to be made, the answer is under their public liability policy. That is, for that second purpose, he was not the employee of the drilling company but, rather, a member of the public.

    In short, two different purposes in one case lead to two different results. Great stuff. But rather fatal for the hunting approach.
16. [1936] OR 290, [1936] 2 DLR 438.
17. *Ibid.*, Justice Middleton (emphasis added).

Now, let me finish by introducing you to what might be a very radical - and potentially radically important legal decision. It is a relatively recent decision of the Supreme Court of Canada: *British Columbia Human Rights Tribunal v. Schrenk* in 2017.[18] *Schrenk* is a typically nasty case of harassment at work. It happened on a construction project (Note: this is quite interesting in itself as such projects often have multiple employers and sub-contracting and sub-sub-contracting arrangements. They are, in a word, fissured, to an exquisite degree. Solving problems in this context may be very instructive in other non-construction fissured workplaces).

Mr Schrenk conducted a campaign of anti-Muslim and homophobic harassment against his victim at the worksite - the site of a road construction project in British Columbia. Such conduct was clearly prohibited by the British Columbia Human Rights Code - the issue was not about the conduct - but about the relationships or lack thereof among the many players on the construction site. Against whom did the victim have a remedy? The perpetrator? The perpetrator's employer? The perpetrator's employer's employer? His own employer?

The owner of the project and the top-of-the-chain contractor was the local municipality, Delta. The municipality hired Clemas as the general contractor to actually carry out the project and Omega, an engineering firm, to supervise Clemas. The contract between Delta and Clemas specified that Omega had certain supervisory powers over the construction employees of Clemas, including the right to ask for the removal of any Clemas worker who appeared 'to be incompetent or to act in a disorderly or intemperate manner'.[19]

Clemas, the construction company, employed Mr Schrenk as a site foreman and superintendent. The victim of the harassment campaign was Mr Sheikhzadeh-Mashgoul, a civil engineer working for Omega whose work gave him supervisory powers over Schrenk.

The victim and perpetrator were employed by two different employers on site. Both employers were contractors with Delta, the municipality at the top of the contracting pyramid. Very interestingly, no employer-employee relationship exists between victim and perpetrator. No contractual relationship of any sort. Nor any relationship between the two immediate employers who contracted separately with the municipality.

Moreover, the victim is not subordinate to the perpetrator - just the reverse - the victim, as a consulting engineer on the project, has workplace power over the construction workforce, including the perpetrator.

All very interesting. No employment contract - or contact of any sort. Instead, the de facto power dynamic is the reverse of the standard idea of subordination - this is a case of the subordinate party harassing a person with power over him.

At the Supreme Court of Canada, the majority held that the victim had a remedy under the Human Rights Code against the perpetrator and the perpetrator's employer. Leaving aside lots of details, we can simply remark this is a purposive view - the object is a harassment-free workplace. The victim was clearly entitled to that. The duty

18. 2017 SCC 62 [*Schrenk*].
19. *Ibid.*, [5].

extended not just to the victim's employer (who had committed no wrong at all) – but to other employees on site. That is very interesting in itself. But there was more. The duty extended not only to other employees but also to employees of other employers. Note – if your purpose is a harassment-free workplace – this seems pretty much a requirement in a multiemployer workplace. What we see here is a horizontal liberation from the idea of contract.

The dissent held the victim could not have a remedy against the perpetrator – but only a remedy against the perpetrator's employer (Clemas – the construction company, and possibly/logically, also against top contractor Delta, the employer of the perpetrator's employer, although the claim was dropped). This too is a very interesting and quite radical holding.

The idea here is based on the pragmatic approach; the question is who can advance the purpose of a harassment-free workplace (what we used to call the 'who is the employer question?'). The answer is the entity that can prevent violations in advance (through contracting, training, and hiring practices) and deal with them when they occur (through contractual and disciplinary measures, etc.) This is a very important idea in the world of supply chains. Here, the parties liable are one or two links up the chain. Here is how the dissent put it:

> It is meant to cover *all* forms of workplace discrimination to which a worker is susceptible. However, it trains its regulatory guns on those responsible for intervening and halting the events in question. Where those responsible for guaranteeing discrimination-free workplaces fail to intervene to prevent or correct discrimination ... (the Code) ... is engaged. Since there will always be an entity in any work context that is responsible for ensuring that workers enjoy a discrimination-free environment, this reading ... does not thwart the purpose of the Code.[20]

This is a terrific demonstration of the correct, non-field guide approach to what we used to call the 'who is the employer?' question. It must be because there is no contract of any sort here. Note that its logic applies not only to Clemas but also to Delta. If Clemas refused to clean up the mess created by Schrenk, then Delta could 'clean up' Clemas. Consider the import of the highlighted passage for supply chain liability – and replace anti-discrimination with employment standards. This is a horizontal escape from the contract plus a vertical escape as well.

But both the majority and dissent spend a lot of time on technical legal analysis. So, perhaps the most interesting judgment is the solo concurring opinion of Abella – who is now retired but for decades Canada's leading labour law judge. Holding, with the majority but for different reasons, that both the perpetrator and perpetrator's employer were responsible, she wrote:

> The purpose ... is to protect employees from the indignity of discriminatory conduct, verbal or otherwise, in a workplace. *Discrimination can and does occur in the absence of an economic power imbalance. It cannot depend on technical lines of authority which may end up defeating the goals of human rights legislation.* While employment discrimination is often, not surprisingly, focused on the ability of

20. *Ibid.*, [123].

> employers to subject complainants to discriminatory conduct as a condition of employment, *all* individuals have the right to be protected from discrimination in the workplace, including those in a position of authority.[21]

I suggest that the highlighted remark be taken seriously. It is an invitation to pursue the thoughts in this paper. The way I read that invitation is that we combine both the majority and the dissent. If we do, we end up with a purposive and functional approach to both who is covered by and who is responsible for this labour law purpose. Note also – we are very much on track for a human-centred approach to the law of work. All without a field guide. All without a category mistake. And all without a mistaken view of how categories work.

21. *Ibid.*, [90] (emphasis added).

CHAPTER 4

The Global and Local Approach

Antoine Lyon-Caen

Sometimes, it's good to hold up a mirror and see what image it reflects.

The mirror is at a distance. It is not certain that it will give an exact image. But the distance makes it possible to reflect on the subject or object whose image the mirror reflects. It is tempting to say, in the words of a French playwright who had his moments of glory over half a century ago, that the mirror thinks before returning the image.

When the mirror is held up to a discipline – such as labour law – it enables an epistemological effort to be made. This, it seems to me, is the gamble of those who conceived this book and the seminar from which it emerged.

In this epistemological endeavour, it is not surprising that we come across categories.

We are not talking about the categories used in the language of law, categories that are usually reduced to notions. Rather, we are interested in the categories used by the language of lawyers. And it is not so much the language of dogmatic jurists, concerned with describing and classifying, as the language of jurists concerned with providing a greater understanding of the law, that needs to be analysed.

It is in this language that the expressions 'global' and 'local', often identified with 'national', appear. The pair they form is singular. It unites adjectives, which invites us to specify the objects that we claim to qualify with these adjectives 'global' and 'local'.

It is proposed that these objects be identified as regulations (or possibly governance) to bring them closer to labour law.

At first sight, 'global' and 'local' in relation to regulation or governance refer to scales.

At first sight, they seem to describe very different conceptions of regulation. The pair is said to be driven by tension.

However, in a second movement, the combination of the two scales corresponds to more harmonious and promising conceptions of regulation.

1 OPPOSITION

Over the last twenty or thirty years, abundant literature has examined the advent and manifestations of global governance. Books have been published, and courses taught under the title Global Law.

It is probably more accurate to speak of a movement, a trend, or a process of globalisation, which is the result of two main factors. On the one hand, the movement has been driven by a new configuration of capitalism, emphasising what it is enlightening to call a 'deterritorialisation' of markets, whether for goods, services or financial markets. It is the production processes themselves that have become deterritorialised with the emergence of value chains.

This trend towards the abolition of borders, or rather a change in the meaning of borders, affects people only very sparingly, except undoubtedly in certain regional areas such as the area corresponding to the European Union. This movement would not have produced the results it has without the other factor: the support of States for the dismantling of activities whose regulations their institutions were trying to ensure.

It soon became quite clear that this change of scale, which underlies globalisation, has not led to the institutions inherited from national experiences being reproduced at a global level.

In other words, this change of scale marks a profound change in the way regulation is conceived. Instead of governments based on elective legitimacy, specialised international organisations or public or private agencies are taking charge of regulation, if not self-regulation.

As for standards, they are, to a large extent, of private creation. When they are the product of international organisations, they are imprecise, open to diverse interpretations and not very effective.

The move towards globalisation of regulation has met with resistance. National regulation persists. It is even asserted, sometimes forcefully.

The social state – the welfare state – was built within the framework delimited by national borders in consideration of the territory they circumscribe. A distinction is drawn between those who are entitled to social rights and those who are excluded.

Globalisation has highlighted both the impossibility of establishing social protection at an international level and the need to preserve the protection that was then enshrined in the framework of the nation-state, especially when it came to meeting the basic needs of vulnerable people.

It is true that globalisation has been accompanied by an erosion of social protection systems. But this erosion has fuelled criticism of the globalisation movement. This is the most striking example of the tension between the 'global' and the 'local'.

Europe is experiencing, to its detriment, calls for the restoration of national control over economic and social developments. Few Member States of the European Union are immune to these demands. These demands for a return to the sovereignty of national states often blossom into frenzied demagoguery. When they were followed up, they did not bring economic and social progress or guarantee respect for freedoms.

Unlike this aggressive return to the 'local', there is another movement that deserves attention.

It seems that the time has come to see the global and the local no longer as opposites but rather as a combination.

2 COMBINATION

To conceive of a combination of levels of regulation, we must first distance ourselves from the most radical positions: the future cannot be drawn as a promise of either the necrosis of the State or the restoration of the State.

How can we articulate the 'global' and the 'local' in such a way that their combination is virtuous?

The main way is to integrate globalisation into national territories and institutions. In other words, to 'denationalise' local regulation. This is the only way to express a sense of solidarity or, at best, an awareness of interdependence.

Three areas can be used to illustrate this 'denationalisation' of national regulation. The area that speaks for itself is that of migration, thanks to the findings of numerous research studies. Migration is a chain, a process that can only be understood and regulated if we take into account both the countries of emigration, their situation and difficulties, and the countries of immigration. Unilateral national regulation is bound to fail sooner or later.

Another eloquent area is the regulation of the Internet.

But the area where innovation is most remarkable is that of controls on the activities of multinational companies. The recognition by certain courts and, from now on, by certain national laws of a duty of vigilance on the part of the head company of a group or network, which is not limited to the national territory, is a good illustration of this virtuous link between the 'local' (creation of the obligation) and the 'global' (extent of the obligation).

The ecological imperative also highlights the urgent need for a new way of linking the 'global' and the 'local'.

To put it simply, the temptation is to say that nothing is possible without global regulation, given that climate, air and water issues are so intractable that they cannot simply be dealt with locally, but that nothing is possible without local regulation.

Just think of the need not only to establish shorter value chains but also of the growing need for local arrangements to guarantee urgent transitions.

Isn't combining the 'global' and the 'local' a plea for complexity? It certainly is. But isn't making complexity felt and understood the first step towards simplicity?

CHAPTER 5

Do the Categories of Labour Law Still Exist?: Labour Law Versus Civil Law – Contractual Autonomy in Labour Law

Mariella Magnani

1 LABOUR AND CIVIL LAW: A UNIVERSAL SUBJECT

The decision to devote an international seminar to the categories of labour law, in the light of the changes that have taken place and those that are in progress, is very timely.

Indeed, I have not been asked to talk about differing or opposing categories of labour law (for instance, self-employment versus employment) but rather to discuss the relationship between labour law as a whole and civil law or private law, or the general law of contract to make the subject more understandable even to common law scholars.

This relationship is everywhere[1] a classic subject of reflection for labour lawyers, who are continually in search of their own identity. And the debate resurfaces regularly, albeit with new perspectives. I will deal with the subject from the point of view of the Italian legal system because it is the one I know best, but I believe that most of my observations can be applied to all countries, especially those of continental Europe.

2 MANDATORY RULES AND FREEDOM OF CONTRACT

Modern labour law, which here is taken to encompass employment law and collective labour law, arose from a protesting stance against civil law, notably against the

1. Including common law systems: *see* H. Collins, *Contractual Autonomy*, A. Bogg et al. eds, *The Autonomy of Labour Law*, London, Hart Publishing, 2015, 45 ff.

reduction of labour relations to the category of commercial contracts, which regard labour as a market commodity.

In employment relationships, it is not just workers' assets that are at stake but also they themselves as people. It is precisely the inseparability of the worker's person from the work performed that demands special regulation which subjects individual autonomy to certain limits (to the extent required by the need to protect the worker). Hence, the set of rules that constitute labour law characterised by the inderogability of most of its norms.

If civil law is the realm of individual autonomy and freedom of contract – the norms are merely default and seldom mandatory – labour law is the realm of mandatory rules, both in the form of laws and collective agreements, which, in principle, are also inderogable.

Obviously, we can find a series of further aspects which mark the key features of the discipline.[2] But the one mentioned above is the founding marker of its autonomy.

In modern labour law, however, the framework is more complex because the mandatory rules governing the employment relationship are increasingly delegated by the law to collective agreements.

This is a further characteristic of labour law compared to civil law, i.e., the pluralistic system of the sources since, alongside the law, we have collective agreements whose rules are, as already said, mandatory, just as the rules prescribed by the law. This opens the fascinating chapter of collective labour law which has at its centre the hybrid entity of the collective agreement, which is indeed both an agreement and a normative act.

For many scholars, trade union law is (or perhaps was) the essence of labour law and so it was (UK) and still is (USA) in Anglo-Saxon countries, consistent with the procedural conception of law typical of those systems.

It is significant that in the United States, the term 'labour law' is reserved for the legislation regulating trade union organisations and their characteristic activities.

The core of American labour law is the process of collective bargaining: it therefore contains the procedural provisions for the establishment of the rules governing the employment relationship rather than the substantive provisions.

The Anglo-Saxon theory of industrial pluralism conceives (or rather conceived, as it is in reality outdated) industrial relations as a self-governing process in which management and labour act like political parties in a representative democracy.

In this model, collective bargaining represents an autonomous 'realm', resistant to the intrusion of statutory rights, and this explains why the model of legislative protection of individuals (which became widespread in the US from 1980 onwards, under the Reagan and Bush administrations) is seen as an alternative to the model of

2. I will not discuss the role of contract as a technical means to legitimise and, at the same time, limit managerial power. For a recent defence of the benefits of the contract as a source of the limits of subordination, in contrast to those who consider the employment contract as marking the inferiority of the employee, *see* A. Viscomi, *Autonomia privata tra funzione e utilità sociale: prospettive giuslavoristiche*, Diritti Lavori Mercati, 2012, 441 ff. *See also* L. Mengoni, *L'influenza del diritto del lavoro sul diritto civile*, Giornale di Diritto del Lavoro e di Relazioni Industriali, 1990, 5 ff.

collective rights protection (and in particular to the process of collective bargaining). The same difficulty was felt in the UK, when, from the 1960s onwards, a considerable amount of legislation regulating the employment relationship was passed, so much so that it was even difficult to base the rights deriving from protective legislation on the contract. Consequently, their violation was treated as a tort rather than as a breach of contract.

Something different happened in continental Europe, and in Italy in particular, where law and collective agreements have complemented each other in the regulation of labour relations, and this can be considered one of the elements characterising the European social model.

3 THE EROSION OF THE PRINCIPLE OF INDEROGABILITY IN LABOUR LAW

Since the 1980s, in the Italian system, we have observed the erosion of the principle of inderogability either directly or indirectly.

In many cases, the legislature has assigned the task of flexibilising the mandatory legal rules in specific fields to collective bargaining (in the field of transfer of undertakings, part-time employment contracts, fixed-term contracts, annual leave, temporary work, collective dismissals, etc.); it has been considered possible to derogate from the provisions of collective agreements in the context of labour disputes being resolved by arbitration; the possibility for the parties to enter into a non-standard contract, such as a fixed-term contract, has been enlarged.

Obviously, widening the possibility of using non-standard contracts is not a direct attack on the principle of inderogability. However, there is no doubt that, although not on a formal level, the broad freedom to resort to flexible types of work breaks up the monolithic character of mandatory regulation.[3]

Moreover, following the profound crisis that Italy experienced in 2011, through the controversial Law No. 148/2011, company (or plant) and local collective agreements, signed by the most representative trade unions, allowed to derogate not only from national collective agreements but also from the mandatory provisions of the law in a wide range of matters. The only limits provided by the law are that these agreements have 'specific' aims (like increasing or protecting employment, improving the quality of employment contracts, tackling undeclared work, increasing competitiveness and wages, etc.) and that, above all, they comply with the provisions of the Italian Constitution, as well as European Union (EU) law and international labour conventions.

This provision is controversial because, according to some scholars, it has reversed the hierarchy of labour law sources, as company agreements prevail over national collective agreements, and company and local agreements prevail over the law in the broad fields where the provision applies.

3. On the implications of using different types of contract in Anglo-Saxon systems *see* G. Davidov, *Non-waivability in Labour Law*, Oxford Journal of Legal Studies, 2020, Vol. 40, No. 3, 482 ff. https://doi.org/10.1093/ojls/gqaa016.

It's worth underlining that such 'power' is attributed only to the lower level of collective bargaining, not to national agreements, thus expressing a sort of preference for this level of bargaining. The same has happened in some other countries of continental Europe.

4 CIVIL LAW PROTECTION TECHNIQUES IN 'ASYMMETRIC' CONTRACTS

On the other hand, civil/private law has also changed: we can observe protection techniques that, while not identical to those of labour law, mimic them, not only in the field of consumer protection (*see* the Italian consumer code) but also in contracts signed by businesses with unequal bargaining power (*see*, for instance, the case of sub-contracting).

'Asymmetric' contracts are contracts in which, due to imbalances in information or other weaknesses, a business, due to its size, suffers from a lack of bargaining strength in its relations with a dominant business.[4]

The impetus for change here, as we know, comes principally from the European institutions. The European Commission, in its Green Paper issued between 2006 and 2007, states 'some businesses, such as individual entrepreneurs and small businesses may sometimes be in a similar situation as consumer when they buy certain goods or services, which raises the question whether they should benefit to a certain extent from the same protection provided for to consumers'.[5]

And it is interesting to note that a similar protection provided for in the case of businesses with unbalanced bargaining power in some countries has been extended to the self-employed. In Italy, for example, the so-called Statute of Self-Employed Work (Law No. 81 of 2017) protects the self-employed in commercial transactions by prohibiting the abuse of economic dependence and providing for the nullity of clauses resulting from it.

Another example is the law (Law No. 49/2023 – which recently amended Law No. 172/2017) on 'fair remuneration' for professionals who negotiate with banks and insurance companies, with companies with more than fifty employees or with public administrations, on the assumption of an imbalance in bargaining power.

Incidentally, the European Commission[6] itself, for the purpose of recognising a right to collective bargaining, is oriented to consider as a specific category – distinct from false self-employed workers (as defined by the Court of Justice of the European

4. *See* E. Roppo, *From Consumer Contracts to Asymmetric Contracts: A Trend in European Contract Law?*, European Review of Contract Law, 2019, 304 ff. https://doi.org/10.1515/ercl.2009.304.
5. European Commission, *Green Paper on the Review of the Consumer Acquis*, 8 February 2007, COM (2006) 744 final, Brussels.
6. *See Communication from the Commission* of 30 September 2022 (2022/C 374/02), Guidelines on the application of Union competition law to collective agreements regarding the working conditions of solo self-employed persons.

Union (CJEU))[7] – 'solo self-employed' workers because they 'may lack sufficient bargaining power'.[8]

The aim of the above-mentioned legislation is to preserve the benefits resulting from the contract for the weaker party: unfair clauses are null and void while the contract remains otherwise valid.

It is interesting to observe that, as scholars have underlined, these provisions, in particular the provision for the nullity of unfair clauses, as determined by a court, are not considered to be in conflict with the contractual autonomy of the parties; rather, they are intended to ensure its effectiveness.

As scholars observe,[9] in order to safeguard contractual autonomy, the law may not limit it *ex ante* but requires a court to evaluate *ex post* its actual exercise through scrutiny of the balance of the arrangement that the parties have given to their mutual interests.

In essence, in relations governed by civil law, 'contractual justice' is pursued not through limitations *ex ante* of the content of the contract but through the intervention of a court to remove *ex post* any unfairness deriving from abuses of bargaining power.

5 RETHINKING THE REASONS FOR LABOUR LAW INDEROGABILITY

The aim of protecting the weaker party emerging in private law leads us to go deeper into the reasons for labour law inderogability. Well, there are two reasons for the rationale behind the inderogability of labour law: one is 'subjective' and is linked to the unbalanced bargaining power of the workers; the other is 'objective' and is linked to the importance of the goods and interests involved in labour relations (for instance, the health and safety of the worker)[10] which are not negotiable.[11]

This justifies us in rethinking the true paradigm of labour law – its inderogability – and the tendency to distinguish the rules that must remain mandatory because they safeguard the person of the worker from those designed to protect the weaker party which can instead be waived where the asymmetry of power is eliminated, perhaps also thanks to the achievements of collective bargaining.

7. CJEU, 4 December 2014, C-413/13, *FNV Kunsten Informatie en Media v. Staat der Nederlanden*.
8. A 'solo self-employed person', as defined by the European Commission, is '*a person who does not have an employment contract or who is not in an employment relationship and who relies primarily on his or her own personal labour for the provision of the services concerned*'. For a discussion on the Commission's guidelines *see* A. Perulli, *Il 'lavoro personale' nel prisma del diritto dell'Unione Europea*, Rivista Italiana di Diritto del Lavoro, 2023, I, 63 ff.
9. *See* A. Albanese, *L'uguaglianza formale e sostanziale nel mercato tra libertà e giustizia 'contrattuale'*, AA.VV., *Per i cento anni dalla nascita di Renato Scognamiglio*, Jovene, Napoli, 2022, 3 ff.
10. We could also add the protection of dignity, but this would open Pandora's box, since it would be difficult to define the content of the concept.
11. For a more detailed analysis *see* M. Magnani, *Il diritto del lavoro e le sue categorie. Valori e tecniche nel diritto del lavoro*, Cedam, Padova, 2005, 19 ff.; *see also* Davidov, *Non-waivability in Labour Law*, *supra* n. 3.

6 THE ENHANCEMENT OF INDIVIDUAL AUTONOMY IN LABOUR LAW

In the Italian legal system, there are signs today of an enhancement in individual autonomy, which was previously attempted through the so-called Biagi reform.[12]

One clear example is the worker's right to derogate from the rules which prohibit his assignment to a lower job grade, if interests laid down by law occur (such as job retention in the event of firm restructuring, health reasons, changing personal objectives) and with the assistance of a third party (union representative or public official) who guarantees the authenticity of her or his consent.

We could also add the individual agreement that, in part-time contracts, allows the employer, in exchange for greater remuneration, and, again, with the assistance of a third party, to increase working hours or change their scheduling (so-called flexibility clauses). Recently, Decree Law No. 48 of 2023, significantly adopted on Labour Day by the Italian government, allows the parties, where there is no relevant provision in a collective agreement, to agree on the continuation or the renewal of a fixed-term contract (for up to 24 months).[13]

An additional, very oft-cited example of greater recognition of individual autonomy is the provision (Article 19, Law No. 81/2017) related to remote working, which requires a specific individual agreement not only to authorise it but also to regulate it. This agreement governs the performance of work outside the workplace also with regard to the exercise of the employer's managerial power, rest periods and the technical and organisational means of securing disconnection.[14]

Notwithstanding these examples, we are far from the recognition of freedom of contract[15] or the general possibility for an individual to derogate from legal rules or collective agreement terms (not even with the assistance of a third party, as some legal scholars propose).[16]

Rather, we are in the field of a kind of regulatory 'customisation' in specific matters, such as working time, that forsakes standardisation resulting from mandatory rules.

12. The White Paper of 2001, published prior to the reform, envisaged the need to modify, through such techniques as multiple-choice collective bargaining, the existing legal order which *'prevents an employer and a worker from agreeing working conditions which derogate not only from the law but also from collective agreements, except in the ambiguous case of more favourable conditions'*: *See 'Libro Bianco sul mercato del lavoro in Italia. Proposte per una società attiva e per un lavoro di qualità'* Rome, October 2001, 35.
13. Even the 24-month limit can be extended individually up to a maximum of 36 months if the agreement is reached in front of a third party, who guarantees the authenticity of the consent.
14. In this case it is also held that, since the manner in which managerial power is exercised outside the company forms part of the agreement, subordination too is subject to individual negotiation with a view to ensuring the worker's greater capacity/freedom: *see* A. Perulli, *'La soggettivazione regolativa' nel diritto del lavoro*, Diritto delle Relazioni Industriali, 2019, 153, who considers remote working as the recognition of a special form of subordination.
15. As I have pointed out in my above-mentioned monograph in n. 11, labour law would no longer be recognisable as such without a core set of imperative norms. *See* Magnani, *supra* n. 11.
16. *See* Viscomi, *supra* n. 2.

In fact, an influential number of legal scholars[17] have begun to argue in favour of a shift in mindset and political philosophies, such as the capability approach as well as the non-domination approach[18] (which are also being discussed in the Italian system), suggesting the need for greater individual autonomy.

There is an interesting debate in the international literature on the philosophical foundations of labour law. This discussion from the Anglo-Saxon world[19] is moving to the countries of continental Europe and particularly to Italy, albeit taking on a different connotation.

In the Anglo-Saxon world, where freedom of contract should be the rule and neo-liberal economic doctrine is very much supported, it is aimed at identifying the justification of labour law. By contrast, in countries like Italy, where labour law, thanks to mandatory rules of law and collective agreements, is well rooted, it seems to me that it leads, paradoxically, to the affirmation of a need to increase the spaces for individual autonomy.

7 HOW TO RECONCILE EQUALITY AND FREEDOM IN LABOUR LAW

Arguments in favour of 'a shift in mindset' regarding contractual autonomy are not new in labour law scholarship. Since the 1990s, we have been witnessing attempts to enhance individual autonomy against the 'colonization' of the individual by the apparatus of the welfare state: mention can be made, for example, of Massimo D'Antona's seminal essay of 1991,[20] along the lines of Spiros Simitis.[21]

However, scholarly debate has not really progressed since then due, on the one hand, to the opposition of more radical legal scholars, who see in this 'challenge' a neo-liberal return to contract; but also, on the other hand, due to the difficulties in finding ways and means to reconcile equality and freedom in labour law. This is the main issue underlying the recognition of individual autonomy in labour law.

17. *See* R. Del Punta, *Labour Law and the Capability Approach*, IJCLLIR, 2022, 383 f. https://doi.org/10.54648/ijcl2016020; Perulli, *La 'soggettivazione regolativa' nel diritto del lavoro, supra* n. 14; B. Caruso & L. Zappalà, *Il diritto del lavoro 'tridimensionale': valori e tecniche di fronte ai mutamenti dei luoghi di lavoro*, R. Del Punta ed., *Valori e tecniche nel diritto del lavoro*, Firenze University Press, 2022, 29 ff.
18. On the importance of domination theory *see* D. Cabrelli & R. Zahn, *Theories of Domination and Labour Law: An Alternative Conception for Intervention?*, International Journal of Comparative Labour Law and Industrial Relations, 2017, 339 ff. https://doi.org/10.54648/ijcl2017015 as well as G. Davidov, *Subordination vs. Domination: Exploring the Differences*, International Journal of Comparative Labour Law and Industrial Relations, 2017, 365 ff. https://doi.org/10.54648/ijcl2017016.
19. *See* H. Collins, G. Lester & V. Mantouvalou eds., *Philosophical Foundations of Labour Law*, Oxford University Press, 2018.
20. *See* M. D'Antona, *L'autonomia individuale e le fonti del diritto del lavoro*, in Giornale di Diritto del Lavoro e di Relazioni Industriali, 1991, 455 ff.; more recently, along the same lines *see* Viscomi, *supra* n. 2.
21. *See* S. Simitis, *Il diritto del lavoro e la riscoperta dell'individuo*, Giornale di Diritto del Lavoro e di Relazioni Industriali, 1990, 87 ff.

So, what are these *ways* and *means*? Is waivability assisted by a third party a model which can be generalised (as some have suggested)?[22] Or should it be accompanied by a catalogue of non-waivable rights?[23] And what are these rights? And their sources? In this respect, does the above-mentioned Article 8 of Italian Law No. 148/2011 suggest a possible way forward?

In brief, labour law scholars should go beyond the 'if' perspective and address the 'how' perspective, as seems to me to be the case in the Anglo-Saxon world where, if one discusses the philosophical foundations of labour law or precisely thanks to this debate, one also discusses the boundaries of imperative protection.[24]

22. *See* Viscomi, *supra* n. 2.
23. *See* C.R. Sunstein, *Human Behavior and the Law of Work*, Virginia Law Review, 2001, Vol. 87, No. 2, 205 ff. https://doi.org/10.2307/1073888; C. Estlund, *Between Rights and Contract: Arbitration Agreements and Non-Compete Covenants as a Hybrid Form of Employment Law*, University of Pennsylvania Law Review, 2006, 379 ff. https://doi.org/10.2307/40041310.
24. *See* Davidov, *supra* n. 3, for an interesting discussion of the benefits and conditions of 'tailored arrangements' that should replace the 'one size fits all system'.

CHAPTER 6

Collective Redundancies in European and Italian Jurisprudential Interpretation

Alberto Pizzoferrato

1 THE EUROPEAN AND ITALIAN CONCEPT DEVELOPMENT

The conceptual landscape in Europe and Italy has evolved in a contrasting yet highly productive manner, focusing on the concepts of workers, employers, public administration, and public sector employees, along with business and branch transfers and, most recently, collective redundancies. The European legal system, after an initial phase of self-restraint and definitional abstention with reference to notions formulated at the national level, has taken on an increasingly interventionist position, both at the legislative level and through authentic interpretation by the Court of Justice. The sphere of influence of European Union law has therefore strengthened, and the level of convergence of protective disciplines has expanded. However, not always in the direction set by European law, as demonstrated by the extension of the notion of a worker as an economically dependent subject for the application of various European regulations (transparency, non-discrimination, equal remuneration, non-competition, etc.), where our legal system has deviated, at least conceptually, from the European context.

The difference in concepts and cases between European Union (EU) law and national law, particularly in the application of protective measures, is currently quite clear in the context of collective redundancies. There has been a significant misalignment between European and domestic frameworks in this area over the last two years. In particular, an irreconcilable conflict has arisen between the Union notion of termination of the employment relationship assimilated to dismissal for the purpose of verifying the minimum parameters for the application of the collective redundancy procedure and the notion adopted at the national level based on the interpretation provided by case law from the Supreme Court and lower Courts in their examination of individual cases. The outcome is not only significant practical uncertainty due to the conflicting nature of national court rulings but also a clash between European law and domestic law that notably narrows the application of European Union regulations.

2 COLLECTIVE REDUNDANCIES IN THE EUROPEAN

2.1 Definition

It is well understood that the concept of collective redundancies defined by the European Council Directive 98/59/EC of 20 July 1998 (Article 1, paragraph 1, letter A), refers to 'dismissals effected by an employer for one or more reasons not related to the individual workers concerned where, according to the choice of the Member States, the number of redundancies is: (i) either, over a period of 30 days: at least 10 in establishments normally employing more than 20 and less than 100 workers; at least 10% of the number of workers in establishments normally employing at least 100 but less than 300 workers; at least 30 in establishments normally employing 300 workers or more, (ii) or, over a period of 90 days, at least 20, whatever the number of workers normally employed in the establishments in question; ... For the purpose of calculating the number of redundancies provided for in the first subparagraph of point (a), terminations of an employment contract which occur on the employer's initiative for one or more reasons not related to the individual workers concerned shall be assimilated to redundancies, provided that there are at least five redundancies'.

The eighth Whereas (recitals) of the Directive confirms and strengthens the principle: 'in order to calculate the number of redundancies provided for in the definition of collective redundancies within the meaning of this Directive, other forms of termination of employment contracts on the initiative of the employer should be equated to redundancies, provided that there are at least five redundancies'.

The position assumed by the Court of Justice of the European Union (CJEU) is clear, even though it is quite difficult to apply in every single specific case. The reference principles are uncontroversial: on the one hand, 'with a view to calculating the thresholds set in Article 1(1), first subparagraph, (a)(i) and (ii) of Directive 98/59, it should be recalled that that directive cannot be interpreted as meaning that the methods for calculation of those thresholds, and therefore the thresholds themselves, are within the discretion of the Member States, since such an interpretation would allow the latter to alter the scope of that directive and thus to deprive it of its full effect (judgments of 18 January 2007, Confédération générale du travail and Others, C-385/05, paragraph 47, and of 11 November 2015, Pujante Rivera, C-422/14, paragraph 31)' (Judgment of 11 November 2020, Marclean Technologies, C-300/19); on the other hand, 'the condition laid down in the second subparagraph of that provision that "there [be] at least five redundancies" must be interpreted as relating not to terminations of employment contracts that may be assimilated to redundancies but only to redundancies stricto sensu' (Judgment of 11 November 2015, Pujante Rivera, C-422/14, paragraph 46).

However, what precisely are redundancies in the strict sense? Do they encompass only the dismissals resulting from a unilateral decision made by the employer, or do they also include decisions that are mutually agreed upon or initiated by the worker in response to significant changes in employment conditions, such as organizational transformations within the company or redistributions of tasks and functions?

The CJEU solves the issue by stating that: 'the Directive 98/59 must be interpreted as meaning that the fact that an employer – unilaterally and to the detriment of the employee – makes significant changes to essential elements of his employment contract for reasons not related to the individual employee concerned falls within the definition of "redundancy" for the purpose of the first subparagraph of Article 1(1)(a) of the directive' (Judgment Pujante Rivera, paragraph 55). This implies that the critical factor in classifying a termination of an employment contract as a collective redundancy is not whether the termination is unilateral or mutually agreed upon, or unopposed by the employee. Rather, it is whether the termination results from significant changes implemented by the employer that adversely affect the employee.

Based on the CJEU jurisprudence, therefore, the scope of application of the EU Directive includes not only a resignation or a mutual termination subsequent to a transfer of the employee in different productive units, functionally or geographically far from the original workplace, but also a mutual termination subsequent to the employer communication of the intention to proceed with an employee dismissal on objective reasons, or a mutual release of the employment contract to a new company due to restructuring and transfer of assets not founding (configurating) a transfer of undertaking.[1]

3 COLLECTIVE REDUNDANCIES IN THE ITALIAN

3.1 Definition

Collective redundancies definition for the regulation protective purposes, according to the Italian interpretation, is wider than the one embraced at the European level and includes, pursuant to Article 24 legislative decree No. 223/1991, all the undertakings 'which employ more than 15 employees, including managers, and who, in as a result of a reduction or transformation of activity work, intend to make at least five redundancies, over the time of one hundred and twenty days, in each productive unit, or in more than one production within the territory of the same province'.

The Directive does not therefore distinguish between redundancies and terminations that are akin to redundancies, in the sense that what is relevant for the applicability of the Italian law is only the occurrence of a minimum of five redundancies (in each productive unit, or in more than one productive unit within the territory of the same province), within 120 days, in an undertaking of more than 15 employees. This has led the Italian jurisprudence to consider assimilated terminations not included

1. Barnard C., *The Substantive Law of the EU*, 7th edn, Oxford University Press, 2022, p. 736; Aleksynska M. & Muller A., *The Regulation of Collective Dismissals: Economic Rationale and Legal Practice*, ILO Working Paper 4, 2020, p. 40.

in the legal parameter of five minimum dismissals, and so far, the procedural discipline of collective redundancies is not applicable in cases in which the minimum requisite of five is also reached through assimilated terminations. Assimilated terminations, not included in the calculation base of the number of redundancies, have been therefore considered by the Italian jurisprudence as equivalent to redundancies for the applicability of the selection criteria and the involvement of the corresponding positions in the collective procedural steps.

The advent of CJEU Pujante Rivera has pushed back the Italian judicial acquiring, and the Supreme Court, dealing with the new precedent, has had to admit that also consensual termination, stemming from a failure to accept a transfer or other negative substantial changes in labour conditions, should be taking into account in the calculation of the number of dismissals required for the application of the discipline concerning collective redundancies (Supreme Court, 20 July 2020, No. 15401). In particular, the Supreme Court has stated that: 'Based on a correct interpretation of Article 1, paragraph 1, subparagraph a) of Council Directive 98/59/EC of 20 July 1998, the notion of "dismissal" includes the fact that an employer unilaterally and to the detriment of the employee proceeds with a substantial modification of the essential elements of the employment contract for reasons not inherent to the employee's person, resulting in the termination of the employment contract, even at the employee's request (CJEU, 11 November 2015, Case C-422/14, points 50 to 54). Such an interpretation, in line with the aforementioned case law of the Court of Justice, implies the overcoming of the previous provision of Law No. 223 of 1991, Article 24, also in light of Legislative Decree No. 151 of 1997, implementing Community Directive No. 56 of 26 June 1992, in the sense that different types of employment termination, even if attributable to the employer's initiative, could not be included in the minimum number of five dismissals, which was considered sufficient to constitute a collective redundancy (Supreme Court, 6 November 2001, No. 13714; Supreme Court, 22 January 2007, No. 1334).'

The Italian trial judges, following this shift by the Supreme Court to align the Italian concept with the evolving jurisprudence of the CJEU, moved towards a broader definition, noting that: 'For the purposes of the directive, any act capable, in advance, of determining a substantial unilateral change in working conditions, from which it can be deemed reasonable to expect the termination of the employment relationship, falls within the scope of application' (Tribunal Napoli, 4 January 2022); 'In other words, for the purpose of the numerical calculation indicated by the directive, the community notion of "dismissal" includes, alongside those formally considered as such, (also) acts of termination of the employment relationship that may seem to result from the employee's consent (such as consensual terminations), but are actually causally attributable to a prior substantial unilateral modification made by the employer to a substantial element of the employment contract for reasons not related to the employee's personal circumstances' (Tribunal Firenze, 23 July 2021, No. 563; *see also*, to the same effect, Appeal Court, Milano 26 August 2021, No. 1030).

Unfortunately, the Supreme Court ruling consistency was overturned only one year later, by the judgment of 31 May 2021, No. 15118. Though in the different case of a consensual termination following the opening of the dismissal procedure for objective reason set up by the employer according to Article 7, Law No. 604/1966, the Supreme Court has stated the opposite principle, i.e., a consensual termination, even if coming up after the beginning of an individual dismissal procedure, should not be considered a redundancy and should not be counted for the reaching of the legal threshold ('the minimum number of five dismissals, considered sufficient to constitute a collective redundancy, cannot include other different types of termination of the employment relationship, even if initiated by the employer'). And the Supreme Court has done so on the (wrong) assumption of giving an interpretation of the internal provision consistent with the European notion, which is not, as above-mentioned.

The previous trend in Italian jurisprudence appears to be resurfacing, reasserting the interpretation that the term 'dismissal' should be understood in a technical sense. This interpretation does not equate dismissals with any other type of employment relationship termination, such as resignations, mutually agreed terminations, or early retirements, even if these terminations are prompted by the same need to reduce excess labour force that justifies dismissals (Supreme Court, 22 February 2006, No. 3866; Supreme Court, 29 March 2010, No. 7519). A confirming case in this regard is the judgment of the Tribunal of Milano dated 10 June 2022, No. 1459, which, referring to the judgment of the Supreme Court of Cassation No. 15118/2021, denies that settlements resulting from an individual dismissal procedure under Article 7 of Law No. 604/1966 can be classified as collective redundancies within the meaning of the Directive and the implementing domestic legislation.[2]

4 EUROPEAN AND ITALIAN FRAMEWORKS NEED TO BE

4.1 Reconciled

The present conflict of interpretation as regards the notions of 'redundancy' and 'assimilated termination' between EU law and domestic law is creating a serious situation of uncertain application in Italy, which greatly challenges both companies and workers and fuels a new and costly litigation process with unpredictable outcomes. Besides, it is also not possible to rely on a clarifying intervention from the Supreme Court, given the current division within the Court and the risk that the

2. Blasi M., *La 'missione di civiltà' del diritto sociale europeo e il nuovo assetto dei licenziamenti collettivi in Italia: rileggendo Mario Grandi*, Variazioni su Temi di Diritto del Lavoro, 2020, pp. 1229-1262; Cosio R., *La nozione di licenziamento collettivo. Le precisazioni della Corte di Giustizia*, Il Lavoro nella Giurisprudenza, 2021, Vol. 5, pp. 502-508; De Luca M., *I licenziamenti collettivi nel diritto dell'Unione europea e l'ordinamento italiano: da una remota sentenza storica della Corte di giustizia di condanna dell'Italia alla doppia pregiudizialità per il nostro regime sanzionatorio nazionale (note minime): prima parte*, Labor, 2020, Vol. 2, pp. 149-164; De Luca M., *I licenziamenti collettivi nel diritto dell'Unione europea e l'ordinamento italiano: da una remota sentenza storica della Corte di giustizia di condanna dell'Italia alla doppia pregiudizialità per il nostro regime sanzionatorio nazionale (note minime): seconda parte*, Labor, 2020, Vol. 3, pp. 267-286; Limena F., *I licenziamenti collettivi nei più recenti orientamenti della giurisprudenza italiana e UE*, Il Lavoro nella Giurisprudenza, 2022, Vol. 7, pp. 760-767; Vidiri G., *L'infinita storia del licenziamento collettivo tra incertezze e sentenze creative*, Il Lavoro nella Giurisprudenza, 2021, Vol. 11, pp. 1021-1028; Perulli A., *La disciplina del licenziamento e le Alte Corti*, Lavoro Diritti Europa, 2023, Vol. 2, pp. 1-7.

fragmentation of decisions may be exacerbated by the multitude of concrete cases that may fall within the aforementioned notions, with the risk of differentiated solutions depending on the specific case at hand.

A legislative amendment of Article 24 of Law No. 223/1991 seems therefore to be urgently needed in order to clarify, beyond any reasonable doubt and in line with the jurisprudence of the CJEU, what is meant by 'collective redundancies' and what is meant by 'assimilated terminations,' as well as determining the applicable regime of effects for each category. A definitional dualism such as the one depicted above cannot exist based on the principle of the primacy of EU law and conforming interpretation. Should the Italian jurisprudence be unable to adopt a clear position that safeguards the primary good of legal certainty, then it will be the legislator's responsibility to address it by specifically intervening in the legislative text and aligning it with the European definitional framework.

From the given example, it is evident how, on the one hand, labour law categories remain vibrant and dynamic through constant updates ensured by the creative contribution of jurisprudence. On the other hand, the process of aligning the domestic legal system with the European Union framework is influenced by the often-extended time required for internal awareness of the renewed European arrangements, as well as the lengthy duration of legal proceedings. As a result, it suffers from cyclical phases of misalignment and conceptual opposition that must be addressed through appropriate legislative measures when judicial responses are delayed or contradictory.

Such measures should ensure the application of European protective regulations within the domestic legal system and preserve their proper and homogeneous scope of application while respecting the discretionary implementation space reserved for the domestic legal order by the European Act. It is no coincidence that the reference by the EU legal system to internal labour law categories is increasingly rare and residual, and European categories tend to assert their primacy and conforming influence. The European and Italian categorical pairing, however, persists and evolves according to unpredictable patterns and yet is based on a case-by-case and sectoral approach. There is no homogeneous descriptive model on the categorization side that applies to all European/National relationships, which unfold along their own paths depending on the specific characteristics of each case and the socio-economic context of reference.

CHAPTER 7

Dogmatic Categories and Labour Law: When Labour Law Looks in the Mirror

Elena Gramano

1 INTRODUCTION

The notion, role, function, and endurance of dogmatic categories in labour law comprise a topic that has remained the focus of scholarly reflections for many years.[1] Indeed, labour law scholarship questions its own method of research and comprehension of labour law and, ultimately, its own identity and role in approaching labour law as a field of scientific investigation.

Amidst this wide-ranging debate, scholars question themselves on the methodology of their legal research, the suitability of the traditional instruments used to conduct legal research to face contemporary challenges, the need to embrace new methodological schemes to interpret and apply the law, and labour law more specifically.

1. In the Italian debate, a renewed debate has been triggered by the article of the jurist Natalino Irti exactly on the crisis of categories (in Italian *fattispecie*): *see* N. Irti, *La crisi della fattispecie*, in Riv. Dir. Priv., 2014, 38. More recently, the debate involved labour lawyers as well. On the topic, *see* A. Zoppoli, *Prospettiva rimediale, fattispecie e sistema nel diritto del lavoro*, Editoriale Scientifica, 2022, and *ivi* for further references. *See also* references under *infra* n. 2.

   The scholarship on this topic is immense, inside and outside labour law. For some essential references, *see* H. Collins, G. Lester & V. Mantouvalou, *Does Labour Law Need Philosophical Foundations?*, in H. Collins, G. Lester & V. Mantouvalou (eds), *Philosophical Foundations of Labour Law*, Oxford University Press, 2018, 1; M. D'Antona, *Labor Law at the Century's End: An Identity Crisis?*, in J. Conaghan, R. Michael Fischl & K. Klare (eds), *Labor Law in an Era of Globalization*, Oxford University Press, 2000, 31; M. D'Antona, *L'anomalia post positivista del diritto del lavoro e la questione del metodo*, in Riv. Giur. Lav., 2009, 3, 401; A. Supiot, *Beyond Employment: Changes in Work and the Future of Labor Law in Europe*, Oxford University Press, 2001.

In this context, we might ask ourselves whether the categories of dogmatics still exist in labour law within a broader reflection that focuses on the very identity of labour law. 'Labour Law in the Mirror' is the title of this volume, which – from different perspectives and through the voices of various authors – touches upon categories, values and interlocutors of labour law and labour lawyers.

When investigating the very identity of the subject that constitutes the labour lawyers' bread and butter, and when reflecting upon the foundations of labour law, we might first ask ourselves why we also consider the existence and role of categories of dogmatics as part of the discussion. Indeed, the debate on the role, relevance and existence of categories of dogmatics has engaged legal scholars for quite some time now. Dogmatic categories and their related attributes form a theme that has always attracted the attention and scientific work of labour lawyers, especially regarding subordination.

However, it is essential to clarify why the discourse on dogmatic categories is part of the problem of the identity of labour law in general. The answer to this question is integral to the main focus of this chapter: Do the dogmatic categories of labour law still exist?

In order to tackle the problem, I believe it is useful to start from two premises, which will structure the following paragraphs.

First, it is essential to set a basic taxonomy in order to identify and distinguish the meaning of the concept of dogmatic categories for the purpose of this brief chapter (without providing for a general notion of dogmatic categories that is valid or relevant outside the perimeter of these pages).

Second, some attention will be paid here to the origins and rationales of the dogmatic categories of labour law, at least in the legal traditions of continental Europe.

These two premises shall guide a reflection on the core of this contribution: the question of the endurance (or not) of the dogmatic categories of labour law, as well as a subsequent reflection on their actual (or lost) role in the field of labour law.

2 A BASIC TAXONOMY: LEGAL CATEGORIES AND DOGMATIC CATEGORIES

As a first premise, for the purpose of this chapter, we might employ and distinguish the following two expressions: *legal categories* and *dogmatic categories*. The distinction between the two is related to the subjects that construct these two types of categories and to the function for which they are made.

If we consider the perspective of the production of the law, the lawmaker often employs legal categories as a regulatory technique by which to identify the scope of application of certain rules. In this sense, legal categories are general, abstract constructions that describe human facts and situations and identify certain legal effects upon them. In other words, when the conditions represented in the legal categories (as constructed by the lawmaker) occur, certain legal effects will occur. The need to rely on the subsumptive method when interpreting and applying legal categories is a logical consequence of the adoption of this regulatory technique in order to ultimately verify whether the human event or fact that occurred in reality can be traced back to what is abstractly represented by the legal category and thus to determine whether and what legal effects are produced, which rules shall be applied and to whom. From a functional point of view, legal categories are premises for the deduction of particular rules or criteria for the legal characterisation of facts for the purpose of subsumption under a general, abstract norm.

In this sense, legal categories are a method of production of the law (in Italian, '*per fattispecie*').

However, categories can also serve to study and systematise the law. Traditionally, jurists and scholars identify, study and bring norms and rules into an ordered system, thus forming *dogmatic categories*.

Indeed, in legal terminology, the term 'dogmatics' can be interpreted with different meanings. Following a distinction made in Riccardo Guastini's '*Legal dogmatics*'[2] in the first sense, dogmatics denotes, in general terms, the doctrinal study of law or, in other words, legal science in its broad sense. According to a second meaning, legal dogmatics constitutes a particular method of interpreting the law. Finally, the term legal dogmatics can also be understood as that sub-sector of legal doctrine devoted to the study or elaboration of so-called legal dogmas. Indeed, if we were to use the expression 'dogmatic' here to mean legal science as a whole, we would be making a questionable choice of conception of law and legal science; that is, we would be referring to a formalistic or merely normativistic approach to legal science, which understands the object of its study as a mere set of norms to the exclusion of any relevance of human facts.

Instead, in the context of this chapter, we refer to dogmatic categories as the product of legal science, which does not limit itself to the exegesis or the interpretation of norms but aims at the elaboration of a system not exclusively, but also by means of the construction of general and abstract categories, the dogmatic categories precisely. In this sense, dogmatic categories are those abstract concepts that describe and translate into a legal order the norms and legal categories adopted by the lawmaker. Reflecting the dual semantic valence of the Greek word 'dogma', which stands for both the disposition of authority and a doctrine or teaching formulated on the basis of normative texts, dogmatic categories can be elaborated on the basis of a set of norms and then condensed into doctrinal formulae; Roman jurists called these *regolae juris*.

An example within the field of labour law is *subordination*, which often builds and elaborates on the legal notion of a worker or employee.

There is also the dogmatic category of *power*, or *authority*, as the prerogative of the employer, who is understood not only as the subject who receives the working activity but also as the organisation within which the worker's activity is inserted, in the light of directives emanating from the owner or the person responsible for the organisation and with reference to which the working activity finds its utility. More generally, within labour law, we find the dogmatic category of *mandatory rule*, a category in certain labour law systems – including the Italian one – which is strictly

2. R. Guastini, *Dogmatica giuridica (voce)*, in A. Belvedere, R. Guastini, P. Zatti & V. Zeno Zencovich, *Glossario*, Giuffrè, 1994, 121.

functional to the protection of the employee and which has traditionally functioned not only as a barrier to the employer's power within the employment relationship but also the dogmatic category of *collective will*, of *representativeness* in relation to that of representation and collective proxy, and the list could go on.

3 ON THE ROOTS OF CERTAIN DOGMATIC CATEGORIES: LABOUR LAW AND THE LAW OF CONTRACTS

As a second premise for this brief chapter, we need to clarify, at least partially (the theme is indeed immense), the roots or genesis of certain dogmatic categories that remain fundamental to labour law.

In many legal systems, at least in continental Europe, labour law was born from the progressive combination and reciprocal contamination of two main types of legislative interventions on the matter of labour. On the one hand, the first – few and limited – legislative interventions were introduced in the 19th century to protect the physical health of workers and provide basic essential welfare support in a context of almost pure exploitation of personal labour by the first industrialists; we might think of the first laws on labour as those of children or pregnant women.

As labour law took shape and became more organic, at least in the continental European systems, it was technically constructed through the provision of mandatory constraints on private autonomy as a counter-limit to market capitalism in order to restrict its freedom of action *vis-à-vis* workers.[3] This occurred within the framework of historical circumstances that made it necessary to tackle the social question head-on and to limit the (hitherto limitless) authority and power of the employer, usually the head of the industries within which labour was performed and often exploited.

Labour law came into being *per differentiam* with respect to the general law of contracts because an apparatus of rules was needed to address the social issue of the protection of workers at the time, by separating and distinguishing the employment contract from other contracts, and by building an apparatus of rules that broke away from contract law, in order to capture the specificity of a relationship – that between an employer and a worker – which is characterised by two essential elements: the *person* who works, and thus the strictly personal nature of the working activity, and the direct unavoidable involvement of the person of the worker in the daily performance of the employment contract, on the one hand; and the *authority* exercised over him or her by the person who receives the working activity, and who exercises this power to transform such an activity into an economic utility through the business organisation; namely, the employer, the head of the undertaking, or owner of the business organisation.[4] All of this takes into account the fundamental collective dimension in which the employment contract is placed, which externally affects the regulation of the employment relationship itself.

3. R. Del Punta, *Valori del diritto ed economia di mercato*, in B. Caruso, R. Del Punta & T. Treu, *Il diritto del lavoro e la grande trasformazione*, Il Mulino, 2020, 34.
4. M. Persiani, *Diritto del lavoro e sistema di produzione capitalistico*, in Riv. It. Dir. Lav., 2019, 1, 279.

It is within the context of this genesis of the labour law, on the basis of this axiological status that deemed the employment relationship to be separated and worthy of a specific dense protection, that the dogmatic categories of labour law – starting with that of subordination – were progressively created and developed, thus distinguishing them from the general principles and categories of the law of contracts.[5]

After the challenge of separating labour law from contract law, labour law scholars then had to deal with an equally important intellectual operation: to provide labour law with an identity, comprehend its specific needs and features and fit it into the legal discourse.

In order to proceed with such a complex operation, the whole discourse on subordination, its notion, the methodology used to identify it and to detect a subordinate employment relationship, and so on, started and has never yet reached an end.

However, in this chapter, we are not concerned with a reflection on the single specific dogmatic categories, their resilience, actuality or their suitability to be part of labour lawyers' daily interpretative tools. More generally, we are concerned with a question that lies at the root of this reflection: what is the use of dogmatic categories in labour law at all?

It is a question that not only forces us to touch upon the roots of labour law and its foundation but also to address the problem of its usefulness and, thus, ultimately, its survival.

4 ON THE EXISTENCE OR PERSISTENCE OF DOGMATIC CATEGORIES: DO WE (STILL) NEED DOGMATIC CATEGORIES IN LABOUR LAW?

Subordination is not the only dogmatic category of labour law, but it is certainly the one on which the entire solar system of labour law has mainly revolved, according to the assumption that has never been completely disproved by any legal system, according to which subordination is the sole means of access to the protection provided by labour law.

The example of the dogmatic category of subordination might allow us to clarify the function performed, at least to date, by the dogmatic categories of labour law in general: that of identifying the perimeter of application of labour law and defining some of the essential features of that discipline which serves to rebalance the asymmetry/difference in contractual power within the employment relationship by providing specific protections for the person who works for someone else, i.e., the weaker party of the contract.[6]

5. M. D'Antona, *La subordinazione e oltre. Una teoria giuridica per il lavoro che cambia*, in M. Pedrazzoli (ed.), *Lavoro subordinato e d'intorni*, Il Mulino, 1989, 43.
6. B. Langille, *A Question of Balance in the Legal Construction of Personal Work Relations*, Jerusalem Review of Legal Studies, 7, 2013, 99 https://doi.org/10.1093/jrls/jlt020; M. Freedland, *The Segmentation of Workers' Rights and the Legal Analysis of Personal Work Relations: Redefining a Problem*, Comparative labor law and policy journal, 36, 2015, 241.

Having clarified these functions of the labour law dogmatic categories, it remains to determine whether or not they still exist and whether or not we (still) need them. In order to achieve this, we could carry out reverse reasoning; that is, we could ask ourselves whether those same functions could be achieved by a different method capable of providing more efficient and coherent responses to the transformations of work and therefore more responsive to new protection needs. In essence, are there alternative methodological options? If so, what are they? Is it possible to offer greater protection for workers without passing through the construction of dogmatic categories?

At this point, our thoughts might turn to the rich debate that has interested legal scholarship, among others, for years, on the opposition between formal categories and remedies, between the formal approach and the material approach.[7]

With respect to this broad, limitless issue, the European legal system might serve as a benchmark against which to prove the *a contrario* test, which we considered above, to verify whether concrete methodological alternatives to the construction and use of dogmatic categories do indeed exist.

In fact, we might consider an example. Under European law, there is no specific or formalised notion of subordination or of the subordinate worker. None of the directives and regulations that refer to the notion of the worker, in order to identify their scope of application, provide for a specific autonomous definition of the notion of worker; in some cases, the directives contain a reference to the national notion of the worker adopted in the single Member States.

However, precisely by means of the rich interpretation of the term 'worker', which constitutes a legal category as it is named and employed in several norms, the European legal system is acquainted with the dogmatic category of subordination. In fact, a consolidated case law of the Court of Justice of the European Union (CJEU), albeit still evolving, has provided for the notion of the worker and, moreover, has gone beyond the very letter of the directives which refer to national notions of workers by affirming that, when applying European Union (EU) law, we must rely on and adopt an autonomous European notion of the worker, which is once again that of the CJEU (the essential reference is to the Lawrie Blum doctrine[8] and its further developments in many decisions of the Court).[9]

7. A. Zoppoli, *Prospettiva rimediale, fattispecie e sistema nel diritto del lavoro*, Editoriale Scientifica, 2022.
8. Case C-66/85 *Deborah Lawrie-Blum v. Land Baden- Wurttemberg* [1986] ECR 02121.
9. On the notion of worker under European law, *see* A. Perulli, *A New Category Within European Union Law: Personal Work*, European Labour Law Journal, 15(1), 2024, 184 https://doi.org/10.1177/20319525231221225; A. Perulli, *The Legal and Jurisprudential Evolution of the Notion of Employee*, European Labour Law Journal, 11(2), 2020, 117 https://doi.org/10.1177/2031952520905145; N. Countouris, *The Concept of 'Worker' in European Labour Law: Fragmentation, Autonomy and Scope*, Industrial Law Journal, 47, 2018, 192 https://doi.org/10.1093/indlaw/dwx014; E. Menegatti, *The Evolving Concept of 'Worker' in EU Law*, Italian Labour Law e-Journal, 12, 2019, 71; E. Menegatti, *Taking EU Labour Law Beyond the Employment Contract: The Role Played by the European Court of Justice*, European Labour Law Journal, 2, 2020, 26 https://doi.org/10.1177/2031952519884713; S. Giubboni, *Being a Worker in EU Law*, European Labour Law Journal,

Lastly, and surprisingly, it is precisely the European lawmaker, with the proposal for a directive on platform work,[10] that aims at introducing a presumption of subordination at the occurrence of certain conditions in a system that formally does not recognise or provide for any legal notion of subordination or of the worker.

Is this proof that the system can work without dogmatic categories? Is there concrete evidence that one can regulate and protect work without passing through the dogmatic category of subordination or any other category? Is it now proven that one can indeed adopt a purely remedial or material approach?

In my opinion, the example offered by the European system of subordination suggests quite the opposite. Indeed, the European legal system confirms that protection today necessarily passes through the definition of who the recipient of that protection is and also by identifying these subjects by means of a rebuttable presumption. Therefore, it proves that the construction of a dogmatic category (of subordination) to select the recipients of a certain regulation or to define its scope of application is needed, even if there is not a formal legal category (of worker). The relevant dogmatic category is contracted by means of interpretation and exegesis of the existing norms, their systematic connection and the rationales pursued by European lawmakers when regulating certain areas.

Even in a legal system that lacks a formal legal category (of worker), a dogmatic category (of subordination) is built and is needed to complement that which the formal regulations lack. Nothing could demonstrate more clearly the fact that, somehow, dogmatic categories still exist.

The question now is whether dogmatic categories still work or whether they have been put to such a test that, in the end, they have become merely empty formal containers or limitations rather than enablers of protection.

On this point, we shall make a *caveat*; that is, the invitation to maintain the separation between the reflection on the existence and function and general role of dogmatic categories in the system and the reflection on their suitability and persistent effectiveness in fulfilling their function. Indeed, it is important to resolve a potential misunderstanding here. Asking which is the role and purpose of the dogmatic categories is conceptually different from asking ourselves whether the dogmatic

---

9, 2018, 223 https://doi.org/10.1177/2031952518791828; E. Gramano, *On the Notion of 'Worker' under EU Law: New Insights*, European Labour Law Journal, 12(1), 2021, 98 https://doi.org/10.1177/2031952521998812.

10. M. Kullmann, *'Platformisation' of Work: An EU Perspective on Introducing a Legal Presumption*, European Labour Law Journal, 13(1), 2021, 66 https://doi.org/10.1177/20319525211063112; A. Alosi, *Platform Work in Europe: Lessons Learned, Legal Developments and Challenges Ahead*, European Labour Law Journal, 13(1), 2022, 4 https://doi.org/10.1177/20319525211062557; A. Aloisi & V. De Stefano, *European Commission Takes the Lead in Regulating Platform Work*, Social Europe, 9 December 2021.

    For some essential readings on platform work, J. Adams-Prassl, *Humans as a Service: The Promise and Perils of Work in the Gig Economy*, Oxford University Press, 2018; V. De Stefano, *The Rise of the Just-In-Time-Workforce: On-Demand Work, Crowdwork and Labor Protection in the 'Gig-Economy'*, Comparative labor law and policy journal, 2016 37, 471 https://doi.org/10.2139/ssrn.2682602; A. Aloisi, *Commoditizied Workers: Case Study Research on Labour Law Issues Arising from a Set of 'On Demand/Gig Economy' Platforms*, Comparative Labor Law and Policy Journal, 37, 2016, 653.

categories (e.g., the dogmatic category of subordination) are fit for their purpose – that of identifying the recipients of the protections that labour law offers or offering specific protection to workers.

The two points must be kept distinct; we can question the suitability of the current dogmatic construction of subordination (or of other dogmatic categories) to identify, and thus select, who is protected by labour laws and who is not, to provide for a certain level or type of protection, and so on. However, this is a logically different operation from the one we are now addressing and which is a precursor to any other question on dogmatic categories.

In my opinion, the weakness of the system with which we are struggling is not a structural logic problem regarding dogmatic categories, as categories still fulfil their original purposes as a formal construction.

As Norberto Bobbio reminds us, it was precisely labour lawyers who were among the first to abandon the 'splendid isolation' of legal science in order to move ashore and recognise legal science as a part of a larger continent or, even more so, as one of the maps that, together with others, concur to help the interpreter on her journey through a territory to be explored.[11]

The jurists' abandonment of their scientific isolation was accompanied by a profound (self)criticism of the legal method proper to the positivists, the 'legists', and by an overall rethinking of the function and role of the legal scientist, no longer the preserver and transmitter of a body of rules already given, of which she is the depositary and custodian, but also and above all the creator of rules, an active participant in the formation of the legal system through the research of law.[12]

Even when constructing dogmatic categories, labour law scholars have always somehow distinguished themselves to some extent from other legal scholars.

If we look at the profile of the study of labour law, and thus the role of labour law scholarship, we realise it has never embraced an exclusively normativistic notion of the law, whereby law would be made up only of the norms produced by the positive lawmaker, nor has it ever limited its role to extrapolating dogmatic categories from norms (i.e., from legal categories), as if categories were *in rerum natura*.

On the contrary, labour law scholars have always held a more all-encompassing and multidimensional notion of the legal system and, above all, they have never embraced a purely formalistic method of studying, interpreting and systematising the law, whereby the jurist would look at the norms but not at the human or natural facts (as the social or natural sciences would do). On the contrary, labour lawyers have always – perhaps more than any other type of jurist – looked at human facts before looking at the norms and dogmatic categories of labour law.

Today, the problem of the suitability of dogmatic categories in enabling the application of the law and its protection of workers arises in an institutional context that has changed both at the normative level and at the level of interpretation and the

11. N. Bobbio, *Diritto e scienze sociali*, in N. Bobbio, *Dalla struttura alla funzione. Nuovi studi di teoria del diritto*, Edizioni di Comunità, 1977, 56.
12. N. Bobbio, *Diritto e scienze sociali*, in N. Bobbio, *Dalla struttura alla funzione. Nuovi studi di teoria del diritto*, Edizioni di Comunità, 1977, 47.

application of the law: positivism has been succeeded by a conception that could be called constitutionalist of the legal system.[13] At the same time, legal argumentation no longer exhausts itself in logical formal operations of an inferential, axiologically neutral type but rather involves evaluative operations that elaborate reasons in favour of one or another of the possible solutions of the case to be decided, which is possible within the limits imposed by the constraints to which the discourse of jurists must be subject.

The complexity of the legal system's surroundings and the multiplicity of viewpoints it introduces into legal argumentation call for a restructuring of the system along the lines of differentiating categories in such a way as to provide a combination of variables that facilitates an understanding of the external complexity. It is a matter of elaborating what has been defined as 'responsive dogmatic'; that is, a dogmatic system that is capable of providing articulate and selective answers to the growing mass of questions and expectations that society pours into the legal system.

We might think of the debate between economics and labour law, in reference to which the ultimate problem depends on the emptying of the (dogmatic) category of subordinate employment from its traditional set of protections. However, economics has given up fighting dogmatics. Although it has accepted the instrument of dogmatics, it empties protection from within. Herein lies the problem of labour law: categories still exist, but what do they bring with them? What protection do they entail?

When the category no longer corresponds to the protections for which it was originally created, its usefulness is brought into question. Ultimately, though, the problem is misplaced. The actual problem lies in the substantial answers and protections attached to the category rather than in the category per se.

In my opinion, the problem is not in the container – and thus in the method – but in the content – and thus in the discipline.

Self-evidently, dogmatic categories are consigned to history as equally as the values that law pursues and protects.[14] Dogmatic categories therefore change and shall be called into question periodically, but their function – not only that of systematising the law but also their heuristic function of driving knowledge and research – cannot be radically challenged.

13. L. Mengoni, *I principi generali del diritto e la scienza giuridica*, Dir. Lav., 1992, 3.
14. R. Del Punta, *Valori del diritto ed economia di mercato*, in B. Caruso, R. Del Punta & T. Treu, *Il diritto del lavoro e la grande trasformazione*, Il Mulino, 2020, 34.

Part II Justify Labour Law: Philosophies, Values, Policies

CHAPTER 8

Sustainability and Human Rights

Tonia Novitz

When placing labour law 'in the mirror' and reflecting on its categories, values, and interlocutors, we are confronted with questions regarding how the creation of labour law has been vindicated previously and how it may be justified in our current circumstances.

In this chapter, I seek to reconcile the older treatment of labour rights as 'human rights' with the contemporary drive to understand regulation of work in terms of what may be understood to be 'sustainable'. These are often juxtaposed as conflicting aspirations, but my suggestion is that they can be reconciled and that it is possible to do so by viewing human rights as a basis for protection of individual and collective worker voice and influence while understanding the significance of participatory engagement for any viable sustainable development policies.

In this way, we can move beyond how we seek to justify existing labour law, looking towards the normative base on which we could establish the further extension and flourishing of our discipline. It is suggested that in this context, we can retain and develop facets of human rights law while also shaping the contours of labour law and other laws which impact work in ways that are sustainable for people and the planet in ways that foster prosperity and peace through partnership. In this context, my concern lies primarily with the development of international law which could enable the United Nations (UN) 2030 Agenda to be realised.[1]

The first part of this chapter introduces the complex relationship between human rights and labour law to date, as reflected in international law and practice. The second part considers how a sustainable development agenda challenges conventional approaches to labour law, not only presenting potential constraints on the potential influence of collective labour objectives but also potentially expanding the legitimate

1. UN (2015) General Assembly Resolution Transforming our world: the 2030 Agenda for Sustainable Development, 25 September 2015 A/Res/70/1 (the 2030 Agenda).

aims which workers could seek to pursue and further bolstering their claims to do so. The third part analyses the evolution of climate and environmental strategic litigation under a human rights rubric and considers whether this is a route which workers and their representatives can and should also pursue to achieve sustainable development.

1 LABOUR LAW AND HUMAN RIGHTS

There have been various attempts to justify labour law in human rights terms. As Virginia Mantouvalou has observed, these include a positivistic assertion that human rights discourse is, in practice, used in ways that protect labour standards.[2] It may also be claimed that protection of labour standards as human rights is of instrumental use, given that this will highlight the importance of the claims being made by workers.[3] Arguably, it is in this way that labour activists can highlight that national laws do not tally with the text of regional or international human rights instruments or their interpretation by various supervisory bodies so as to initiate a process of reform or improvement.[4] Mantouvalou also asserts that the human rights of workers are best understood in a normative sense, namely as compelling moral claims, which are universal, stringent and timeless in nature.[5] The latter may be a more virtuous route for legal theorists to pursue from a philosophical perspective, but as a labour lawyer, perhaps it is inevitable that the discussion in this chapter centres on the positive law and its tangible uses. The normative enters when we evaluate the adequacy of legal norms and practices. In this respect, as has been reported by many commentators, the successful protection of workers' interests has been mixed.[6]

1.1 The Emergence of International Human Rights Norms Relevant to Labour

Following the Second World War, the emergence of human rights protections under international law had an impact on how certain labour standards were protected. A key initial instrument was the UN Charter 1945, its preamble stating the commitment 'to reaffirm faith in fundamental human rights, in the dignity and worth of the human person, in the equal rights of men and women and of nations large and small', such that the UN institutions would 'establish conditions under which justice and respect for the obligations arising from treaties and other sources of international law can be

2. Virginia Mantouvalou, 'Are Labour Rights Human Rights?' (2012) 3 *European Labour Law Journal* 151 https://doi.org/10.1177/201395251200300204. *See* especially at 152-156.
3. *Ibid.*, 156-163.
4. Alan Bogg, 'Can We Trust the Courts in Labour Law? Stranded Between Frivolity and Despair' (2022) 38(2) *International Journal of Comparative Labour Law and Industrial Relations* 103 https://doi.org/10.54648/ijcl2022006; and Lord John Hendy KC, 'Reflections on the Role of the Trade Union Lawyer' (2022) 38(2) *International Journal of Comparative Labour Law and Industrial Relations* 91 https://doi.org/10.54648/ijcl2022005.
5. Mantouvalou, *supra* n. 2, at 163-169.
6. Colin Fenwick & Tonia Novitz (eds), *Human Rights at Work: Perspectives on Law and Regulation* (Hart/Bloomsbury/Oñati International Series in Law and Society, 2010).

maintained', alongside 'social progress and better standards of life in larger freedom'. In the Universal Declaration of Human Rights (UDHR), 1948, slavery, servitude and the slave trade were prohibited (under Article 4, reflecting the terms of the earlier 1926 Slavery Convention), protecting freedom of association (via Article 20), the right to work and to fair terms and conditions, including equal remuneration and to form and join trade unions (in Article 23), the right to 'reasonable limitation of working hours and periodic holidays with pay' (through Article 24) and to a standard of living adequate for 'health and well-being' (as set out in Article 25).[7]

The politics of the Cold War led to a distinction recognised in the international community between civil and political rights of individuals and collective socio-economic rights, with the latter being more controversial.[8] This problematic separation explains the parallel adoption of, for example, not only the European Convention on Human Rights of 1950 and the European Social Charter of 1961 (now both subject to further Protocols and amendments) but also in the same vein the International Covenant on Civil and Political Rights (ICCPR) and the International Covenant on Economic, Social and Cultural Rights (ICESCR) adopted in 1966 (which together with the UDHR are often referred to as 'the International Bill of Human Rights'). In this problematic and rather artificial split, slavery, servitude and forced labour, as well as freedom of association (including the right to form and join trade unions), came to be recognised as 'civil and political' rights, while more tangible work-related entitlements such as pay, hours, holidays and health and safety, as well as collective bargaining and rights to take strike action, were viewed as 'socio-economic' and suitable for policy-making rather than judicial enforcement.[9] The superiority of supervisory mechanisms on the international (and regional) stage regarding the former led to some neglect of the latter, which received attention from various commentators who were disappointed at the outcomes for working people.[10]

1.2 The Role of the International Labour Organization

The International Labour Organization (ILO) was the UN agency whose establishment, having preceded the UN Charter,[11] offered a more nuanced standard-setting and advisory role, identifying the connections between the two species of rights and their relevance for workers.[12] The ILO also had some impact on the drafting and interpretation

7. *See* Nicolas Valticos, 'International Labour Standards and Human Rights: Approaching the Year 2000' (1998) 138 *International Labour Review* 135.
8. *Ibid.*, 138.
9. For an example, *see* Ivan Hare, 'Social Rights as Fundamental Human Rights', in Bob Hepple (ed.), *Social and Labour Rights in a Global Context: International and Comparative Perspectives* (Cambridge University Press, 2002).
10. *See* Virginia Leary, 'The Paradox of Workers' Rights as Human Rights', in Lance Compa & Stephen Diamond (eds.), *Human Rights, Labour Rights and International Trade* (University of Pennsylvania Press, 1996); and Judy Fudge, 'The New Discourse of Labor Rights: From Social to Fundamental Rights' (2007) 29(1) *Comparative Labor Law and Policy Journal* 29.
11. The ILO constitution dates from the 1919 Treaty of Versailles.
12. Lee Swepston, 'Human Rights Law and Freedom of Association: Development Through ILO supervision' (1998) 137 *International Labour Review* 169.

of the 1966 Covenants, both of which deferred to ILO Convention No. 87 on Freedom of Association and the Right to Organise, stating that nothing in Article 22 of the ICCPR or Article 8 of the ICESCR 'shall authorize States Parties to the International Labour Organisation

Convention of 1948 concerning Freedom of Association and Protection of the Right to Organize to take legislative measures which would prejudice, or to apply the law in such a manner as to prejudice, the guarantees provided for in that Convention'.

Arguably, ILO assertions of indivisibility and interdependence arguably influenced revision of these instruments and their supervision after the end of the Cold War.[13] It was, for example, obvious that collective labour rights could be viewed as connected, so that freedom of association and the right to form and join trade unions must be linked to the right to engage in collective bargaining and to take strike action. This led to a shift in the jurisprudence of the European Court of Human Rights (ECtHR) accordingly.[14] There has also been a change in supervisory mechanisms for enforcement of socio-economic rights, enabling individual complaints.[15]

On the one hand, a human rights discourse offers a large and inclusive narrative, suggesting rights for all as human beings, which does not require 'worker' or 'employee' status, which are too often used to exclude those who are most vulnerable from protection under national labour laws.[16] At the same time, a focus on only individual human rights, such as protection from slavery and child labour or personal rights to non-discrimination, has its limitations in the world of work. Amartya Sen, for example, argued for the 'decent work' expansion of ILO objectives beyond 'fundamental principles and rights at work'.[17] He did so on the basis that this would be a broader and more far-reaching human rights approach, which enabled the building of capabilities of all people and their agency to act individually and collectively: A universalist understanding of work and working relations can be linked to a tradition of solidarity and commitment.[18] If this element of individual and collective agency is given

13. Tonia Novitz, 'Are Social Rights Necessarily Collective Rights? A Critical Analysis of the Collective Complaints Protocol to the European Social Charter' (2002) *European Human Rights Law Review* 50; Ariel Zylberman, 'The Indivisibility of Human Rights' (2017) 36(4) *Law and Philosophy* 389 https://dx.doi.org/10.1007/s10982-017-9296-2.
14. In the ECHR context, *see Demir and Baykara v. Turkey* Application No. 34503/97, 12 November 2008; discussed in Keith Ewing & John Hendy, 'The Dramatic Implications of Demir and Baykara' (2010) 39 *Industrial Law Journal* 2 https://dx.doi.org/10.1093/indlaw/dwp031. *See* more recently, 'Freedom of Association, Including the Right to Form and Join Trade Unions', Joint statement by the Committee on Economic, Social and Cultural Rights and the Human Rights Committee, 23 October 2019, E/C.12/2019/3-CCPR/C/2019/1.
15. Optional Protocol (GA resolution A/RES/63/117) to the ICESCR which provides the Committee competence to receive and consider communications, and Additional Protocol to the American Convention on Human Rights in the area of Economic, Social and Cultural Rights 'Protocol of San Salvador', available at: http://www.oas.org/es/sedi/ddse/documentos/Protocolo%20San%20Salvador/English/1.%20Protocol.pdf.
16. Valerio De Stefano, 'Non-Standard Work and Limits on Freedom of Association: A Human Rights-Based Approach' (2017) 46(2) *Industrial Law Journal* 185 https://dx.doi.org/10.1093/indlaw/dww034.
17. Amartya Sen 'Work and Rights' (2000) 139(2) *International Labour Review* 119 https://dx.doi.org/10.1111/j.1564-913x.2000.tb00406.x.
18. *Ibid.*, 128.

prominence in a human rights discourse, that could also have considerable positive implications for the expansion and further development of a human rights approach, as well as one which, as we will see, may have more to contribute to the achievement of sustainable development objectives. In this sense, the normative approach to human rights treatment of labour standards identified by Mantouvalou persists in its relevance.

It is also noteworthy that the human rights approach to labour standards has in an era of decolonisation been extended from a narrow preoccupation with limited definitions of civil, political and socio-economic rights to the recognition of the rights of people, including rights to self-determination, cultural preservation and to development.[19] The ILO has, for example, sought to promote the rights of indigenous peoples in the context of labour through Conventions Nos 107 and 169, which provide for rights to participation, consultation and self-management for indigenous peoples.[20] Notable is the generous understanding of 'work' or 'labour': 'the consideration of land-based livelihoods reminds us that industrial labour is not the only "work" that merits attention'.[21] The 2007 United Nations Declaration on the Rights of Indigenous Peoples (UNDRIP)[22] further recognises rights of indigenous peoples 'to free, prior and informed consent' (if not veto), alongside entitlement to develop priorities and strategies for the exercise of the right to development.[23] In these ways, the voices of those at work from indigenous communities and their participatory and autonomous decision-making have achieved respect in some international legal form, if not always in domestic practice.[24]

1.3 Finding Agency in a Human Rights Approach for Labour

Arguably, the difficulty and danger of a human rights approach for labour is that it ultimately depends on appeals to judges in courts or experts in international supervisory bodies, such as those established under the 1966 Covenants or in the Council of Europe or the Organization of American States (OAS), such as the ECtHR or the Inter-American Court of Human Rights (IACtHR) respectively. This creates a top-down

19. James Crawford, *The Rights of Peoples* (Oxford University Press 1988); Peter Jones, 'Human Rights, Group Rights, and Peoples' Rights' (1999) 21 *Human Rights Quarterly* 80 https://dx.doi.org/10.1353/hrq.1999.0009.
20. *See* the 'Convention No. 169 Toolbox', available at: https://www.ilo.org/global/topics/indigenous-tribal/toolbox/lang--en/index.htm.
21. Sara Seck, 'Transnational Labour Law and the Environment: Beyond the Bounded Autonomous Worker' (2018) 33(2) *Canadian Journal of Law and Society* 137, 141 https://doi.org/10.1017/cls.2018.15; also Ania Zbyszewska & Flavia Maximo, 'Rethinking the Labour-Environment (Land) Nexus: Beyond Coloniality, Towards New Epistemologies for Labour Law' (2023) 39(3&4) *International Journal of Comparative Labour Law and Industrial Relations* 293 https://doi.org/10.54648/ijcl2023021.
22. *See* text and resources, available at: https://www.un.org/development/desa/indigenouspeoples/declaration-on-the-rights-of-indigenous-peoples.html.
23. Sarah A. Radcliffe, 'Geography and Indigeneity III: Co-articulation of Colonialism and Capitalism in Indigeneity's Economies' (2020) 44(2) *Progress in Human Geography* 374, 383-384 https://dx.doi.org/10.1177/030913251982738.
24. *See* John Knox reports UN Doc A/HRC/25/53 (2014) and UN Doc A/HRC/37/59, (2018); discussed by Seck *supra* n. 21, at 146-148.

system where the entitlements of workers are determined less by collective bargaining and active agency in negotiation and more by the political opinions (and prejudices) of an elite.[25]

One way to counter this concern is to focus on the ways in which human rights can enable voice and participatory engagement in decision-making, for example, via the right to freedom of speech and also freedom of association. For example, Grainne de Búrca has documented how agency can be achieved through 'human rights experimentalism', in which appeal to human rights norms can be helpful where the project is a dynamic one, which is 'activated, shaped, and given its meaning and impact through the ongoing mobilization of affected populations, groups and individuals, and through their iterative engagement with an array of domestic and international institutions and processes over time'.[26] She has also identified what could be a 'multiple boomerang effect' of human rights litigation, for while it may be difficult for civil society and social movements (including workers and their representatives) to accomplish their goals through a single judgment in their favour, by engaging with human rights standards in courts and public policy debates, they may be able to regenerate and reshape those norms, refashioning their content and the ways in which court findings are then implemented at multiple levels: nationally, regionally and internationally.

2 SUSTAINABILITY AND HUMAN RIGHTS

This second part of the chapter examines the wide-ranging promise of sustainability, the significance of the content of the Sustainable Development Goals (SDGs) in unpacking what sustainability might mean in practice and the relevance of human rights to both. As is the case from a human rights perspective, there is positive law and potential instrumental use of a sustainable development approach to consider,[27] but it may be preferable to start from the point of principle, namely the origins and character of this normative concept, before considering more concretely the UN SDGs adopted in 2015 as a key facet of the 2030 Agenda[28] alongside their relationship to other human rights instruments.

2.1 Defining Sustainable Development

It is common to identify three 'pillars' of sustainable development: economic, environmental and social.[29] This raises the question – where does labour fit? Arguably, labour

25. Kevin Kolben, 'Labor Rights as Human Rights' (2009) 50 *Virginia Journal of International Law* 449; and Conor Gearty & Virginia Mantouvalou, *Debating Social Rights* (Bloomsbury Publishing, 2010).
26. Grainne de Búrca, *Reframing Human Rights in a Turbulent Era* (Oxford University Press, 2021), 3-4.
27. Cf. Mantouvalou, *supra* n. 2.
28. *See* 2030 Agenda, *supra* n. 1.
29. Ben Purvis, Yong Mao & Darren Robinson, 'Three Pillars of Sustainability: In Search of Conceptual Origins' (2019) 44(3) *Sustainability Science* 681.

law is concerned with the social dimension of sustainability, and this is where it is usually placed.[30] After all, labour is a vital part of participation in a wider social community; work offers access to the necessities of life and, thereby, human well-being overall. In this context, connections have been made between the capabilities approach espoused by Sen and subsequently Martha Nussbaum, which has been aimed at empowering local communities and especially those at work who suffer systemic disadvantage.[31]

I would also argue that labour standards are as concerned with environmental and social objectives as with social objectives. Labour contributes to the economy, being the basis for employer profit[32] but also because workers' wages are spent in the economy and keep it afloat.[33] Further, the close relationship between those at work and their wider environment has been explained in relational terms by Sara Seck, Ania Zbyszewska and others.[34] In considering the application of capabilities theory to work, Simon Deakin has observed the sources of agency underlying human functionings and thereby moulding capabilities will depend on 'their society (such as social norms, legal rules and legal political institutions) and their *environment* (which could include climate, physical surroundings and technological infrastructure)'.[35] Paolo Tomassetti has also made the point that the wider environment is also of considerable relevance to many of those at work in different sectors, whether this be delivery or transport or remote work of some other kind.[36] This was demonstrated subsequently in the COVID-19 pandemic and its aftermath,[37] so that we can observe that health and safety at work therefore requires clean and healthy environments beyond factory walls or the shop or office. Moreover, it is evident that how work is carried out will have a profound impact on the environment, as Tomassetti's recent analysis of energy sources for

30. Erich Grießler & Beate Littig, 'Social sustainability: A Catchword Between Political Pragmatism and Social Theory' (2005) 8(1-2) *International Journal of Sustainable Development* 65 https://dx.doi.org/10.1504/ijsd.2005.007375; Konstantinos Alexandris Polomarkakis, 'The European Pillar of Social Rights and the Quest for EU Social Sustainability' (2020) 29(2) *Social & Legal Studies* 183 https://dx.doi.org/10.1177/0964663919829199.
31. As discussed in Grießler & Littig, *supra* n. 30. *See* Sen, *supra* n. 17; also Amartya Sen, *Development as Freedom*, (Oxford University Press, 1999); and Amartya Sen, 'Human Rights and Capabilities' (2005) 6(2) *Journal of Human Development* 151 https://dx.doi.org/10.1080/14649880500120491. *See* further Martha Nussbaum, *Creating Capabilities: The Human Development Approach* (Harvard University Press, 2011) and Martha Nussbaum, 'Labour Law and the Capabilities Approach', in Brian Langille (ed.), *The Capability Approach to Labour Law* (Oxford University Press, 2019).
32. From a Marxist material explanation of exploitation in contemporary capitalism, for which *see* Karl Marx, *Capital* (Wordsworth, 2013); Anne-Laure Fayard, 'Notes on the Meaning of Work: Labor, Work, and Action in the 21st Century' (2021) 30(2) *Journal of Management Inquiry* 207, 209 https://dx.doi.org/10.1177/1056492619841705.
33. *See* for e.g., Florence Jaumotte & Carolina Buitron, *Inequality and Labor Market Institutions* (IMF Staff Discussion Note 15/14, 1 July 2015).
34. *See* Seck, *supra* n. 21; and Ania Zbyszewska, 'Regulating Work with People and "Nature" in Mind: Feminist Reflections' (2018) 40 *Comparative Labor Law and Policy Journal* 9.
35. Simon Deakin, 'Social Rights in a Globalized Economy', in Philip Alston (ed.), *Labour Rights as Human Rights* (Oxford University Press, 2005), 56.
36. Paolo Tomassetti, 'Labor Law and Environmental Sustainability' (2018) 40 *Comparative Labour Law and Policy Journal* 61, 63.
37. Lina Vyas, '"New Normal" at Work in a Post-COVID World: Work–life Balance and Labor Markets' (2022) 41(1) *Policy and Society* 155 https://dx.doi.org/10.1093/polsoc/puab011.

production illustrates.[38] His dissection of legal and social labour history illustrates how the three pillars of sustainability are not neatly distinguishable but intersect and interact.

Beyond these conceptual dimensions of sustainable development, there is also a temporal aspect to consider. What also may be considered distinctive regarding a sustainability approach is a concern with both inter-generational and intra-generational justice. In other words, sustainable development is concerned with meeting 'the needs of the present without compromising the ability of future generations to meet their own needs' (inter-generational justice), which entails consideration 'of the long term as well as the short- term advantages and disadvantages of alternative actions'.[39] Simultaneously, attention is also to be paid to *intra*-generational justice addressing, for example, relative poverty or other forms of injustice within a current generation.[40] In this way, sustainability as a broader objective mirrors the universal, stringent and timeless features that Mantouvalou considers to distinguish human rights.[41]

If we accept this normative basis for labour standards, then workers and their representatives are entitled to seek to improve conditions not only for their immediate workplace in economic terms but also in broader environmental ways, with attention to concerns of the entire community. They may also be able to pursue cross-border concerns, given that environmental issues do not stop at national boundaries. Further, they may be able to make the case that any collective agreement should serve not only the immediate interests of current workers but also in inter-generational terms, workers who will be hired in the future. The scope of labour law in this way has immense potential not to contract but rather to expand.

2.2 Aligning Sustainability and Human Rights

Sustainability or sustainable development has been a paradigm favoured by business in preference to a human rights approach. As the 'business and human rights' guiding principles gained momentum, a sustainability approach seemed less intrusive, and a 'softer' line was pedalled by business interests which were heavily represented in the consultative process that led to the drafting of the 2015 SDGs.[42] However, a bolder (and

38. Paolo Tomassetti, 'Energy Transition: A Labour Law Retrospective' (2023) 52(1) *Industrial Law Journal* 34 https://dx.doi.org/10.1093/indlaw/dwac008.
39. World Commission on Environment and Development (WCED), *Our Common Future* (Oxford University Press, 1987), 51.
40. For discussion, *see* William M. Lafferty & Oluf Langhelle, 'Sustainable Development as Concept and Norm', in William M. Lafferty & Oluf Langhelle (eds), *Towards Sustainable Development* (Palgrave Macmillan, 1999).
41. *See* Mantouvalou, *supra* n. 2.
42. Regina Scheyvens, Glenn Banks & Emma Hughes, 'The Private Sector and the SDGs: The Need to Move Beyond "Business as Usual"' (2016) 24(5) *Sustainable Development* 371 https://dx.doi.org/10.1002/sd.1623; Thomas Pogge & Mitu Sengupta, 'The Sustainable Development Goals (SDGs) as Drafted: Nice Idea, Poor Execution' (2015) 24(3) *Washington International Law Journal* 571, 574-575; and Lou Pingeot, *Corporate Influence in the Post- 2015 Process* (2014)

arguably preferable) claim is that sustainable development policies and human rights are not severable but have to be aligned. A failing of the Millennium Development Goals (MDGs) was said to be that they 'sidestepped rather than aligned with human rights obligations', such as equality and non-discrimination.[43] However, the SDGs embedded in the 2030 Agenda do seem to incorporate human rights (and workers' human rights) in palpable and important ways.

For example, the preamble to the UN 2030 Agenda Resolution states that SDGs 'seek to realize the human rights of all and to achieve gender equality and the empowerment of all women and girls' – no one to be left behind. While the Introduction (in paragraphs 3 and 8) again restates that aim. Paragraph 10 claims grounding in the UDHR and 'international human rights treaties'. It has been asked whether this means that these SDGs (or particular targets and indicators that include them) 'are symmetrical to or a deviation of present obligations set out in law'.[44]

The difficulty lies potentially in including human rights norms set out in other international instruments while contemplating their dilution. Seeking to prevent any disparity, the UN Office of the High Commissioner for Human Rights (OHCHR) has set out the links between various SDGs and associated targets with existing human rights protections.[45] For example, in relation to SDG 8 which seeks promotion of 'sustained, inclusive and sustainable economic growth, full and productive employment and decent work for all', SDG targets 8.5, 8.6 and 8.8 on working environment are linked expressly to Article 23 of the UDHR, Articles 6, 7 and 10 of the ICESCR, as well as Article 27 of the UN Convention on the Rights of Persons with Disabilities, alongside ILO Core Conventions and ILO Declaration on Fundamental Principles and Rights at Work. Similarly, prohibition of slavery, forced labour, and trafficking of persons in SDG target 8.7 is linked to Article 4 of the UDHR, Article 8 of the ICCPR, Article 6 of the Convention on Discrimination Against Women (CEDAW) and Articles 34-36 of the Convention on the Rights of the Child.

Mention of freedom of association is missing from the text of SDG 8 and associated targets in a way that might seem to obstruct the realisation of 'decent work'. At least since 2017, SDG indicator 8.8.2 requires attention to any 'increase in national compliance of labour rights (freedom of association and collective bargaining) based on ILO textual sources and national legislation', with reference to 'sex and migrant

---

working paper, https://www.cidse.org/wp-content/uploads/2014/02/Misereor_Corporate_influence_in_the_Post-2015_process_Jan_2014.pdf.

43. Diane F. Frey & Gillian MacNaughton, 'A Human Rights Lens on Full Employment and Decent Work in the 2030 Sustainable Development Agenda' (2016) 6(2) *Sage Open*, available at: https://doi.org/10.1177/2158244016649580.
44. Duncan French & Louis J. Kotzé (eds), *Sustainable Development Goals: Law, Theory and Implementation* (Edward Elgar Publishing, 2018), 3; *see also* for examination of this concern, Tonia Novitz & Margherita Pieraccini, 'Agenda 2030 and the Sustainable Development Goals: "Responsive, Inclusive, Participatory and Representative Decision-Making"?', in Margherita Pieraccini & Tonia Novitz (eds), *Legal Perspectives on Sustainability* (Bristol University Press, 2020).
45. *See* https://www.ohchr.org/sites/default/files/Documents/Issues/Development/SR/AddisAbaba/SDG_HR_Table.pdf.

status'.[46] Further, the UN Special Rapporteur on the Rights to Peaceful Assembly and Association UN Special Rapporteur has taken the view that reference to 'fundamental rights' in SDG target 16.10 can be understood to include freedom of association, collective bargaining and a right to strike.[47] There is also a reference in SDG indicator 16.10.1 to 'killing, kidnapping, enforced disappearance, arbitrary detention and torture of [inter alia] trade unionists', which speaks of a desire to protect workers' representatives. I have also argued that the importance of collective worker representation and agency follows from SDG target 16.6 that sets out the commitment to 'develop effective, accountable and transparent institutions at all levels' and target 16.7 which aims to '[e]nsure responsive, inclusive, participatory and representative decision-making at all levels'.[48]

This raises the issue of just transition and the role of social dialogue (relying on individual and collective worker voice and influence) to achieve 'transformations of contemporary working practices to pre-empt and mitigate environmental harms while preserving social justice'.[49] This strategy has an extensive history, derived from the concerns of Canadian and United States unions in the 1970s,[50] now reflected in the ILO Guidelines on Just Transitions 2015[51] and the preamble to the 2015 Paris Agreement, which takes 'into account the imperatives of a just transition of the workforce and the creation of decent work and quality jobs'.[52] A further Just Transition Declaration was adopted by a selection of countries at the UN Climate Change Conference COP 26, held in Scotland in 2021.[53]

3 WHAT CAN BE DONE TO UTILISE HUMAN RIGHTS MECHANISMS TO PROMOTE SUSTAINABILITY AT WORK?

This final part of the chapter considers what human rights bodies and other actors have done to recognise the connections between sustainability and human rights in the

46. IISD, *Policy Brief: Getting to 2030: Tracking SDG Indicators for Evidence of Implementation Progress* (2018), http://sdg.iisd.org/commentary/policy-briefs/getting-to-2030-tracking-sdg-indicators-for-evidence-of-implementation-progress/.
47. Report of the Special Rapporteur on the rights to freedom of peaceful assembly and association, 7 August 2018, A/73/279, paras 6 and 58, also paras 87-89.
48. Tonia Novitz, 'Engagement with Sustainability at the International Labour Organization and Wider Implications for Collective Worker Voice' (2020) 159(4) *International Labour Review* 463, 472-478 https://dx.doi.org/10.1111/ilr.12181.
49. Cf. Alexandra R. Harrington, *Just Transitions and the Future of Law and Regulation* (Palgrave Macmillan 2022); David J. Doorey & Ann Eisenberg, 'The Contested Boundaries of Just Transitions', in Consuelo Chacartegui Jávega (ed.), *Labour Law and Ecology* (Thomson Reuters Arazandi, 2022).
50. Dimitris Stevis, Edouard Morena & Dunja Krause, 'Introduction: The Genealogy and Contemporary Politics of Just Transitions', in Edouard Morena, Dunja Krause & Dimitris Stevis (eds), *Just Transitions: Social Justice in the Shift Towards a Low-Carbon World* (Pluto Press, 2020), 9.
51. ILO Guidelines for a just transition towards environmentally sustainable economies and societies for all (ILO, 2015).
52. *See* Navraj Singh Ghaleigh, *Just Transitions for Workers: When Climate Change Met Labour Justice*, Edinburgh School of Law Research Paper No. 2019/30 (University of Edinburgh, 2019).
53. *See* information available at: https://www.ilo.org/global/about-the-ilo/newsroom/news/WCMS_826717/lang--en/index.htm.

context of work, which is as yet remarkably little. This process seems to be just beginning and evolving. Human rights institutions in regional and UN systems are initiating forms of change. Moreover, lessons may be learnt from strategic human rights litigation based on climate change and also from recent findings of regional Courts of Human Rights on the question of freedom of association and worker voice.

3.1 Initiatives Taken by Human Rights Mechanisms

We are now witnessing a greater determination to address environmental concerns for workers in human rights terms. For example, the Inter-American Commission on Human Rights adopted a resolution on the Climate Emergency and the scope of Inter-American Human Rights Obligations, noting the 'right to work', as well as obligations to respect trade union rights and adapt social protection.[54] In perhaps a similar vein, in 2022, the UN General Assembly recognised 'a right to a clean, healthy and sustainable environment', underscoring the obligation of states 'to respect, protect and promote human rights, including in all actions undertaken to address environmental challenges', but making no mention of work.[55]

What has been perhaps more significant is the determination at the ILO International Labour Conference in 2022 to incorporate into the ILO Declaration on Fundamental Principles and Rights at Work an entitlement to 'a safe and healthy working environment' while giving 'fundamental' status also to Conventions Nos 155 and 187.[56] At the same 2022 ILC, a further Resolution was adopted on employment policy,[57] seeking to facilitate 'the just transition towards environmentally sustainable and inclusive economies and societies in accordance with the Guidelines for a just transition towards environmentally sustainable economies and societies for all of the International Labour Organization (ILO)'.[58] The vehicle for realisation of those ambitious objectives was to be 'social dialogue', stated to include 'collective bargaining and tripartite cooperation', which is regarded as 'essential in promoting peace, enabling recovery and building resilience'.[59] This is consistent with the assertion of the International Labour Office (the ILO secretariat) in 2019 that freedom of association and collective bargaining would be crucial to realisation of the SDG 8 targets.[60]

54. Inter-American Commission on Human Rights Resolution No. 3/2021 Climate Emergency: Scope of Inter-American Human Rights Obligations.
55. UN General Assembly Resolution A/76/L.75 2022.
56. *See* Resolution on the inclusion of a safe and healthy working environment in the ILO's framework of fundamental principles and rights at work, ILC.110/Resolution1, 10 June 2022 available at: https://www.ilo.org/wcmsp5/groups/public/---ed_norm/---relconf/documents/meetingdocument/wcms_848632.pdf. For background, *see* Zahra Yusifli & Colin Fenwick, 'Workers' Rights and Human Rights: Toward a New Fundamental Principle?', in Kimberley Elliott (ed.), *Handbook on Globalisation and Labour Standards* (Edward Elgar, 2022).
57. ILC.110/Resolution IV, adopted 11 June 2022. Available at: https://www.ilo.org/wcmsp5/groups/public/---ed_norm/---relconf/documents/meetingdocument/wcms_848637.pdf.
58. *Ibid.*, para. 10.
59. *Ibid.*, paras 13-16.
60. International Labour Office, *Time to Act for SDG 8: Integrating Decent Work, Sustained Growth and Environmental Integrity* (Geneva: ILO, 2019).

These initiatives have had further springboard effects, such that a new strategy on just transition was endorsed at the ILC in 2023,[61] while the advocacy of the current ILO Director-General, Gilbert F. Houngbo, of a 'Global Coalition for Social Justice' has been expressly linked to sustainable development objectives.[62] The need for the Global Coalition has been justified by Houngbo in terms of 'growing inequalities', which are 'threatening the achievement of the 2030 Agenda for Sustainable Development'.[63] This proposal is also intended to chime with the vision presented by the UN Secretary-General in 2021 of a 'Common Agenda' and a renewed social contract.[64]

In other words, the right to a healthy environment is now recognised as a free-standing human right at the ILO and in the UN, with potentially positive implications for workers, while freedom of association and collective rights have been recognised as vital human rights to enable sustainability objectives. Additionally, ongoing collaborative global partnership in terms of SDG 17 is envisaged to achieve the kinds of institutions contemplated under SDG 16 to 'promote just, peaceful and inclusive societies'.

3.2 Human Rights Litigation on Sustainability, Labour and Just Transition

The 'universal' dimension to human rights claims, namely the underlying assumption that that 'everyone' matters in a way that spans national borders (no one is to be left behind), has provided a useful foothold for litigants seeking to resist climate change and other environmental harms. That idea of universality and cross-border relevance resonates with the determination to resist the impact of ecological disruption and pollution, which also has no respect for national boundaries.[65] An example is the *Duarte Agostinho* case,[66] submitted to the ECtHR by a group of young persons challenging the lack of action on greenhouse gas emissions by 33 states, which they observe is leading to climate change which will affect their right to life and quality of life under Articles 3 and 8 of the European Convention on Human Rights. At the time of writing, this case is due to be heard at the Grand Chamber but has yet to be determined (or judgment issued). There is, however, some prospect of success, given recent observations in the Court. For example, the recent majority judgment in *Pavlov v. Russia* indicates that failure to act to address air-borne pollution which has a

61. ILO Resolution concerning a just transition towards environmentally sustainable economies and societies for all 2023, ILC.111/Resolution V, ILC, 111th Session.
62. *Update on the Global Coalition for Social Justice* GB.347/INS/4, 20 February 2023; *Report of the Director-General: Advancing Social Justice* (ILO 2023).
63. *Update on the Global Coalition for Social Justice* GB.347/INS/4, 20 February 2023, 4, para. 8.
64. *Ibid.*, 5, para. 10; *Report of the Director-General: Advancing Social Justice* (ILO 2023), 30, para. 107.
65. Tonia Novitz, 'Sustainability as Solidarity Unbound: Labour Rights and Collective Voice in the United Nations Sustainable Development Goals and the European Union', in Julia López López (ed.), *Inscribing Solidarity* (Cambridge University Press, 2022), 27.
66. *See* Appn No. 39371/20 *Cláudia Duarte Agostinho and others v. Portugal and 32 other States* pending at the time of writing.

significant risk of damaging human health can constitute a breach of Article 8.[67] Further, in a concurring opinion, Judge Serghides recognised that 'the protection of the environment and human rights are ... closely interconnected',[68] also citing findings of the European Committee of Social Rights under the European Social Charter relating, *inter alia*, to health and safety at work.[69] However, other statements by the ECtHR do not yet make that connection.

At the IACtHR, comparable claims have been successfully presented, and judgment has been given accordingly. For example, the Court's Advisory Opinion OC-23/17 established the responsibility of OAS Member States to address transboundary harms and to be proactive in doing so, recognising and safeguarding the human right to a healthy environment, acting as a harbinger for subsequent resolutions.[70] Further, in another case decided in 2020, the Inter-American Court has recognised the rights of indigenous peoples to a healthy environment and communal property and associated with this adequate food, water, and preservation of their cultural life, as well as agency in the forms of consent (and refusal of consent) to any interferences by the state with the same.[71] The entitlement to a healthy working environment is also well-established for workers,[72] whether hired through the formal or informal labour market.

More explicitly on the subject of work, the jurisprudence of the IACtHR can fairly be described as 'transformative'.[73] The universal dimension of human rights has been utilised to extend the entitlement of those in precarious or unconventional work to basic socio-economic and civil and political rights, as well as coverage under labour laws which protect these at a national level. Indeed, structural poverty which impedes access to formal work is a basis for the Court's intervention.[74] Hence, in the Brazilian *Fireworks Factory* case, in which 64 workers were killed, the government had an obligation to monitor the activities of private actors regardless of the informality of the workers' employment situation, so that there should have been supervision and control ensuring safety, health and hygiene in the workplace under Article 26 of the American Convention on Human Rights 1969.[75]

67. Appn No. 31612/09 *Pavlov v. Russia*, 11 October 2022.
68. *Ibid.*, Concurring Opinion of Judge Serghides, para. 4.
69. *Ibid.*, para. 5; citing *Marangopoulos Foundation for Human Rights (MFHR) v. Greece* Complaint No. 30/2005, 6 December 2006.
70. IACtHR Advisory Opinion OC-23/17 of 15 November 2017 requested by the Republic of Colombia. *See* Belem Olmos Giupponi, 'Just Transition in the Global South: Alternative Approaches from Latin America' (2023) 39(3&4) *International Journal of Comparative Labour Law and Industrial Relations* 381, 389 https://dx.doi.org/10.54648/ijcl2023025.
71. *Ibid.*, discussing IACtHR, *Case of The Indigenous Communities of the Lhaka Honhat (Our Land) Association v. Argentina*, Judgment of 6 February 2020.
72. IACtHR, *Case of Spoltore v. Argentina*, Judgment of 9 June 2020.
73. Julieta Lobato, 'Labour Law and Transformative Constitutionalism: Toward Transformative Labour Law in Latin America' (2023) MPIL Research Paper Series No. 2023-24, forthcoming in (2024) *International Journal of Comparative Labour Law and Industrial Relations*, available at: https://papers.ssrn.com/sol3/papers.cfm?abstract_id=4628560.
74. IACtHR, *Case of the Employees of the Fireworks Factory of Santo Antônio de Jesus and their families v. Brazil*, Judgment of 15 July 2020. Series C No. 407, cited by Lobato, *supra* n. 73, 18-19.
75. *Ibid.*, para. 176.

Moreover, access to freedom of association is generously construed by the IACtHR and very clearly protects not only collective bargaining but also the right to strike, again for women and others in atypical work. In Advisory Opinion OC-27/21, the Court adopted a multidimensional perspective on the right to freedom of association, the right to collective bargaining, the right to strike, and their relation to other rights. The Opinion concluded that: 'The rights to freedom of assembly and freedom of expression, as they relate to freedom of association, the right to collective bargaining and the right to strike, are fundamental rights for allowing workers and their representatives to organize and express their specific demands concerning working conditions and for them to be able to take part in matters of public interest with a collective voice.'[76] Moreover, the Court observed that 'states have the obligation to adapt their laws and practices to new conditions in the labor market, regardless of the type of technological developments that bring about such changes, and in consideration of the obligations to protect worker rights under the terms of international human rights law'.[77] This Opinion thereby prompts attention to the process of just transition, with respect to workers' rights, alongside mere protection of civil and political rights, such as freedom of speech and association. Indeed, the IACtHR offers a way of considering how such workers' rights could be combined to promote voice more actively rather than prevent egregious breaches while also prompting states to act as regulators. In a comparable way, the IACtHR required a programmatic response to the *Fireworks Factory* judgment, which was exceptionally far-reaching, including further investigations, psychological counselling and medical assistance for all those affected, creation of an ongoing inspection programme (to be designed in collaboration with workers and their representatives) as well as compliance with UN Guiding Principles on Business and Human Rights obligations.[78]

This is a stark contrast to the ECtHR, which seeks to establish an 'employment relationship' as a precondition for claiming Article 11 rights under the Convention that can then be defeated by other secondary considerations associated with public policy.[79] Further, while in *Straume v. Latvia,* a right to freedom of speech has now been established for trade union representatives on matters pertinent to their members' interests,[80] this looks likely to be restricted. It seems that such an entitlement cannot be claimed in the same way for individual workers unless they can rely on the additional requirements for whistleblower status,[81] since the free speech entitlements of the employer can be balanced against the employer's entitlement to defend their commercial self-interest.[82] 'Employees have a duty of loyalty, reserve and discretion to their

76. IACtHR Advisory Opinion OC-27/21 on request of the Inter-American Commission of Human Rights, 5 May 2021.
77. IACtHR Advisory Opinion OC-27/21, para. 202. *See also* in support of a wide-ranging right to strike in another judgment, IACtHR *Case of the Former Employees of the Judiciary v. Guatemala*, Judgment of 26 July 2022.
78. *Case of the Fireworks Factory, supra* n. 73, paras 267-291, discussed by Lobato, *supra* n. 73, 20.
79. Appn No. 2330/09 *Sindicatul 'Pastorul Cel Bun' v. Romania* judgment of 9 July 2013, paras 57 and 142.
80. Appn No. 59402/14 *Straume v. Latvia*, Judgment of 2 June 2022.
81. *Ibid.*, paras 91 and 101.
82. *Ibid.*, paras 100 and 103.

employer and certain expressions that may be legitimate within other contexts are not appropriate in labour relations.'[83] In a similar fashion, the ECtHR now regards as inadmissible individual claims relating to a right to strike under Article 11 of the European Convention on Human Rights, which are not supported by officially recognised trade unions.[84] The refusal to hear these cases might seem to be based on the wording of Article 11, which refers to freedom of association, including 'the right to form and join trade unions'.[85] As I have observed elsewhere, this seems an odd and unnecessary interpretation, given that freedom of association is stated in Article 11 to include those rights rather than excluding others.[86] Also, official trade union representation is not available in many European legal systems where access to membership is demarcated in restrictive ways, such as stringent employment status. This approach of the ECtHR restricts access to inclusive speech and association contemplated by SDGs 8 and 16.[87]

What is less clear in either Court is how human rights institutions will respond when collective labour interests and other environmental concerns are in conflict. Belen Olmos Giupponi has cited in this respect the *Somarco* case brought in the Chilean courts, where workers contested a decree that had been issued by the Ministry of Energy to phase out coal-based electricity generation.[88] The Chilean Supreme Court ruled not only in favour of the decarbonization programme but also in reliance on Article 19 of the Chilean Constitution that upheld workers' claims to equality under the law, the right to work and trade union freedoms, requiring the Ministry to put in place a programme supporting the workers affected, which reflects the wider remedial response of the IACtHR to past labour rights cases.

A cursory examination of these two regional human rights courts therefore indicates that human rights claims will not inevitably serve workers' interests or further the demands of a sustainable development agenda for labour. However, what the findings of the IACtHR indicate is that there remains scope for this to happen. Arguably, the Court's judgments are sending a message to other constitutional courts in the region as to how this transformational approach can be realised, even if this

83. *Ibid.*, para. 108.
84. Appn No. 66828/16 *Bariş v. Turkey*, 14 December 2021; Appn No. 52051/17 *Ateş and Others v. Turkey*, Decision 28 February 2023; and Appn No. 46183/12 *Ekelik and Others v. Turkey*, Decision 28 February 2023.
85. *See* Filip Dorssemont, 'Bariş and Others v. Turkey (ECHR, 66828/16): How Wild Are Spontaneous Strikes?' *European Human Rights Updates Annotations*, Annotation to European Court of Human Rights, 14 December 2021, ECLI:CE:ECHR:2021:1214DEC006682816 (ECHR-2022-00 94*)*, para. 13.
86. Tonia Novitz, 'Exploring a Human Rights Approach to "Decent" Digital Work: What Happens When Freedom of Association and Expression Are Combined?' (2023) 2 *Hungarian Labour Law e-Journal* available at: https://hllj.hu/.
87. For more detailed criticism of this line of reasoning, *see* Tonia Novitz, 'Collective Labour Rights for Working People: The Legal Framework Established by the International Labour Organization', in Sanjukta Paul, Shae McCrystal & Ewan McGaughey, *The Cambridge Handbook of Labor in Competition Law* (Cambridge University Press, 2022), 11-26.
88. Olmos Giupponi, *supra* n. 70, 389-390, citing the Judgment of the Chilean Supreme Court (Rol No. 25.530–9 August 2021, 2021), https://climate-laws.org/geographies/chile/litigation_cases/company-workers-union-of-maritima-commercial-somarco-limited-and-others-v-ministry-of-energy.

approach has yet to be adopted by the ECtHR. There are, however, likely to be certain preconditions for human rights claims to assist and reinforce sustainability and the associated process of just transition.

4 CONCLUSION

To conclude, this chapter has reviewed the ways in which human rights claims and labour standards can connect and coalesce. It has been suggested that human rights need not be viewed as antagonistic to labour rights but can offer a way to highlight their universality and significance while also fostering the access to voice and association needed for the realisation of these essential entitlements. A sustainable development approach based on inter- and intra-generational justice, traversing social, economic and environmental facets of sustainability, also requires engagement in social dialogue, the prerequisites of which are freedom of speech and association for workers and their representatives. The OHCHR has observed the necessity of compliance with established international human rights, including ILO Conventions, with respect to achievement of the SDGs. Additionally, the UN Rapporteur for the rights to assembly and association has emphasised the importance of these entitlements in relation to SDGs 8 and 16. Further, the importance of the voices of workers and that of their representatives in collective bargaining and other forms of social dialogue and global partnership continues to be stressed by the ILO as a prerequisite for achievement of SDG 8 and the other SDGs. Indeed, the ILO is seeking to foster a global partnership aligned with SDG 17 with respect to just transitions and a Global Coalition for Social Justice.

It would seem that we could be seeing a melding of human rights and environmental concerns on the global stage, both in terms of initiatives taken by international organisation and human rights litigation. In this respect, the protection of labour rights has more relevance than currently seems to be contemplated by the ECtHR. However, the IACtHR offers an example of the ways in which a regional human rights court could foster protection of workers' rights as human rights in the context of sustainable development. Much will depend on the impact of the Court's findings and whether its influence extends beyond OAS Member States to places like Europe. There is genuine potential for the multilevel human rights experimentalism and civil society engagement contemplated by de Búrca,[89] but we have yet to see whether it will be realised.

89. de Búrca, *supra* n. 26.

CHAPTER 9

Cosmopolitan Solidarity; Equality in Social Rights as the Agenda

Julia Lo'pez Lo'pez

1 SOLIDARITY AS A FOUNDATION TO PURSUE AN EQUALITY AGENDA

How to advance the construction of labour regulation by decommodifying labour,[1] underscoring workers' dignity as a philosophical foundation for labour law,[2] is the main challenge facing social law today. In this sense, labour law as a contribution to fortifying democracy should be recognizable as an instrument to cut contractual imbalances that foster inequalities - especially between employer and worker. Doing so requires structures of workers' representation and collective voice[3] as well as solid systems of social protection geared toward advancing the protection against vulnerability. The idea animating this chapter is to develop the notion of inclusive solidarity as a *cosmopolitan* concept that moves from individual to collective subjects, that interconnects transnational and national multilevel sources of regulation, and that brings together hard law, soft law and hybrid management instruments.[4] A fundamental claim of this essay is that the principles of solidarity and equality can best be translated into effective forms of regulation when they are woven together in ways that fortify both standards.

---

1. On the person of the worker as a subject of law, *see* Supiot A. (1994), Critique du droit du travail, ed. Quadrige, PUF, p. 44.
2. Collins, H., Lester, G. & Mantouvalou, V. eds (2018), Philophical Foundations of Labour Law, OUP.
3. Bogg, A. & Novizt, T. (2014), Voices of work. Continuity and Change in Common Law World, OUP.
4. On cosmopiltan legal order, *see* Stone Sweet, A. & Ryan, C., (2018), A Cosmopolitan Legal Order. Kant, constitutional justice and the Convention on Human Rights, Oxford University Press.

Why is it important, as advocated here, to continue to raise equality and non-discrimination as an objective and to include solidarity-oriented policies in the pursuit of that objective? An initial point of departure is the basic observation that no country presents a situation where there are no gaps of inequality between large groups - for example - between men and women.[5] The best data on gender outcomes are presented by Iceland (where women obtain 91.2% of male outcomes), followed by Norway, Finland, New Zealand, Sweden, Germany, Nicaragua, Namibia and Lithuania (80%). In the labour market, in 2022-2023, the participation of women has gone from 63% to 64%, remaining below the level of 2009 when it was 69%.

As a starting point for identifying the usefulness of the solidarity principle and its 'inscriptions' in forms of regulation, it is helpful to note that the implementation of solidarity can be pursued by differentiating several angles in its analysis: solidarity as resistance,[6] solidarity as construction of spaces of democracy[7] and solidarity as collective action.[8] An increasingly present component in the development of an inclusive solidarity model is the one that builds the concept of sustainability.[9]

Leon Bourgeois (1902) asked in his classic book *Solidarité* whether this concept represents a variant of the term fraternity or, on the contrary, should be seen as a new idea.[10] More recent theoretical work points out how solidarity allows us to visualize the need to reconstruct the links between individual and social action, between interests and values and between behaviour and rules, as Rodota has advocated.[11]

2 REGULATORY POLICIES IN THE CONSTRUCTION OF AN INCLUSIVE AND COSMOPOLITAN SOLIDARITY

In elaborating the discourse of solidarity (and its inscriptions in legal instruments), it is crucial to emphasize the constitutionalization of rights and principles[12] in a globalized world where conflicts are created between the notion of fundamental rights and market logic; those conflicts mean that the market's logic cannot prevail exclusively. The role of fundamental rights, both in the International Labour Organization (ILO) and in the European Union (EU), plays an important role in labour regulation, as highlighted by Bob Hepple in the context of the globalization of markets and their management[13]

5. Global gender Gap Report (2023), World Economic Forum.
6. *See* Chenoweth, E. (2021), Civil Resistance. What Everyone Needs to Know, Oxford University Press.
7. *See* De Sousa Santos, B. & Cesar Rodriguez-Garavito, A. eds (2005), Law and Globalization from Bellow. Towards a Cosmopolitan Legality, Cambridge Studies in Law and Society.
8. Doellgast, V., Lillie, N. & Pulignano, V. eds (2020), Reconstrucitgn Solidarity. Labour Unions, Precarious Work and the Politics of Institutional Change in Europe, Oxford University Press.
9. *See* Novitz, T. (2022), Sustanaibility as Solidarity Unbound. Labour Rights as Collective Voice in the United Nations Sustainable Development Goals and the European Union in Lopez Lopez, J. ed., Inscriptions of Solidarity: Labour Law and Beyond, CUP.
10. *See* Bourgeois, L. (1902), Solidarité, Classic Reprint Series, Forgotten Books, Troisieme edition.
11. Rodota, S. (2011), Elogio del moralismo, Editori Laterza, p. 12.
12. Rodotà, S. (2014), Solidarietà, editori Laterza, p. 93.
13. *See* Hepple, B. (2005), Labours Laws and Global Trade, Hart Publishing, pp. 238-249.

within the challenges posed by new forms of industrial relations[14] and specifying the role of the State.[15]

The constitutionalization of fundamental rights has a major impact on the normative shaping of the de-commodification of labour policies. This impact is reflected in important documents such as the ILO's Declaration on Fundamental Principles and Rights (1998),[16] its Declaration on Decent Work and its 2030 Agenda, and the European Union's Charter of Fundamentals Rights. These important texts set the guidelines for cosmopolitan and inclusive solidarity policies to be implemented for all.[17]

I argue that the interactions between, on the one hand, the regulation of equality and non-discrimination, and on the other hand, inscriptions of the solidarity principle provide advantages that are decisive in achieving the objectives that the United Nations has defined for globalization and justice. Indeed, those interactions can serve to enhance the pursuit of both principles: equality and solidarity.

At the ILO level, the management of what has been called a solidarity economy presents modest results, but they are still of interest. The defence of alternative business organization models such as cooperatives has included three international labour standards instruments: Recommendation 193(2002) on the promotion of cooperatives, Recommendation 204(2015) on the transition from the informal to the formal economy and Recommendation 205(2017) on employment and decent work for peace and resilience. In these documents, the role of cooperatives and other social economy initiatives is recognized, and they are viewed as important institutions for achieving solidarity.

At the level of the EU, the first mention of solidarity is found in the original law. Thus, Article 2 of the Treaty declares[18] that the EU is founded on the values of respect for human dignity, freedom, democracy, equality, the rule of law and respect for human rights. These values are common to the Member States in a society characterized by pluralism, non-discrimination, tolerance, justice, solidarity and equality between women and men. The right to equal pay and non-discrimination is enshrined in Article 153 of the Treaty of the Functioning of the European Union (TFEU), and Article 157 of the TFEU authorizes positive action to empower women.

Equality and solidarity have both been developed or 'inscribed' in specific formulations in the Charter of Fundamental Rights of the European Union. Equality as the principle has been legally developed at the level of both international and

14. *See* Finkin, M.W. & Mundlak, G. (2015), Comparative Labour Law, Research Handbooks in Comparative Law, Elgard.
15. *See* Perulli, A. & Bellomo, S. (2019), New Industrial Relations in the Era of Globalization, Universitat Ca' Foscari Venezia – Dipartamento di Economia Collna del Centro Studi Giuridici 15, Wolters Kluwer, Cedam.
16. Adopted at the 86th session of the International Labor Conference in 1998 and in its latest version at the 110th session in 2022.
17. Conceptualizing transnational labour law, Blackett, A. & Trebilcock, A. (2015), Blackett, A. & Trebilcock, A. eds, Research Handbook on transnational labour law, Elgard, pp. 3-31.
18. Solidarity appears in the Treaty in the Preamble, values and in the objectives, *see* Barnard, C. (2006), Labour Market Integration: Lessons from the EU in Globalization and the Future of Labour Law, Craig, D.R. & Lynk, S. eds, CUP, p. 232.

community norms can potentially transmit its strength to objectives linked to the solidarity principle and more specifically can serve as the basis for an audit system assessing compliance once solidarity policies have been implemented. More specifically, the standard of equality can be used to verify the results of policies in their effects on equality and non-discrimination, a potentially tangible way to promote the enforceability of efforts to obtain solidarity-oriented objectives. At the same time, the solidarity principle can be used to expand the range of themes addressed beyond what is directly implied by explicitly equality-oriented standards. Alongside this interaction and in line with the identification of institutions, policies and actors connecting solidarity and equality, the analysis of the contents of solidarity-oriented matters in the Charter of Fundamental Rights raises a new reading of the principle of subsidiarity. Calls and referrals to the national level of development, rooted in a cooperative reading of subsidiarity with regard to the pursuit of solidarity, can exert positive effects.

The principle of subsidiarity plays a significant role in the distribution of competences both at the international level[19] and at the human rights level,[20] marking certain dimensions in the interrelations of the subjects involved. In this regard, Community case law maintains that the requirements of both the uniform application of Union law and the principle of equality mean that a provision of Union law which does not contain an express reference to the law of the Member States to determine its meaning and scope must normally be the subject throughout the Union of an autonomous and uniform interpretation (judgment of 2 June 2022, HK/Danmark and HK/Privat, C587/20, EU:C:2022:419, paragraph 25 and case law cited).

Given this understanding of subsidiarity in the EU, it follows that provisions on equality and solidarity contained in the Charter of Fundamental Rights of the European Union will be applied when community rules are being activated by the member countries. This principle radiates the contents of the Charter to the legal systems of the member countries.

The Charter of Fundamental Rights includes in Chapter 3 equality and non-discrimination as a fundamental right in the EU: All persons are equal before the law (Article 20), prohibition of discrimination (Article 21), cultural, religious and linguistic diversity (Article 22), equality between men and women, equality between men and women shall be guaranteed in all areas, including employment, work and remuneration. The principle of equality does not prevent the maintenance or adoption of measures offering specific advantages in favour of the underrepresented sex (Article 23), the rights of minors (Article 24), the rights of the elderly (Article 25) and the integration of disabled persons (Article 26).

The development of equality policies has been pursued through Directives mainly on gender equality and non-discrimination[21] and, to a lesser extent, on other discrimination factors.[22] The latest directives connect the principle of equality and non-discrimination with the solidarity policies developed in Chapter V of the Charter. Among

19. *See* Supiot ed. (2015), La solidarité. Enquete sur le príncipe juridique, Collège de France, Odile Jacob. p. 344.

these, it is useful to mention Directive 2022/2381 of the European Parliament and of the Council of 23 November 2022 on a better gender balance among directors of listed companies and on related measures with regard to participation rights, and Directive 2023/970 of the European Parliament and of the Council of 10 May 2023, reinforcing the application of the principle of equal pay for equal work or work of equal value for men and women through pay transparency measures and mechanisms for compliance with the right to fair working conditions. However, the role of the ECJ has been very important in the development of the principle of equality and non-discrimination based on gender,[23] and the ECJ has also ruled on the application of solidarity on multiple occasions.[24]

---

20. Paolo G. Carozza, Subsidiarity as a Structural Principle of International Human Rights Law, 97 Am. J. Int'l L. 38 (2003). Available at: https://scholarship.law.nd.edu/law_faculty_scholarship/564, https://doi.org/10.2307/3087103.
21. Among others, Directive 2004/113, equal treatment for men and women in the access to and supply of goods and services, Directive 2006/54, equal treatment for men and women in employment and occupation, including social security schemes, Directive 2010/41, equal treatment for men and women engaged in an activity in a self-employed capacity, Directive 2019/1158, relating to the reconciliation of family and working life for parents and carers, and repealing Council Directive 2010/18/EU.
22. *See* Fredman, S. (2016), Past and Futures: EU Equality, in Bogg, A. & Novitz, T., Research Handbook on EU Labour Law Elgard.
23. ECJ of 8 April 1976, Defrenne II, C 43/75, recognized the direct effect of the principle of equal pay for men and women and declared that it is applicable not only to the actions of public authorities, but also to all collective bargaining agreements; ECJ of 13 May 1986, Bilka C 170/84, considered it 'indirect discrimination' to exclude part-time workers from pension funds, as it affected more women than men; ECJ of 17 May 1990, Barber C 262/88 defined pay within the meaning of Art. 119 of the Treaty as all forms of occupational pensions; CJEU of 11 November 1997, Marschall C 409/95 declared that Community law did not preclude a national rule requiring priority promotion of female candidates in cases where there were fewer women than men in a sector, provided that the advantage was not automatic and that male candidates were guaranteed an examination of their candidacy without being excluded a priori; ECJ of 1 March 2011, Test-Achats C-236/09, declared invalid Art. 5(2) of Council Directive 2004/113/EC as contrary to the principle of equal treatment between men and women in the access to and supply of goods and services; the same actuarial calculation system must be applied to men and women when determining premiums and benefits for insurance purposes; ECJ of 8 May 2019 C-161/18 Cioleta Villar, held in a Spanish case that the rules on the calculation of retirement pensions for workers hired part-time is contrary to EU law if it is considered to be particularly unfavorable to female workers; ECJ of 8 May 2019, C-486/18, on discrimination, part-time work and severance pay and its calculation. ECJ of 7 October 2019, Safeway C-171/18 on the equalization of retirement benefits in the context of a company pension plan; ECJ of 18 September 2019, Ortiz Mesonero, C-366/18, the father was denied authorization to work fixed shifts in order to better care for his children and held that Community rules do not contain any provision obliging Member States, in the context of a request for parental leave, to grant the worker the right to work fixed hours when his usual working regime is a shift regime with a variable schedule; ECJ of 20 June 2019, Hakelbracht, C-404/18, the CJEU established the need to protect in discrimination claims colleagues who may formally or informally support the victim so that they cannot be harmed by the employer. ECJ of 3 June 2021, Tesco Stores C-624/19, in the judgment, the CJEU first recalled its judgment in the Praxair MRC case (C-486/18), in which the prohibition of discrimination between male and female workers also extends to collective agreements, as well as to private contracts intended to regulate remuneration.
24. Schiek, D., Solidarity in the Case Law of the European Court of Justice, Opportunities Missed?, in Krunde, H., Petersen, H. & Manners, I. eds, Transnational Solidarity. Concept, Challeges and Opportunities.

In the frame to interconnect equality and solidarity, Chapter IV on Solidarity of the Charter of Fundamental Rights includes the contents or inscriptions[25] in a broad and ambitious way as a decent work agenda.

Solidarity is read here in a collective way: Collective rights are part of the framing of solidarity, from the right to information and consultation of workers within the company, which is guaranteed at appropriate levels and with sufficient notice, to the right to negotiate and engage in collective action in cases of conflict of interests, the conception of solidarity-oriented rights includes collective actions including strikes to defend worker interests. The Charter's conception of solidarity also includes the right to employment, as is reflected, for example, in free job placement service.

The Charter's 'inscriptions' of the solidarity principle in more specific guarantees or provisions include the promise of fair and equitable working conditions[26] with rights to health, safety and dignity, as well as limited working hours and vacations. Also included is the commitment that young people admitted to work must have working conditions adapted to their age and be protected against economic exploitation or any work that may be harmful to their safety, health, physical, mental, moral or social development or that may jeopardize their education. These commitments have promoted complementary legislation and regulation. It is noteworthy that the new Directive of the European Parliament and of the Council on the improvement of working conditions at work on digital platforms of 8 March 2024 refers to the implementation of a set of rights contained in the Charter of Fundamental Rights, as well as Article 8 (right to the protection of personal data concerning him/her); Article 12 (everyone has the right to freedom of peaceful assembly and freedom of association at all levels); Article 16 (guarantees the freedom to conduct a business); Article 21 (the right to non-discrimination); Article 27 (the right of workers to information and consultation within the company). Article 31 (every worker has the right to just and equitable working conditions) expressly mentions that the aim is to prevent the application of new mechanisms of surveillance and counter-monitoring of workers from leading to a further increase in corporate powers. As this essay argues, the development of a cosmopolitan solidarity involves a complex set of (often multilevel) interactions between instruments of legislation and regulation.

A very important point in the interconnections between the Chapter on Equality and Solidarity refers to the policies of reconciliation of family and work life within the Chapter on Solidarity. Thus, Article 33.2 establishes that in order to be able to reconcile family and professional life, everyone has the right to be protected against any dismissal for a reason related to maternity, as well as the right to paid maternity leave and parental leave on the occasion of the birth or adoption of a child. Family protection is thus guaranteed at the legal, economic and social levels in order to be able to

25. *See* Lopez Lopez, J. (2022), Incriptions of Solidarity: Debates on Labor Law and Beyond, ed. Cambridge.
26. The advantages to not only workers but also employers of paying fair wages are many in the interactions between the two, *see* Akerlof, G.A. & Shiller, R.J. (2009), Animal Spirits, How Human Psychology Drives the Economy, and Why It Matters for Global Capitalism, Princenton, p. 106.

reconcile family and professional life. Reconciliation policies are not integrated into the Equality Chapter but as part of the Solidarity Chapter.

Another inscription of inclusive solidarity refers to protection by age, ranging from the prohibition of child labour to the protection of young people at work. The solidarity agenda for young people connects with their right to education, thus establishing that the minimum age for admission to work may not be lower than the age at which compulsory schooling ends.

Solidarity in the contents of the Charter of Fundamental Rights appears as the responsibility of the State in both social protection and the fight against poverty.[27] Article 34 on Social Security and Social Assistance recognizes and respects the right of access to social security benefits and social services that guarantee protection in cases such as maternity, illness, accidents at work, dependency or old age, as well as in the event of loss of employment, according to the modalities established by Community law and national legislation and practices. The provision also integrates the principle that any person residing and moving legally within the Union is entitled to social security benefits and social advantages in accordance with Community law and national laws and practices.[28]

In order to combat social exclusion and poverty, the right to social and housing assistance to ensure a decent existence is recognized and respected for all those who do not have sufficient resources, in accordance with the procedures established by Community law and national laws and practices.

The principle of subsidiarity plays a determining role in the implementation of social protection, and if we take, for example, the Green Paper on Ageing[29] (2021), it articulates, years later, the reality of an ageing population as a challenge and set of opportunities to respond to growing necessities. These necessities include health care, long-care mobility, connectivity and well-being, life-long learning, active ageing, volunteering in retirement and fair pension systems. All of these challenges need to be confronted through the multilevel set of instruments available. The combination of the regulatory framework linked to the subsidiarity principle and the articulation of soft and hard law instruments sets down a complex panorama. This has generated a range

27. In addition to the above, the European Pillar of Social Rights states under Social Protection that 'irrespective of the type and duration of their employment relationship, employed persons and, under comparable conditions, self-employed persons, are entitled to adequate social protection'. The European Pillar of social rights should not prevent Member States or their social partners from setting more ambitious social standards. In particular, none of the provisions of the European Pillar of Social Rights should be interpreted as restricting or adversely affecting the rights and principles recognized, in their respective fields of application, by Union law or by international law and international conventions to which the Union or the Member States are party, including the European Social Charter, signed in Turin on 18 October 1961, and the conventions and recommendations of the ILO. The European Pillar of Social Rights recognizes unemployment benefits (No. 13), minimum income (No. 14), pensions and old age benefits (No. 15), health (No. 16), inclusion of people with disabilities (No. 17), long-term care (No. 18), housing (No. 19) and access to essential services (No. 20).
28. Directive 2009/52/EC of the European Parliament and of the Council of 18 June 2009, establishes minimum standards on sanctions and measures applicable to employers of illegally staying third-country nationals.
29. Towards adequate, sustainable and safe European pension systems European Commission 27 January 2021.

of differing results at the national level with a strong impact on equality and non-discrimination policies.[30]

Another important inclusive solidarity policy is the one that refers to health protection. In the content of this solidarity policy, the Charter of Fundamental Rights establishes that everyone has the right to health prevention and to benefit from health care under the conditions established by national legislation and practices. The right to occupational health understood as the integral health of workers provides a normative framework that, through the protection of especially vulnerable groups, also reinforces inclusive solidarity policies by interpreting them as equality policies. The development of occupational health rights once again connects the chapters on equality and solidarity with a broad development through Directives; attention to vulnerable groups is concentrated in Directives both on health and on equality and non-discrimination. Additionally, the Framework Directive establishes a notion of working environment in line with ILO Convention 155.

The Directive introduces the principle of risk assessment as a fundamental element and defines its main components (e.g., risk identification, workers' participation, adoption of appropriate measures giving priority to eliminating the risk at source). It has been developed through a number of other instruments, in particular Directive 89/391 EEC (Framework Directive), Directive 89/654 EEC (workplaces), Directive 89/655 EEC (work equipment), Directive 89/656 EEC (personal protective equipment), Directive 90/269 EEC (manual handling of loads) and Directive 90/270 EEC (equipment including display screens). It is through Directives that the right to health is developed with special reference to sectors and the most vulnerable groups. In addition to these rules implementing Article 153 of the Treaty, the Pillar of Social Rights recognizes the right to occupational health as one of the key principles for the development of social rights.

Inclusive solidarity also appears in its content in the Charter of Fundamental Rights as access to services of general economic interest. The Union maintains, recognizes and respects access to services of general economic interest, as provided for in national laws and practices, in accordance with the Treaty establishing the European Community, in order to promote the social and territorial cohesion of the Union.

The defence of cosmopolitan and inclusive solidarity also presents another angle, and that is, within the system of sources, the analysis of the connection between the instruments that consecrate equality, hard law, and those that design solidarity. It is interesting in this sense to analyse the STJCE of 12 January 2023, case C-356/21,[31] from the connection between equality and solidarity as objectives of the EU. Thus, it holds that:

30. *See* Beyond methodological nationalism in explanations of gender equality. The impact of EU policies on gender provisions in national collective agreements in Belgium (1957-2020), European Journal of Industrial Relations 2022, Vol. 28, pp. 47-64.
31. The reference for a preliminary ruling concerns the interpretation of Art. 3(1)(a) and (c) and Art. 17 of Council Directive 2000/78/EC of 27 November 2000 establishing a general framework for equal treatment in employment and occupation (OJ 2000 L 303, p. 16, corrigendum in OJ 2021 L 204, p. 49).

> Discrimination jeopardizes the achievement of the objectives of the EC Treaty, in particular the attainment of a high level of employment and social protection, the raising of the standard of living and quality of life, economic and social cohesion, solidarity and the free movement of persons.

The protection conferred by Article 16 of the Charter of Fundamental Rights of the European Union, the freedom to conduct a business does not constitute an absolute prerogative but must be taken into account in relation to its function in society (judgment of 22 January 2013, Sky Österreich, C-283/11, EU:C:2013:28, paragraph 45).

One content of solidarity that is developed, among other sources of management in the 2030 Agenda and its Sustainable Development Goals, is its sustainability content which is based on cooperation, multilateralism and a transformative will to eradicate poverty, reduce inequalities, and achieve sustainable development with no one left behind. Thus, inclusive solidarity is becoming part not only of the normative content – as reflected, for example, in Directives – but also of Community jurisprudence, although still in a modest way, but with some results to be highlighted for self-employed workers.[32] The interactive construction of a cosmopolitan solidarity includes judicial findings articulated at both the EU and Member State levels.

3 THE CHALLENGES FOR THE CONSTRUCTION OF MATERIAL EQUALITY THROUGH SOLIDARITY POLICIES: A SOLIDARITY-BASED MIGRATION POLICY

A very significant point of connection established between solidarity and equality is that of cooperation and shared responsibility in migration and asylum policies, which are a clear case of the challenges faced and of how the subjects involved can construct policies in the future.

The Global Compact for Migration presents a non-legally binding framework for cooperation based on the commitments agreed upon by Member States in the New York Declaration for Refugees and Migrants[33] The Global Compact is based on international human rights law and upholds the principles of non-retrogression and non-discrimination regardless of migration status, at all stages of the migration cycle. There are two basic supranational principles at play here: on the one hand, the application of the human rights framework, but on the other hand, the principle of subsidiarity, which allows for a great deal of diversity among EU Member States in the development of migration policies.

In the framework of the EU, the EU Action Plan against Smuggling 2021-2025 addresses the need to amend Directive 2011/36/EU on preventing and combating trafficking in human beings and protecting victims. The most criticized aspect of the EU

32. *See*, for example, the STJCE of 12 January 2023, (case C-356/21) on the prohibition of discrimination based on sexual orientation of an independent Employer working on the basis of a contract for the provision of services regarding the termination and non-renewal of a contract.
33. The objective is to foster international cooperation on migration, recognizing that no State can address migration alone, and respecting the sovereignty of States and their obligations under international law.

Strategy on voluntary return and reintegration[34] is its Recommendation for the issuing and mutual recognition of return decisions. The proposed Regulation on Asylum and Migration Management also proposes return sponsorship as a solidarity measure whereby the Member States can assist other Member States in a situation of migratory pressure. Solidarity is therefore treated from the point of view of cooperation between countries to return migrants with an understanding of the term that is open to criticism from a human rights perspective.

In the context of criticisms of the regulation of migration, articulated from the parameters marking inclusive solidarity, the Spanish Law of Cooperation[35] presents positive aspects of cooperation that are very interesting to highlight. This legislation addresses the situation of migrants from the standpoint of sustainability and cooperation. The aforementioned law maintains that it is necessary from the standpoint of sustainability to promote inclusion and participation, equality and equity, transparency and accountability, considering all factors of discrimination and their intersection from a solidarity-based vision of cooperation. It recognizes the importance of education for sustainable development and global citizenship, as well as the promotion of participation, global justice and solidarity.

Along with the elaboration of a migration policy truly based on human rights and inclusive solidarity, another pending challenge is effective judicial protection and access to justice, which have been highlighted by the Report on the implementation of the Charter of Fundamental Rights 2023. In 2022 and 2023, National Human Rights Institutions identified obstacles to access to justice for vulnerable groups in the EU, in particular for people on low incomes, minors, women, victims of domestic violence, trafficking and labour exploitation, migrants and applicants for international protection, as well as for ethnic minorities.

Similarly, in migration and asylum matters, effective judicial protection plays an important role, as the Court of Justice of the European Union (CJEU) has stated that Member States must respect certain guarantees in decisions on returns, entry bans, expulsion and detention orders, such as the right to be heard and the right of access to files.

In the absence of national provisions explicitly implementing the procedural guarantees of the Charter, claims relating to fundamental rights in matters involving Union law have been based directly on the Charter. The CJEU has endowed Article 47 of the Charter with direct effect, allowing individuals to invoke this right directly before the national courts. Crucially, the increase in case law references to the Charter by the CJEU and national courts shows considerable interest in defining effective judicial protection through the perspective of fundamental rights.[36] In practice, in its legal treatment and thus 'inscriptions', solidarity has mutated from being a right based on

34. 'Towards an operational strategy for more effective returns' in January 2023.
35. Law No. 1/2023 of 20 February 2023 on Cooperation for sustainable development and global solidarity (BOE No. 44 of 21 February 2023).
36. *See* Report from the Commission to the European Parliament, the Council, The European economic and Social Committee and the Committee of the Regions Protecting Fundamental Rights in the Digital Age. 2021. Annual Report on the Application of the EU Charter of Fundamental Rights. COM (2021) 819 final, Brussels, 10 December 2021.

civil law to being a social right[37] developed through complex interactive processes. Central to those processes is the agenda of constructing a cosmopolitan and inclusive solidarity that is articulated through a multilevel interplay between public and private responsibility for implementation in pursuit of the objective of material equality.

37. *See* Supiot, A. (2005), Homo juridicus. Essai sur la fonction antrophologique du droit, Points, p. 307.

CHAPTER 10

Fundamental Rights in the Age of Robotics and Artificial Intelligence*

Massimiliano Delfino

1 INTRODUCTION

The topic of robotics and work empowerment is crucial in current labour law. Moreover, this subject allows me to face the present and, above all, the future of our subject matter since this topic has yet to be well-established, especially with the rise of Artificial Intelligence (AI) enhanced robotics.[1] The paper presents a legal perspective on this complex matter. First, I choose the fundamental rights approach since examining the applicability and adaptability of labour law legislation to robotics is secondary to analysing the issue of fundamental rights in that field, such as the respect for private

---

* *This study was supported by the ROOTS ('gReensOftrOboTicS') and AURORA ('sustAinableaUgmentedpRoducts for spORts and sAfety') projects. ROOTS and AURORA are part of the MICS (Made in Italy–Circular and Sustainable) project and received funding from the European Union Next-Generation EU (PIANO NAZIONALE DI RIPRESA E RESILIENZA (PNRR) – MISSIONE 4 COMPONENTE 2, INVESTIMENTO 1.3 –D.D. 1551.11-10-2022, PE00000004). This manuscript reflects only the authors' views and opinions; neither the European Union nor the European Commission can be considered responsible for them. This paper has also been published in Italian Labour Law e-Journal, 2023, 2.*

1. On AI, *see* M. Biasi (ed.), *Diritto del lavoro e intelligenza artificiale*, Giuffrè, 2024; S. Ciucciovino, *Risorse umane e intelligenza artificiale alla luce del regolamento (UE) 2024/1689, tra norme legali, etica e codici di condotta*, DRI, 2024, pp. 573 ff.; T. Treu, *Intelligenza Artificiale (IA): integrazione o sostituzione del lavoro umano?*, WP Massimo D'Antona.IT – 487/2024; M.A. Boden, *L'intelligenza artificiale, Il Mulino, Bologna*, 2019; S. Borelli, et al., *Lavoro e tecnologie, Giappichelli*, Torino, 2022; M. Peruzzi, *Intelligenza e lavoro. Uno studio su poteri datoriali e tecniche di tutela*, Giappichelli, Torino, 2023. On the interactions between robotics and work, *see, inter alia*, E. Fiata, *Robotica e lavoro*, in Biasi (ed.), *Diritto del lavoro e intelligenza artificiale*, Giuffrè, 2024, pp. 611 ff.; M. Faioli, *Prospects on Risks, Liabilities and Artificial Intelligence, Empowering Robots at Workplaces Level*, Quad. FGB, 2024, n. 24; V. Maio, *Il diritto del lavoro e le nuove sfide della rivoluzione robotica*, in Argomenti di diritti del lavoro, 2018, pp. 1414 ff.

and family life and freedom of expression and information, the right to privacy, the right to non-discrimination and the principle of equality between women and men. Therefore, I intend the environment as the social environment where robotics operate. Second, it is worth reminding that robotics *et similia* are linked to the AI issue since systems based on AI can be easily divided into two types: (1) software operating in the virtual world (vocal assistants, search engines, etc.) and (2) software that can incorporate AI in hardware devices, such as robots and exoskeletons, which are the devices we are interested in this context.

This contribution deals with the issues of AI and the fundamental rights approach to AI. In a broader sense, both are essential to understanding robotics, work empowerment and the environment. Moreover, the Fundamental Rights approach deals with the issue of the environment, intended as the social environment, strictly linked to legal sustainability.

2 ROBOTS *ET SIMILIA*: THE LEGAL IMPLICATIONS AND THE LINK WITH AI

The need for 'laws of robotics' to ensure the peaceful coexistence of humans and robots on Earth comes from the process of robotisation. Robots are part of everyday life (including in areas such as transportation, medical care, education, and agriculture). They assist humans, facilitating tasks that, on their own, they could not easily do. Considering the need to regulate new phenomena that increasingly involve robots acting independently, the European Parliament adopted the Resolution of 16 February 2017, making recommendations to the Commission concerning the Civil Law Rules on Robotics, namely the civil liability profiles for any damage caused by 'autonomously thinking' robots. Robotisation processes, however, can also be considered to have a significant impact on the organisation and labour market, concerning which the resolution highlights not only the problem of the lack of skills to be filled, the need to monitor job losses, the need to ensure respect for fundamental rights in the workplace, and the levels of health and safety in the working environment through the transfer of some dangerous and harmful tasks from humans to robots but also of the risks of deterioration caused by the new threats due to the increasing number of human-robot interactions.

A confirmation derives from this resolution. In one or two points, the European Union (EU) Parliament stresses the link between Robotics and AI: 'A comprehensive Union system of registration of advanced robots should be introduced within the Union's internal market where relevant and necessary for specific categories of robots, and calls on the Commission to establish criteria for the classification of robots that would need to be registered; in this context, calls on the Commission to investigate whether it would be desirable for the registration system and the register to be managed by a designated EU Agency for Robotics and Artificial Intelligence' (paragraph 2); the Parliament asks the Commission to consider the designation of such an Agency 'to provide the technical, ethical and regulatory expertise needed to support the relevant public actors, at both Union and Member State level, in their efforts to ensure a timely, ethical and well-informed response to the new opportunities and challenges ... arising from technological developments in robotics, such as in the transport sector' (paragraph 16).

The European Parliament not only 'notes the great potential of robotics for the improvement of safety at work by transferring several hazardous and harmful tasks from humans to robots', but also 'their potential for creating a set of new risks owing to the increasing number of human-robot interactions at the workplace; underlines in this regard the importance of applying strict and forward-looking rules for human-robot interactions to guarantee health, safety and the respect of fundamental rights at the workplace'. For that reason, in the annexe to the resolution, you can find some recommendations, such as the Code of Ethical Conduct for robotic engineers, where it is underlined that 'robotics research activities should respect fundamental rights and be conducted in the interests of the well-being and self-determination of the individual and society at large in their design, implementation, dissemination and use'. In other words, human dignity and physical and psychological autonomy should always be respected.

Consider, for instance, robots used in surgery to support doctors. Although this technology is now widespread in medicine, there is still little guidance on managing risk and liability during surgery, the doctor's autonomy in conducting the action, the criteria for verifying diligence, and the accuracy required in using a robot.

A following Resolution was passed by the EU Parliament in 2020,[2] which is interesting from many points of view. It highlights the connection between the risk of using AI and other devices with the violation of fundamental rights by saying 'that artificial intelligence, robotics and related technologies should be considered high-risk when their development, deployment and use entail a significant risk of causing injury or harm to individuals or society, in breach of fundamental rights and safety rules as laid down in Union law' (paragraph 14). This approach is confirmed by Article 4, letter e, of the proposal for a regulation on ethical principles for the development, deployment and use of AI, robotics and related technologies annexed to the resolution: '"high risk" means a significant risk entailed by the development, deployment and use of AI, robotics and related technologies to cause injury or harm to individuals or society in breach of fundamental rights and safety rules as laid down in Union law, considering their specific use or purpose, the sector where they are developed, deployed or used and the severity of injury or harm that can be expected to occur'.[3] Under this proposal, 'any artificial intelligence, robotics and related technologies, including software, algorithms and data used or produced by such technologies, shall be developed, deployed and used in the Union in accordance with Union law and in full respect of

2. P9_TA(2023)0236 *Artificial Intelligence Act Amendments adopted by the European Parliament on 14 June 2023 on the proposal for a regulation of the European Parliament and of the Council on laying down harmonised rules on artificial intelligence (Artificial Intelligence Act) and amending certain Union legislative acts* (COM(2021)0206 – C9-0146/2021 – 2021/0106(COD)).
3. European Parliament, *Robotics, Artificial Intelligence, and the Fundamental Rights Approach to AI*, European Parliamentary Research Service, European Parliament resolution of 20 October 2020 with recommendations to the Commission on a framework of ethical aspects of AI, robotics and related technologies.

human dignity, autonomy and safety and other fundamental rights set out in the Charter' (Article1, paragraph 1).

According to the proposal for a regulation on ethical principles annexed to the 2020 resolution, AI comprises two main areas of interest: the technical area in a broad sense (engineering, robotics, computer science, etc.) and the ethical area, including the proper ethics and the legal aspects of AI, which are different starting from the binding force of legal elements, which is not typical of the ethical aspects. This difference is more unclear in other sources (passed or not) regulating AI, such as the AI Act, where those notions are pretty confused. However, it is more evident in the Whereas and Recitals (the preamble) than in the Articles of the AI Act.

3 THE TWO PROPOSALS FOR EU REGULATION

As said, this risk-based social environment approach is crucial[4] and like that used in the two EU regulations, which have recently passed and provide for a more robust intervention of the EU in the field of Robotics and AI after reminding that the 2020 proposal on robotics was substantially absorbed in the 2021 proposal for a regulation on AI. The AI Act[5] and the Regulation on the market for digital services[6] are different, even though the legal basis is similar. Both are based on Article 114 Treaty of the Functioning of the European Union (TFEU), which provides for the adoption of measures aimed at ensuring the establishment and functioning of the internal market, with the objective, for the regulation regarding AI, of 'ensuring the proper functioning of the internal market by establishing harmonised rules, in particular concerning the development the placing on the Union market and the use of products and services using AI technologies or provided as stand-alone AI systems' and, for the proposal on the services market, to 'ensure the smooth functioning of the internal market, in particular about the provision of cross-border digital services (more specifically,

4. This approach has been recently used by the US Administration in the *Executive Order on the Safe, Secure, and Trustworthy Development and Use of Artificial Intelligence*, delivered by President Biden on 30 October 2023. The references to workers and the risk-based approach are many, starting from the eight guiding principles and priorities contained therein, especially n° d, which states as follows. 'The responsible development and use of AI require a commitment to supporting American workers. As AI creates new jobs and industries, all workers need a seat at the table, including through collective bargaining, to ensure that they benefit from these opportunities. My Administration will seek to adapt job training and education to support a diverse workforce and help provide access to opportunities that AI creates. In the workplace itself, AI should not be deployed in ways that undermine rights, worsen job quality, encourage undue worker surveillance, lessen market competition, introduce new health and safety risks, or cause harmful labor-force disruptions. The critical next steps in AI development should be built on the views of workers, labor unions, educators, and employers to support responsible uses of AI that improve workers' lives, positively augment human work, and help all people safely enjoy the gains and opportunities from technological innovation.'
5. Regulation (EU) 2024/1689 of the European Parliament and of the Council of 13 June 2024 laying down harmonised rules on artificial intelligence and amending Regulations (EC) No 300/2008, (EU) No 167/2013, (EU) No 168/2013, (EU) 2018/858, (EU) 2018/1139 and (EU) 2019/2144 and Directives 2014/90/EU, (EU) 2016/797 and (EU) 2020/1828 (Artificial Intelligence Act).
6. Regulation (EU) 2022/2065 of the European Parliament and of the Council of 19 October 2022 on a Single Market For Digital Services and amending Directive 2000/31/EC (Digital Services Act).

intermediary services)'. In addition, considering that the first regulation 'contains certain specific rules on the protection of natural persons concerning the processing of personal data, in particular restrictions on the use of AI systems for "real-time" remote biometric identification in publicly accessible areas for law enforcement purposes', it is appropriate to base it, as far as those specific rules are concerned, on Article 16 TFEU, which precisely involves the protection of personal data.

The choice of regulation as the source of the law is justified by the need for uniform application of the new rules (i.e., the definition of AI), the prohibition of certain harmful practices permitted by AI and the classification of specific AI systems. The direct applicability of regulation, following Article 288 TFEU, will reduce legal fragmentation and facilitate the development of a single market for AI systems. This will be achieved by introducing a classification for high-risk AI systems and obligations for such systems providers and users/deployers. A similar objective characterises the regulation on the market for digital services 'aimed at ensuring harmonised conditions to allow the development of innovative cross-border services in the Union by addressing and preventing the emergence of obstacles to such economic activity arising from the different ways in which national laws are drafted, taking into account that many Member States have legislated or intend to legislate on issues such as the removal of illegal content online, the duty of care, notice and action procedures and transparency'.

The AI regulation confirms the strict connection between robotics and AI since it explicitly refers to the 2017 Resolution on Ethical Aspects of Artificial Intelligence, Robotics and Related Technologies (recital 8), considered one of the bases of AI regulation.

The proposals for a regulation contain some provisions on fundamental rights, even though they differ, at least considering the first version of the AI Act. Both referred to fundamental rights and/or the Nice Charter in their preambles and recitals. Nevertheless, only the regulation on digital market services refers to special fundamental rights in the body of the text. In particular, Article 1(1) aims to establish uniform rules for a safe and reliable online space, protecting fundamental rights as enshrined in the Charter; Article 9(2)emphasises the need for territorial scope limitations in countering illegal content, considering applicable Union and national laws and international principles; Article 22 mandates that intermediary service providers inform users of restrictions on service use, requiring them to act diligently and proportionately, respecting the fundamental rights of all parties involved; Article 34 requires extensive online platforms to identify and assess systemic risks, including those affecting fundamental rights, such as privacy, freedom of expression, non-discrimination, and children's rights; Article 35(3) allows the Commission to issue guidelines on mitigation measures, considering their impact on fundamental rights. The regulation also addresses crisis protocols, specifically in extraordinary circumstances impacting public security or health while safeguarding fundamental rights. In the final version of the AI Act, a more significant role for the fundamental rights approach has been recognised. This is evident in Article 1, paragraph 1: 'The purpose of this Regulation is to promote the uptake of human-centric and trustworthy artificial intelligence and to ensure a high level of protection of health, safety, fundamental rights, democracy and the rule of law, and the environment from harmful effects of artificial intelligence systems in the Union while supporting innovation.' Another example is clear as well. According to Article 3, paragraph 1, n. 49, a '"serious incident" means any incident or malfunctioning of an AI system that directly or indirectly leads, might have led to or might lead to any of the following', among which you cannot only find 'the death of a person or serious damage to a person's health' but also 'a breach of fundamental rights protected under Union law'. As you can see, the death of a person is as severe as the breach of fundamental rights, and this is quite innovative.

The effectiveness of social rights in the AI age depends on the applicability of the sources that contain them. Thus, at the supranational level and beyond, the question of the scope of the Charter of Fundamental Rights is decisive.[7] The first question is whether the Charter applies to the above regulations. The reference is to the rules of the Charter on regulated profiles by European secondary sources of law. The problem concerns the regulation on services in the digital market. For the first time, a legislative act of general scope, binding and directly applicable in the Member States of the Union, makes express reference to the Charter and its rules in at least two cases. Indeed, declaring that digital service providers must act 'with due regard to the rights and legitimate interests of all parties involved, including the applicable fundamental rights of the recipients of the service enshrined in the Charter' and that online platforms must identify systemic risks, including 'any adverse effects on the exercise of fundamental rights to respect for private and family life and to freedom of expression and information, the right to non-discrimination and the rights of the child, as laid down respectively in Articles 7, 11, 21 and 24 of the Charter', it seems to me that it makes the fundamental rights contained in the Charter applicable to internal systems, concerning digital providers and online platforms.

4 THE ISSUE OF APPLYING THE NICE CHARTER

It is necessary to wait how the Court of Justice will decide on them without undermining the role of the doctrine. In this regard, a judgment of the Court of Justice of 17 March 2021, *KO*, C-652/19,[8] weakens the certainties reached up to that point. After recalling that 'the provisions of the Charter apply, under Article 51(1) thereof, to the Member States, only when they are implementing Union law, Article 6(1) TEU and Article 51(2) of the Charter, make it clear that the Charter does not extend the field of application of Union law beyond the powers of the European Union and does not establish any new power or task for the EU, or modify powers and tasks as defined in the Treaties. The Court is, therefore, called upon to interpret, in the light of the Charter, the law of the EU within the limits of the powers conferred on it'; it emphasises that 'for it to be found that Directive 98/59 and, consequently, the Charter, apply to the main proceedings, that directive must impose a specific obligation in respect of the situation

7. *See* M. Delfino, *Article 51 Charter of Fundamental Rights of the European Union*, in E. Ales, M. Bell, O. Deinert, S. Robin-Olivier (eds), *International and European Labour Law*, Nomos, Baden-Baden, 2018, pp. 234 ff.
8. M. Delfino, *Continuity and Discontinuity in the Scope of Social Rights in the Recent Case Law of the Court of Justice*, in *Diritti Lavori Mercati (International)*, 2023, n. 1.

at issue in those proceedings, which has been implemented by the provisions of Italian law concerned'.

However, 'such an obligation is not apparent from the provisions of Directive 98/59. The main objective of that directive is to make collective redundancies subject to prior consultation with the workers' representatives. Prior notification to the competent public authority,' and 'Directive 98/59 provides for only a partial harmonisation of the rules for the protection of workers in the event of collective redundancies, that is to say, harmonisation of the procedure to be followed when such redundancies are to be made' is ensured. In particular, 'the means of protection to be afforded to a worker who has been unlawfully dismissed as part of collective redundancy, following a failure to comply with the criteria based on which the employer is required to determine the workers to be dismissed, are manifestly unrelated to the notification and consultation obligations arising from Directive 98/59. Neither those means nor those selection criteria fall within the scope of that directive. Consequently, they remain within the Member States' competence'.

These declarations of the Court of Justice contrast previous case law (from *Akeberg* to *Florescu* via *Poclava*) that had yet to go into detail. This source has been transposed into national law, and the implementation of Union law allows the Charter of Fundamental Rights rules to enter the Member States' legal systems. In addition to a potential new direction, there is an inconsistency in the reasoning of the recent Luxembourg Court ruling. The argument needs to be differentiated on a case-by-case basis. Article 20 CFREU focuses on equality before the law and does not deal with dismissals, while Article 30 deals with protection against unjustified dismissals. Therefore, on the one hand, implementing the Directive on Collective Redundancies cannot allow the application of Article 20 in domestic law. On the other hand, the application of Article 30 would have been irrelevant here. However, the Court of Justice's interpretation will likely weaken the Charter of Fundamental Rights and the application of social rights in domestic law. The Court of Justice's partial *revirément* also concerns the Italian Constitutional Court, which, in Judgment 194 of 2018, had stood by the Court of Justice's previous positions.

On the EU law profiles, the Constitutional Court argued as follows:

(i) Under Article 51 CFREU, the Court of Justice of the European Union has consistently held that the provisions of the Nice Charter apply to the Member States when they act within the scope of Union law. This is clear to the Constitutional Court, according to which 'for the Charter of Fundamental Rights of the European Union to be invoked in a case of constitutional legitimacy, the case subject to domestic legislation must be governed by European law – in so far as it is inherent in acts of the Union, in national acts and conduct which give effect to EU law – and not by national rules alone which have no connection with that law' (Judgment No. 80 of 2011). In the present case, there is no evidence to suggest that the censured regulation of Article 3(1) of Legislative Decree No. 23 of 2015 was adopted in implementing the EU law.

(ii) For the applicability of the CFREU, Article 3(1) of Legislative Decree No. 23 of 2015 should fall within the scope of a rule of Union law other than those of the Charter itself. However, the mere fact that Article 3(1) of Legislative Decree No. 23 of 2015 falls within an area where the Union has competence within the meaning of Article 153(2)(d) of the Treaty on the Functioning of the EU cannot entail the applicability of the Charter given that, as regards the regulation of individual dismissals, the Union has not exercised that competence. Moreover, it cannot be considered that the legislation censured was adopted in implementing Directive 98/59/EC (on collective redundancies) since Article 3(1) of Legislative Decree No. 23 of 2015 regulates individual redundancies.

(iii) To argue the existence of a 'European case', the respondent claimed that they would fall within the scope of the Union's employment policy and the measures adopted in response to the Council's recommendations. Those recommendations provided for in Article 148(4) TFEU fall within the Council's discretion and have no binding force, so this is the implicit reasoning conducted by the Constitutional Court; they cannot be regarded as Union law. This is also valid beyond labour law.[9]

The immediate direct effect of the regulations (AI and digital market services) means that, if passed, they will apply immediately in such legal systems and be effective against both States and individuals without the need for further action. In addition, regulations can entitle individuals to rights and obligations and, therefore, be invoked by individuals before national courts and used as a reference in relations with other individuals, Member States and Union institutions. Regarding the regulations, we cannot speak of the 'implementation of Union law', which is necessary according to Article 51 CFREU to make the rules of the Charter operational in domestic legal systems. However, since the Regulation has a direct horizontal effect and its implementation is unnecessary, it is usually a *solid bridge* between the Charter and the national legal systems. It thus allows the entrance of the rules (at least those expressly mentioned) in domestic law. In addition, the regulation also strikes a balance between freedoms and fundamental rights.

5 FUNDAMENTAL RIGHTS AND AI: THE RESPONSIBILITIES OF THE PERSONS

The connection between Robotics, AI and fundamental rights is complicated, especially regarding the proposal for the AI Act. In the proposal for a regulation of digital market services, there will not be any problems in applying the Charter of Fundamental Rights since there are some specific references to the provision of the Charter itself,

9. The Constitutional Court, in its Judgment 149 of 2022, stated that there is no doubt that the EU secondary law governs the matter of copyright protection, in particular by Directive 2001/29/EC, and this implies that the domestic regulation falls within the scope of implementation of EU law within the meaning of Art. 51 CFREU, with the consequent obligation to respect the rights recognised by the Charter, including Art. 50 CFREU.

which enter into force into the domestic legal systems thanks to the regulation. On the contrary, some questions could arise about AI regulation, even for the old versions of it. The reference to the Charter in the 2021 proposal for an AI Act was more indirect before the amendments passed by the European Parliament in June 2023. Article 7.1 provided that 'the Commission is empowered to adopt delegated acts … to update the list in Annex III by adding high-risk AI systems where both of the following conditions are fulfilled': (a) the AI systems are intended to be used in the areas listed in Annex III and, above all, (b) 'the AI systems pose a risk of harm to the health and safety or a risk of adverse impact on fundamental rights, that is, in respect of its severity and probability of occurrence, equivalent to or greater than the risk of harm or of adverse impact posed by the high-risk AI systems'. Indeed, according to Article 7, paragraph 2, 'when assessing for the purposes of paragraph 1 whether an AI system poses a risk of harm to the health and safety or a risk of adverse impact on fundamental rights that is equivalent to or greater than the risk of harm posed by the high-risk AI systems already referred to in Annex III, the Commission shall take into account' among other criteria 'the extent to which the use of an AI system has already caused harm to the health and safety or adverse impact on the fundamental rights or has given rise to significant concerns about the materialisation of such harm or adverse impact, as demonstrated by reports or documented allegations submitted to competent national authorities'.

Thus, it did not seem possible that the Charter of Fundamental Rights applied to domestic legal systems. Rights and principles in the Charter could only be used to understand whether AI systems are at risk of hurting them to modify the list of high-risk AI systems provided in Annex III. The fundamental rights (especially those provided in the Charter) only operated at the EU level. Therefore, the previous versions of the AI Act could not be considered a solid bridge to make the fundamental rights of the Charter enter into the national legal systems. Things could change with the passed version of the AI Act. As a matter of fact, according to Article 1, 'the purpose of this Regulation is to improve the functioning of the internal market and promote the uptake of human-centric and trustworthy artificial intelligence (AI), *while ensuring a high level of protection of health, safety, fundamental rights enshrined in the Charter*'. Therefore, thanks to the last sentence, the Charter also applies to the domestic systems. Indeed: (a) 'human agency and oversight' means that AI systems shall be developed and used as a tool that serves people, respects human dignity and personal autonomy, and that is functioning in a way that can be appropriately controlled and overseen by humans; (b) 'technical robustness and safety' means that AI systems shall be developed and used in a way to minimise unintended and unexpected harm as well as being robust in case of unintended problems and being resilient against attempts to alter the use or performance of the AI system so as to allow unlawful use by malicious third parties; (c) 'privacy and data governance' means that AI systems shall be developed and used in compliance with existing privacy and data protection rules, while processing data that meets high standards in terms of quality and integrity; (d) 'transparency' means that AI systems shall be developed and used in a way that allows appropriate traceability and explainability, while making humans aware that they interact with an AI system as well as duly informing users of the capabilities and limitations of that AI system and affected persons about their rights; (e) 'diversity, non-discrimination and fairness' means that AI systems shall be developed and used in a way that includes diverse actors and promotes equal access, gender equality and cultural diversity while avoiding discriminatory impacts and unfair biases that are prohibited by Union or national law; (f) 'social and environmental well-being' means that AI systems shall be developed and used in a sustainable and environmentally friendly manner as well as in a way to benefit all human beings, while monitoring and assessing the long-term impacts on the individual themselves, on the society and the democracy.[10]

A couple of examples of the applicability of social rights can be made. Article 21 CFREU prohibits 'any discrimination based on any ground such as sex, race, colour, ethnic or social origin, genetic features, language, religion or belief, political or any other opinion, membership of a national minority, property, birth, disability, age or sexual orientation'. At the same time, Article 23 declares that 'equality between women and men must be ensured in all areas, including employment, work and pay'. These provisions enter into force in domestic jurisdictions, and human beings must respect them since robots and algorithms cannot be responsible for violating fundamental rights.

The problem is to understand who is responsible for respecting those rights. The AI regulation clearly show that the provisions and the rights of the Charter do not apply to AI in general but to individuals, not robots or AI systems. However, the AI act uses different words (operators, users, deployers, providers) in other contexts.

A good example is Article 4, according to which 'providers and deployers of AI systems shall take measures to ensure, to their best extent, a sufficient level of AI literacy of their staff and other persons dealing with the operation and use of AI systems on their behalf'.[11] Moreover, the AI regulation clearly define the operator, i.e., 'a provider, product manufacturer, deployer, authorised representative, importer or distributor'.[12]

Some other times, reference is made only to the user or, in the to the deployer, which is 'any natural or legal person, public authority, agency, or other body using an AI system under its authority, except where the AI system is used in the course of a personal, non-professional activity' (Article 3). This is also true for the scope of application of the Act, i.e., the deployers (not the users anymore) of AI systems that have their place of establishment or are located within the Union (Article 2, point 1.b). *See also* Article 13, paragraph 1: 'High-risk AI systems shall be designed and developed

10. European Parliament. *Fundamental Rights and Artificial Intelligence in Robotics: A Comprehensive Approach* (https://www.europarl.europa.eu/doceo/document/TA-9-2023-0236_EN.html). S. Aloisi, E. Gramano, *Artificial Intelligence Is Watching You at Work. Digital Surveillance, Employee Monitoring and Regulatory Issues in the EU Context*, in *Comparative Labor Law & Policy Journal*, 2019, vol. 41, n. 1, p. 95; P. Cappelli, *The Consequences of AI-Based Technologies for Jobs*, in *R&I Paper Series*, 2020, n. 4; M. Durante, *Intelligenza Artificiale. Applicazioni Giuridiche*. Utet, Torino, 2007; C.B. Frey, M.A. Osborne, *The Future of Employment: How Susceptible Are Jobs to Computerisation?*, 2013 (cfr. https://www.oxfordmartin.ox.ac.uk/downloads/academic/future-of-employment.pdf).
11. Taking into account their technical knowledge, experience, education and training and the context the AI systems are to be used in, and considering the persons or groups of persons on whom the AI systems are to be used.
12. Article, 3, para. 1, point 8 AI Act.

in such a way as to ensure that their operation is sufficiently transparent to enable deployers to interpret a system's output and use it appropriately.'

In other cases, the provisions refer to the '*importers* and *distributors* of AI systems' (Article 2, point 1.d).

The problem of terminology is crucial. One of the most essential aspects is recognising the personal scope of the application of Fundamental Rights, which, as I have underlined, differs depending on the provisions of the AI Act. All companies, undertakings, and individuals operating in this field must be conscious of that and apply the rights and principles of the Charter depending on whether they are users, deployers, providers, importers, distributors, or authorised representatives of AI systems.

CHAPTER 11

The Value of the Environment and Labour Law

Tatiana Sachs

1 ENVIRONMENTAL VALUE AND THE FUNCTIONS OF LABOUR LAW

What place does environmental value have in labour law? At first glance, the answer to this question might seem straightforward: there is no place for environmental value in labour law. This is because of both the purpose of labour law and its functions.[1] Since its purpose is to govern dependent labour law relationships, labour law, understood as a branch of positive law, is indifferent to environmental issues. As far as its functions are concerned, it is accepted that the aim of labour law is to protect employees. But many analysts have shown that we cannot be content with this somewhat naïve conception of labour law. If we look at the role that labour law actually plays, we see that labour law assumes an economic function and plays a full part in the organisation of the economic system.[2] Thus, authors have shown that labour law, even when it is driven by the objective of protecting employees, is a capitalist labour law. While protecting employees, labour law legally establishes subordination. Other analyses have then shown that labour law assumes a function of company organisation – here it is the link between labour law and human resources management that is highlighted.[3] Finally, analyses have shown that labour law is a law that structures and organises markets: the goods and services markets, where labour law helps to improve the conditions of competition in a sector of activity, and the

1. F. Géa, 'À quoi sert le droit du travail?', *Droit social*, 2020, p. 444.
2. A. Jeammaud, 'Les fonctions du droit du travail', in *Le droit capitaliste du travail*, PU Grenoble, coll. 'Critique du droit', 1980, p. 149.
3. J. Barthélémy, *Le droit du travail, technique d'organisation de l'entreprise*, Editions Liaisons, 2003.

labour market, where it influences the flow of people into and out of employment.[4] In this role, labour law, which is becoming labour market law, tends to focus less on protecting employees in their jobs and more on improving the employment situation in the labour market.

However, like other branches of economic law,[5] labour law, and more broadly, social law, is called upon to take part in the ecological transition. Labour law can make a number of contributions: changes to workplaces, setting up professional transition processes to accompany changes in the production system, sharing the burden of the ecological transition, and so on. We therefore need to look at how labour law can incorporate environmental value. There are obstacles to this (2). However, there are signs that labour law is becoming more environmental. The example of French labour law will be taken (3). On the basis of this example, a typology of the forms of environmentalisation of labour law may be proposed (4).

2 OBSTACLES TO THE ENVIRONMENTALISATION OF LABOUR LAW

While the environmentalisation of labour law is necessary, we need to gain a better understanding of two difficulties this integration has to overcome: the prevalence of the growth paradigm (2.1) and the weight of the separations that structure the relationship between labour law and the environment (2.2).

2.1 The Weight of the Growth Paradigm in Labour Law

The greening of labour law comes up against one difficulty: the 'growth paradigm' that structures it.[6] Labour law is part of the Fordist compromise, enabling the mobilisation of a subordinate workforce, dispossessed of the product of its labour, to work towards increasing production in the service of the nation's wealth.[7] The background to labour law is the promotion of 'productive' employment. As some authors have pointed out, the 1944 Declaration of Philadelphia, at the same time as liberating labour from the dogma of the market and promoting social justice, 'propagates the narrative that the attainment of these objectives necessarily involves the "fuller and wider utilization of the productive resources of the world" and the "expansion of production and consumption" [Article IV

4. T. Sachs, 'La consolidation d'un droit du marché du travail', *Revue de droit du travail*, 2016, p. 748.
5. On this matter, *see* the project Transition écologique du droit économique.
6. A. Bailleux & F. Ost, 'Six hypothèses à l'épreuve du paradigme croissanciel', *Revue Interdisciplinaire d'Etudes juridiques*, 2016, n° 77, p. 27.
7. E. Dermine & D. Dumont, 'Le droit social et le productivisme. Droit de la croissance ou droit de l'autonomie? Une cartographie du rapport de forces', in *Le droit en transitions. Les clés juridiques*, A. Bailleux (ed.), Presses de l'Université de Saint-Louis, 2021, pp. 207 et seq.; on the place of the productivist paradigm in labour law, *see* F. Géa, 'Droit du travail et écologie', *Revue de droit du travail*, 2024, p. 17.

of the Declaration]'.[8] The logic of accumulation and increasing production is reflected in the representation of work. The 'productivist conception of work' can be seen in many texts, including those promoting decent work, which is seen as 'access to productive and adequately remunerated work'.[9]

The exploitation of nature lies at the heart of economic development based on productivism.[10] The latter is marked by a relationship of domination and exploitation of natural resources, to the point of losing all 'sense of connection and limits in our relationship with nature'.[11] Caught up in the meshes of the 'market society',[12] this domination ultimately goes hand in hand with a commodification - some would say a commodification - of nature, but also of labour.

2.2 The External Environment

The centrality of the 'growth paradigm' is rooted in - and feeds into - a representation of the environment as external to labour law in two ways.

On the other hand, labour law is the repository of a representation of the environment based on a 'radical distinction between human subjects and "non-human" beings'.[13] This historically and culturally situated dualism consists of 'transforming nature into an "environment": a simple setting at the centre of which sits man, who proclaims himself "master and possessor"'.[14] This is accompanied by naturalisation of the environment.[15] The reference to the environment constitutes an 'invocation of nature'[16] and refers to the diversity of the elements that make it up. This 'great divide' between the environment-nature and the cities of man has an extension in the conception of work: 'The imaginary of nature outside work'.

In addition to this initial separation between the human and the non-human, there is also a separation between what falls within the remit of the company and what

8. E. Dermine & D. Dumont, 'Le droit social et le productivisme. Droit de la croissance ou droit de l'autonomie? Une cartographie du rapport de forces', *supra* n. 7, p. 213.
9. ILO, *Decent Work, Report of the Director-General to the International Labour Conference*, 87th session, Geneva, 1999 (quoted by E. Dermine & D. Dumont, 'Le droit social et le productivisme. Droit de la croissance ou droit de l'autonomie? Une cartographie du rapport de forces', *supra* n. 7).
10. The term 'natural resources' refers to the domestication and consumption of nature. The question arises as to whether the exploitation of nature is specific to productivism (which includes the economy of 'communist' countries). In this sense, *see* F. Géa, 'Droit du travail et écologie', *supra* n. 7. Or should we rather consider that it stems from a particular mode of productivism that is capitalism. This is the thesis of P. Guillibert in particular, who goes so far as to consider that the exploitation of labour power, specific to capitalism, is the cause of the climate crisis (*Exploiter les vivants. Une écologie politique du travail*, Éd. Amsterdam, 2023).
11. F. Ost, *La nature hors la loi*, La Découverte, 2003, p. 9.
12. K. Polanyi, *The Great Transformation. Aux origines politiques et économiques de notre temps*, Gallimard, 'Tel' series, 2009.
13. O. Godard, *Environnement et développement durable. Une approche méta-économique*, De Boeck, coll. 'Ouvertures économiques', 2015, p. 55.
14. F. Ost, *La nature hors la loi*, La Découverte, 2003, p. 9.
15. P. Descola, *Par-delà nature et culture*, Gallimard, 'Folio Essais' collection, 2015.
16. C. Lafaye & L. Thévenot, 'Une justification écologique? Conflits dans l'aménagement de la nature', *Revue française de sociologie*, XXXIV, 1993, p. 521.

does not. In France, from the 19th century onwards, the birth of industry and then the development of large companies called for the regulation of what are commonly referred to as industrial risks. This term refers to the dangers posed by economic activities to the health and safety of their environment – people and property. The legal treatment of these risks has been based on a distinction between the effects on people and property within the company, on the one hand, and outside the company, on the other. The extension of this segmentation is the creation of two branches of law: one devoted to protection against industrial risks within the company, the other to safety (of objects and people) and health (of people outside the company). Environmental law, which is devoted to protection outside the company, and labour law, which is designed to protect workers, were born out of a common breeding ground, that of protection against industrial risks, and are gradually drifting apart.[17] The dissociation between the two bodies of law was definitively sealed by the French law of 9 April 1898 on accidents at work.[18] From 1898 onwards, a system of occupational risk was developed, borrowing from both labour law and social security law. Parallel to the emergence of occupational risk and the branches – labour law and social security law – that govern it, environmental law was developed and dedicated to the management of environmental risk.

Highlighting these separations should not lead to the conclusion that it is impossible to green labour law. Rather, it is intended to set the conditions for the latter: to become aware of these separations in order to succeed in overcoming them. The climate crisis is systemic and requires cross-cutting solutions. The legal treatment of the climate issue, and more broadly of the environment and its protection, must go beyond its primary domain, namely environmental law.

Considering that environmental protection is not just the prerogative of environmental law requires us to abandon the naturalistic perception of the environment. The environment cannot be reduced to a set of natural elements worthy of protection. The relationship between human beings and the environment is intertwined with moral, economic, social and other issues. If 'the environment is at the heart of the social question', the converse is also true: the social and the economic are at the heart of the environment, or more precisely, of ecology. The fact that the economic, social and environmental spheres are intertwined puts to the test the division of positive law into object-centred branches. At the heart of the promotion of environmental economic law is the conviction that the pursuit of ecological goals requires us to go beyond these divisions of tasks between legal branches and disciplines. The project of ecological transformation and the quest for the levers of this transformation reinforces this conviction of the need to environmentalise the law – or should we say the rights – that govern economic activities. This is reflected in the fact that environmental protection and climate change objectives are being taken into account in the tools used by the industries concerned. Labour law cannot escape this trend towards environmentalisation, especially as there can be no effective climate action without social justice.

17. L. Jubert, *L'organisation du travail et la prévention des risques professionnels*, Thèse Université Paris Nanterre, C. Wolmark (dir.), 2019.
18. Law of 9 April 1898 concerning liability for accidents at work, JO of 10 April 1898, p. 2209.

3 MANIFESTATIONS OF THE ENVIRONMENTALISATION OF LABOUR LAW: THE EXAMPLE OF FRENCH LAW

Specifically, it can be seen that the environmentalisation of French labour law is progressing, particularly under the effect of the so called Climate and Resilience Act adopted on 22 August 2021 (3.1). Similar developments in positive law are reflected in the work of academics. Works devoted to the greening of labour law are multiplying and diversifying (3.2).

3.1 The Place of Environmental Considerations in Positive Law

Environmental considerations already have their place in labour law. Two areas of labour law have traditionally been their preferred terrain: occupational health and employment. In the first area, labour law and the environment come together in provisions dealing with risks affecting the health and safety of workers and the environment. Such risks are given the adjective 'mixed'.[19] The occupational risk, which affects employees, then has an ecological dimension.[20] An element is thus likely to produce consequences both within the company, on workers, and outside the company, on neighbours, consumers or natural elements. The mixed risk is thus considered to be an 'occupational risk with an ecological dimension'.[21] In this case, labour law contains instruments designed to deal not only with the effects on employees but also with environmental risk, particularly for risk-prone establishments.[22] This is a fundamental trend in employment law.[23]

Employment and its protection is the second area of labour law that is usually 'brought into contact' with environmental concerns, usually to highlight the tension between protecting employment and protecting the environment. The case of *Ilva*, a steelworks located in Taranto, a town in the Italian region of Puglia, is emblematic in this respect.[24] In the name of employment, the Italian government authorised the company not to comply with health and safety standards for the protection of people and the environment. In 2019, the European Court of Human Rights insisted on the need to put an end to the impunity enjoyed by the company and condemned Italy for

19. A. Supiot, 'L'alerte écologique', 'L'alerte écologique dans l'entreprise', *Droit et ville*, 1994, n°37.
20. In this sense, *ibid*; more recently, C. Vanuls, *Travail et environnement. Regards sur une dynamique préventive et normative à la lumière de l'interdépendance des risques professionnels et environnementaux*, PUAM, pref. A. Bugada, 2014; L. Jubert, *L'organisation du travail et la prévention des risques professionnels*, Thèse Université Paris Nanterre, C. Wolmark (dir.), 2019, n° 69 et s.
21. A. Supiot, 'L'alerte écologique dans l'entreprise', art. cit, p. 95.
22. A. Bugada, 'Gestion globale du risque: les apports de la loi du 30 juillet 2003 sur les risques majeurs', in *Droit du travail et droit de l'environnement. Regards croisés sur le développement durable*, cit., p. 105.
23. This movement was already perceptible in 1994 in the observation made by A. Supiot ('L'alerte écologique dans l'entreprise', art. cit.). For a historical perspective, *see* E. Lafuma, 'Comité social et économique: compétences en matière de santé et sécurité', *Rép. Dal.* 2023.
24. On this case, *see* S. Laforgia, 'Se Taranto è l'Italia': il caso Ilva', *Diritto e Lavoro*, 1, 2022.

repeatedly failing to assume responsibility for remedying the violations caused by the heavy pollution produced by the plant.[25]

This concurrence between environmental protection and employment protection is due to the fact that environmental considerations and employment come together through the category of economic risk. Who bears the consequences of a natural phenomenon on the company's activity, the employer or the employee? How should the consequences of a reorganisation made necessary by ecological change be shared between employers and employees? Ultimately, it is around the question of how to share the economic risk created by natural phenomena or by organisational choices that are part of the ecological transformation that the tensions between employment and the environment are exacerbated.[26]

In addition to these two areas where environmental considerations have been taken on board, there are now two others, which the recent French Climate and Resilience Act has helped to highlight and give impetus to social dialogue on the one hand[27] and vocational training on the other.

As far as social dialogue is concerned, it is important to bear in mind that in France, the public authorities play a major role in promoting and organising social dialogue at all levels: at the national level, at the level of business sectors and also at the company level. The 'Climate and Resilience' Act and the national interprofessional agreement of 11 April 2023 on the ecological transition and social dialogue have given a major boost.[28] The law made the 'environmental consequences' of a company's activities the subject of social dialogue, both in terms of collective bargaining with trade union representatives and the involvement of elected representatives in companies. It has thus extended the remit of the social and economic committee, an elected body, to include environmental issues.[29] While the extension of the employee representatives' remit to the environmental field raises a number of questions, it is nonetheless remarkable that the environment has been made the subject of social dialogue for its own sake. What is more, the legislator has provided staff representatives with the resources they need to take on these new responsibilities: enhanced information, expert reports, training hours, etc. While these resources are inadequate, they are not sufficient to meet the needs of the employees. Although the inadequacy of these resources has been highlighted, the foundations have been laid for an environmentalisation of the employee representatives' powers and responsibilities.

Second, with regard to vocational training, the 'Climate and Resilience' Act has explicitly built a bridge between skills management mechanisms and the ecological transition at both industry and company levels. At the branch level, Article L. 2241-12

25. ECHR, 24 January 2019, Nos 54414/13 and 54264/15.
26. On this point, *see* T. Sachs, *La raison environnementale et le droit du travail*, HDR thesis defended on 15 December 2023, Université Paris Nanterre.
27. Environmental social dialogue preceded the Climate and Resilience Act. The latter aims to encourage and stimulate social dialogue in this area. On this point, *see* below.
28. For example, the management of jobs and career paths (GEPP) must respond 'to the challenges of the ecological transition' as well as the accompanying measures likely to be associated with it Art. L. 2242-20 of the Labour Code.
29. On this point, *see*, in particular, the dossier 'La mise en œuvre des attributions environnementales du CSE', A. Casado (coord.), *Bulletin Joly Travail* févr. 2022, n° BJT201a6.

of the French Labour Code requires compulsory three-yearly negotiations on 'forward-looking management of jobs and skills, in particular to meet the challenges of the ecological transition'. At the company level, Article L. 2242-20 of the Labour Code imposes a three-year negotiation obligation on the management of jobs and career paths, 'in particular to meet the challenges of the ecological transition'.[30]

As we can see, French labour law is giving increasing prominence to environmental considerations. This is echoed in the more acute attention paid to them by Labour doctrine.

3.2 The Place of Environmental Considerations in French Labour Law Doctrine[31]

Dogmatico-doctrinal analyses, to use Antoine Jeammaud's terminology,[32] attempt to account for the way in which the categories of labour law deal with legal issues relating to the environment and the ensuing disturbances. In this respect, two pioneering doctrinal approaches can be distinguished, although there is a certain artifice in differentiating between them, given the extent to which some writings mix them. The first category of work focused on the management of health and environmental risks and on the category of 'mixed risk'.[33] A second category took as its starting point the interactions between corporate social responsibility and labour law.[34] Dogmatic and doctrinal analysis was given fresh impetus in the wake of the Climate and Resilience Act. Analyses of the new powers of the employee representatives, their relationship with existing powers and the appropriateness of the new resources conferred have proliferated.[35]

From a more normative point of view, one author argues in favour of a development of labour law that is deliberately geared towards one goal: environmental protection.[36] Based on an analysis of positive law, the author shows that the 'environmental vocation' of labour law already exists and that it only needs to be revealed and amplified.[37] From this perspective, the category of risk can no longer be the cornerstone of labour law's encounter with environmental concerns.[38] Environmental protection in

30. This obligation only applies to companies with more than 300 employees, or more than 150 employees if they belong to a Community-scale group.
31. About the Italian and International doctrine, *see* A. Perulli & T. Treu (dir.), *Labour Law and Climate Change*, Wolters Kluwer, 2023. A. Perulli presents the theoretical issues about greening labour law (A. Perulli, 'Towards a Green Labour Law').
32. A. Jeammaud, 'La part de la recherche dans l'enseignement du droit', *Jurisprudence. Revue critique*, No. 1, 2010, pp. 185 et seq.
33. C. Vanuls, *Travail et environnement. Regards sur une dynamique préventive et normative à la lumière de l'interdépendance des risques professionnels et environnementaux*, *supra* n. 20.
34. *See*, for example, P. Blin-Franchomme & I. Desbarats (eds), *Droit du travail et droit de l'environnement: Regards croisés sur le développement durable*, Lamy, Axe du Droit series, 2010.
35. *See*, for example, the dossier published in *JCP S* (No. 50, 2021).
36. A. Casado, 'Le droit social à vocation environnementale', *D.*, 2019, p. 2425.
37. A. Casado, *Le droit social à vocation environnementale*, LexisNexis, coll. 'Droit et professionnels', 2024.
38. In this regard, *see* A. Casado's contribution to the controversy 'Controverse: Quel droit du travail pour la transition écologique?', *RDT*, 2022, p. 9.

general, and the ecological transition in particular, must be seen as a goal of employment law. Labour law tools must evolve in this direction.

Another doctrinal position should be highlighted: that which advocates a renewed analysis of work understood as an activity. According to Frédéric Géa, 'the hypothesis of an ecological labour law leads to a return to the philosophical foundations of labour law.[39] This is because it is irrevocably a question of inscribing a new grammar of the relationship between work and nature – between work and ecology'.[40] As ergonomists have shown, such an approach requires attention to the conditions in which work activities are carried out, as well as the 'work' which refers to the practices and activities carried out by workers.

Whatever the doctrinal path taken to integrate environmental considerations, it is remarkable that they are based on a call for interdisciplinarity within the law – when it is a question, for example, of reflecting on the relationship between labour law and environmental law – or outside the law – when we think of philosophy, ergonomics, the knowledge needed to assess risks, etc. However, extra-legal knowledge does not always have the same status. As part of a dogmatic-doctrinal approach, it is considered to be an auxiliary science to the law,[41] enriching the analysis of the 'environmental' facts that labour law deals with. The sciences outside the law are used to reformulate the categories of labour law, such as labour. Such an approach seems necessary if we are to overcome the limits encountered by the environmentalisation of labour law.[42]

4 PROPOSAL FOR A TYPOLOGY OF MODES OF ENVIRONMENTALISATION OF LABOUR LAW

4.1 A Reality: The Internalisation of Environmental Considerations

What resources, particularly narrative resources, does labour law have at its disposal to go beyond the productivist narrative? To begin to answer this question, we need to pay particular attention to the theories of sustainable development, which have been inspiring international institutions since 1987, when the Brundtland Report was published.[43] This report is the fruit of a global awareness of the need to rethink our development model. It defines sustainable development as 'development that meets the needs of the present without compromising the ability of future generations to meet

39. F. Géa, *supra* n. 1, p. 17.
40. Stressing that the term 'work' is ambiguous, ergonomists suggest distinguishing between 'work regimes', which refer to the legal and practical conditions under which the activity is carried out, and 'work', which refers to the concrete content of the activity. 'Working' is a 'concrete activity of transforming matter or information, which from an anthropological point of view constitutes an irreplaceable human experience' (C. Casse, M. Pueyo & P. Béguin, 'Développement durable, transitions professionnelles et cadres normatifs et réglementaires', *Revue de Droit du Travail*, 2023, p. 468).
41. O. Leclerc, *Le juge et l'expert. Contribution à l'étude des rapports entre le droit et la science*, LGDJ, coll. 'Blibliothèque de droit privé', No. 443, 2005.
42. In this regard, *see* F. Géa, 'Droit du travail et écologie', *supra* n. 1; T. Sachs, *La raison environnementale et droit du travail, supra* n. 26.
43. M. Pieraccini & T. Novitz, *Legal Perspectives in Sustainability*, Bristol university press, 2020.

their own needs'. The emphasis is on striking a balance between the economic, environmental and social aspects of development. The pursuit of this balance is now an objective promoted by international institutions and incorporated into corporate governance tools.[44] Despite varying, even opposing conceptions, the unchanging core of sustainable development is based on three pillars: environmental sustainability, social equity and economic viability. This is a step towards the decommodification of work and nature: satisfying social needs (e.g., having a job) and preserving the environment are not only just a means to development but also its ends.

However, at the same time as the idea of sustainable development was being promoted, another movement was sweeping through economics: the consolidation of environmental economics, whose programme involves applying concepts and methods from so-called standard economics to so-called environmental problems. Standard economics considers relations with the environment through the category of externality. In this perspective, the positive and negative effects on elements that are not directly involved in economic activities and/or transactions, such as the environment, are therefore only taken into account in a secondary manner. Neoclassical theory has thus developed instruments to force economic decision-makers (companies, investors, consumers) to consider the consequences of their trade-offs on the environment. Foremost among these instruments are taxes, which embody the polluter-pays principle. The prices of goods are then adjusted to reflect their internal and external costs, particularly those associated with the deterioration of the environment. More generally, these economic tools aim to internalise an element that has initially been externalised.

This is the dual movement of externalisation and internalisation that characterises the introduction of environmental economics into neoclassical theory. It has enabled economic theory to address a wide range of environmental issues: greenhouse gas emissions, pollution, and so on. But the presupposition remains unchanged: the separation between economics and the environment. Although it came in for heavy criticism in the 1970s, the neoclassical approach to the environment became 'in the eyes of many, [...] the natural and obvious framework for analysing environmental problems'. This body of theory and the corresponding economic policy instruments have been adopted at both international and national levels. In 1975, for example, the Organisation for Economic Co-operation and Development (OECD) adopted the 'polluter pays' doctrine.

This dual logic of externalisation and internalisation can be found in law when labour law incorporates environmental considerations while continuing to leave unchanged the other dimensions of activities, notably social and economic. This is the case when the law imposes a new area of social dialogue – taking account of 'environmental consequences' – without this addition changing the way in which the

44. T. Novitz, 'Sustainability as Solidarity Unbound: Labour Rights and Collective Voice in the United Nations Sustainable Development Goals and the European Union', in *Inscribing Solidarity Debates in Labor Law and Beyond*, J. Lopez (dir.), Cambridge University press, 2020; T. Novitz, 'The Paradigm of Sustainability in a European Social Context: Collective Participation in Protection of Future Interests?', The International Journal of Comparative Labour Law and Industrial Relations, Vol. 13, 2015, p. 263 https://doi.org/10.54648/ijcl2015014.

other two areas of social dialogue – the social and economic aspects of labour relations – are analysed and dealt with. While an ecological function of labour law is emerging, this function is juxtaposed with its economic and social functions, which otherwise remain unchanged. As a result, these functions sometimes compete with each other. This is the case when employment conflicts with the objective of ecological transformation. This competition results from the fact that internalising the environmental objective does not change the way employment is understood.[45,46] However, as economists and ergonomists have shown, if sustainable development is to be taken seriously, it will be necessary to modify the analysis of work, to take an interest in work rhythms and gestures, the relationship with technology, and so on. Simply internalising environmental concerns without changing the software of labour law hits a glass ceiling. We therefore need to look for ways in which environmental values cannot only be added to other values but can also bring about a genuine transformation of labour law categories.

4.2 A Perspective: The Endogenisation of Environmental Considerations

Endogenisation is a more demanding method of integrating the environment into labour law. This method results in a modification of the whole – in this case, labour law – which integrates the element considered to be external to such an extent that this element loses its status as an external element. This is the case, for example, when the integration of environmental concerns leads to changes in the company's operating rules: its accounting, the way it assesses its performance, and its rules of governance. Only endogenisation can have a truly transformative impact.

At the time of writing, endogenisation is far from being a reality. Rather, it is a perspective, a horizon. At the heart of endogenisation lies the need to rebuild the company. This can take several forms. One possible approach is to use instruments that change the axiological underpinning of the company. The company is no longer seen as a profit centre but rather as a project focused on the pursuit of values that compete with profit. This conception of the company is at the heart of the French provision which allows companies to define a mission or raison d'être. The pursuit of a mission allows managers to relax the short-term constraint of maximising shareholder value. Another possible way of reshaping the company is that taken by the European Union with its two directives: the Corporate Sustainability Reporting Directive and the Corporate Sustainability Due Diligence Directive. Considering the second one, its purpose is to make global value chains accountable in the case of serious violations of fundamental human rights or the environment. What strikes the observer straight away is the symmetrical treatment of violations of human rights, on the one hand, and of the environment, on the other. The provisions relating to the duty of

45. *See* in particular I. Sachs, 'Les temps-espaces du développement', Diogène, October 1980, No. 112, p. 80, republished in Concilier économie et écologie, cit., p. 109. *See also* A. Lyon-Caen & A. Perulli, 'Vers un droit du travail écologique', 2022, p. 429.
46. P. Béguin, V. Pueyo & C. Casse, 'Réflexions sur les liens entre le travail humain et le développement durable', *RDT*, 2021, p. 306.

vigilance address, in one and the same movement, the 'negative impacts' – to use European terminology – both social and environmental, of the activities of global value chains. In the European directive, the qualification of these impacts is determined by the violation of certain treaties mentioned in the annex to the draft directive. International Labour Organization (ILO) conventions feature prominently among these, as do international standards relating to environmental protection. The fact that these two aspects are dealt with symmetrically suggests that the demarketing of the environment and that of labour may reinforce each other. Loosening the constraints exerted by financial capitalism can benefit both workers and environmental protection, as well as even ecological transformation.

In a demanding and ambitious interpretation, which has yet to be developed, the duty of vigilance constitutes an innovative model for controlling the power of multinationals, combining ex-ante accountability (obligation to draw up an action plan) and ex-post liability. These two aspects are more than just two sides of the same coin: they are intended to establish a real dynamic for the control of the power of large companies. This control technique is likely to promote a logic of endogenisation of social and environmental considerations in company management, as it attempts to inscribe environmental concerns in the DNA of economic operators. A similar ambition has been assumed at the European level. Thus, according to point 27 of the preamble to the directive, 'in order to exercise due diligence in relation to human rights and the environment with regard to their operations, subsidiaries and value chains, the companies covered by this Directive should integrate the duty of care into their corporate policies'. This endogenisation is marked by the uncertainty that runs through the climate transition process. Consequently, endogenisation must be based on democratic debate, particularly within companies.

CHAPTER 12

Values and Labour Law Politics: A New Search for Meaning

Marzia Barbera

1 INTRODUCTION

In one of his last writings devoted to the relationship between labour law and values, Riccardo Del Punta wondered whether, when we talk about values, *'we are talking about law, or are we talking, instead, about philosophy, ... more or less idly'*. Riccardo's answer was that lawyers should not hesitate to claim that one can indeed discuss law by discussing values. Not only are values the underlying thread of all narratives of justification of the law (including those concerning labour law) but also the constitutionalisation of labour law has produced 'bridging' principles, perpetually in communication with values. However, he remarked, lawyers must be cautious because the legal discussion on values must always remain anchored to the actual processes to which labour law relates, *'without escaping into the hyperuranium'*.[1]

Del Punta's caution was understandable. The search by labour law scholars for a philosophic foundation for their subject is quite a new thing. While for centuries there has been a lively discussion about the meaning of work, the Nature of exploitation, and just distribution of the product of work, philosophers have rarely been interested in exploring how and why the law regulates or ought to regulate work.[2]

The opposite has also been true. Traditionally, most labour law theories were ascribed to the realist theories of law, and a realist vision of the legal system is rarely preceded by a theoretical and philosophical reflection on what the law is about. Indeed,

1. R. Del Punta, *Diritto del lavoro e lavori,* in R. Del Punta (ed.), *Valori e tecniche nel diritto del lavoro,* Firenze, University Press, 2022, p. 21 ss.
2. H. Collins, G. Lester & V. Mantouvalou, *Introduction: Doers Labour Law Need Philosophical Foundation?* in H. Collins, G Lester & V. Mantouvalou, *Philosophical Foundations of Labour Law,* Oxford, Oxford University Press, 2018, p. 1 ss.

a distinctive trait of many realist positions is precisely the distrust of any philosophical reflection on the Nature of the law. Realists see the law not as a set of rules and principles but as a set of social facts, and, if anything, what distinguishes one thinker from another is the way in which they answer the question of what kind of social facts law is about.[3]

The social facts at which labour lawyers have generally looked are the different historical forms of imbalance of power that govern the employment relationships and the limits set by collective and legislative action, seen as the result of complex economic and social processes and institutional strategies of consent or conflict. Labour law scholars have also been interested in the functions and consequences of the law more than in its moral foundation. This instrumental view of the law has commonly led labour lawyers to lean towards a '*material rationality*,' which starts from the interest at stake and looks at the law as a tool to solve conflicts between those interests.[4]

This attitude is also the reason why law has often been seen as a *pragmatic art*, and lawyers as practitioners of that art who operate by suggestion (we might say by nudge) and never by default choices. Giugni wrote: '*The lawyer, in modern legal systems, proposes models of solutions, does not solve problems; designs, does not decide; operates, normally, exerting influence on the subjects who are legitimised to enact the law.*'[5]

It must be said, however, that even the pragmatic approach favoured by the fathers of modern labour law (I am thinking of Gino Giugni, but the same goes for Otto Kahn-Freund) tended to evolve into a theoretical approach. Pluralism as a doctrine was not only an empirical account of the reality of collective relations but also a *theory* of social action. Nevertheless, there is no doubt that pluralist theories started not from the theorist's own ethical commitments[6] but rather from the recognition of social facts – from the expressions of a spontaneous, living law – that were then translated into a specific, theoretical interpretation of the function of the law.

In more recent years, a new search for meaning started from a perceived loss of authority over the law in the face of the emergence of a deregulatory discourse on flexibility and competitiveness and models of purely experimental regulation. To reassert the autonomy of labour law vis-à-vis the hegemonic claims exercised by the economic sphere, many labour lawyers abandoned realism and functionalism and adopted a decidedly prescriptive and normative approach. They perceived the need to go back to norms whose validity could not be further discussed in consequentialist

3. G. Itzcovich, *Il realismo giuridico ridefinito da Guastini*, in P. Chiassoni, P. Comanducci & G.B. Ratti (eds), *L'arte della distinzione. Scritti per Riccardo Guastini*, Madrid et al., Marcial Pons, 2018,Vol. I, pp. 167-168.
4. M. D'Antona, *L'anomalia post-positivista del diritto del lavoro e la questione del metodo*, in *RTDPC*, 1990, p. 404.
5. G. Giugni, *Il diritto sindacale e i suoi interlocutori*, in *RTDPC*, 1970, p. 369 ss, now in *Lavoro, leggi, contratti*, Bologna, Il Mulino, 1989, p. 191.
6. A. Bogg, *Labour Law and the Trade Unions: Autonomy and Betrayal*, in A. Bogg et al. (eds), *The Autonomy of Labour Law, Oxford and Portland*, Oregon, Hart Publishing, 2015, p. 74.

terms, and those norms could be found only in fundamental principles and rights and in an underlying value-based theoretical framework.

Today, the normative turn holds the field in many areas of labour law discourse. For some authors, a normative justification can provide a moral underpinning of only bits of labour law; for others *'the normative enters as a part of our account of what labour law is. As part of our constituting narrative. It does not simply enter "after the event"'*.[7]

Among the normative theories of law, I include legalistic neo-positivism, according to which the law should be studied and applied by formulating cognitive and objective judgments and not evaluative and subjective ones. While this may seem to be a methodological stance, I include it because it in fact implies a normative choice about the meaning of the law. Remarkably, neo-positivism seems to be embraced, consciously or not, by many members of the young labour law doctrine, at least in Italy. Perhaps one reason for this attitude is that, as Massimo D'Antona observed some years ago, many lawyers have seen in legalistic positivism a point of view that incontrovertibly identifies the law as a point of view independent of the other social sciences, particularly economics.[8]

In this paper, I will deal with the values that should inspire labour politics and norms. In the first part, my approach will be analytical-descriptive; I will look at the discourses of the doctrine as attempts to found or re-found a specific legal culture. I will focus my analysis on the positions of the Italian exponents of today's most favoured streams of thought. I would suggest, however, that these streams represent a common thread that connects this epistemic community at a global level. In the second part, I will provide a critical appraisal of the doctrinal debate and suggest the need for a pluralism of values as a way to escape monism, reconcile the different values on which labour law relies, and mirror the multiple facets of social reality.

2 THE NORMATIVE TURN IN LABOUR LAW DISCOURSE: THE SUCCESS OF THE CAPABILITY APPROACH AND NEW REPUBLICANISM AND ITS REASONS

As I mentioned before, unlike old realists and neo-positivists, many labour lawyers now openly claim the need for a value-based theory capable of rebuilding from the ground up the reasons (someone would say the justification) for labour law. I am referring, in particular, to the scholars who are inspired by the *capability approach* of Sen and Nussbaum[9] and the *new republicanism* of political thinkers such as Philipe Pettit, Quentin Skinner, and Frank Lovett. Both streams of theory rely on the values of individualism, freedom, and autonomy, on the sense of responsibility towards oneself

7. On these two different positions, *see* B. Langille, *What is Labour Law? Implications of the Capability Approach*, in B. Langille (ed.), *The Capability Approach to Labour Law*, Oxford, Oxford University Press, 2019, pp. 125-126.
8. M. D'Antona, *supra* n. 4, p. 403.
9. *See* B. Langille (ed.), *The Capability Approach to Labour Law, supra* n. 7, and the book *Philosophical Foundations of Labour Law*, already quoted at *supra* n. 2, which refers to a diverse bunch of theories.

and towards others, on proceduralism and reasonableness and on justice as equal rights and opportunities in life. According to its proponents, such a theoretical move should lead to a paradigm shift in labour law, not only at a conceptual level but also in terms of political and practical choices. For Italian doctrine, I am thinking especially of Riccardo del Punta, Bruno Caruso, and Adalberto Perulli, but Italian scholars certainly are not alone. Sen seems to have become the guiding spirit not only in the research but also in the political planning of many labour lawyers. Think of the influence that Sen's thought has had on scholars like Simon Deakin, Mark Freedman, Nicola Kounturis, and Brian Langille.

These theories are attractive in many respects, and this might explain their success. First of all, despite starting from the value of freedom (which, Del Punta says, should be able to bring *'the spirit of liberty into the world of labour'*),[10] the two theories enable one to retain the horizon of justice. Second, these models focus not only on the modern values of impartiality and autonomy but also on the post-modern (or perhaps we should say new-modern) values of subjectivity – the desires and aspirations of the person. Finally, they recognise one of the cornerstones that labour lawyers find hard to give up: the existence of unequal power within economic and social relationships.

Capabilities theory refers to the *real* capability of a person to do some fundamental things.[11] Since inequality of power limits the freedoms and substantial capacities of individuals, the theory claims the need for public and collective actions to foster individual empowerment. However, there is an important difference between this approach and what can be considered the basic feature of classical labour law. As Del Punta observed, following Sen's theory, disparity of power loses its existing status as a 'foundational base' of this sector of law and becomes only an 'obstacle to be removed'.

For this reason, some authors have enriched capability theory by making reference to the principle of freedom as non-domination endorsed by Quentin Skinner, Philipe Pettit, and Frank Lovett. In contrast with the classic concept of freedom as the mere absence of interference, this new republican strand defines freedom as absence of domination or dependence on the arbitrary will of another.

The principle of non-domination, Del Punta argues, is far from specific to labour law; it is rather the expression of a more universal ideal that has to do with everyone's freedom with respect to everyone else and with the democratic character of social relationships. It is as an individual citizen, more than as a worker, that the person is entitled to enjoy freedom and a series of basic civil and social rights.

Indeed, according to Del Punta's reasoning, work itself loses its foundational meaning and the centrality that traditionally exists in labour law discourse. Work, according to Del Punta, is, before anything else, the source of production of an income and, therefore, substantially, an economic activity qualitatively similar to any other

10. *See* R. Del Punta, *Is the Capability Theory an Adequate Normative Theory for Labour Law?,* in B. Langille (ed.), *The Capability Approach to Labour Law, supra* n. 7, p. 87. *See also* R. Del Punta, *Leggendo 'The Idea of Justice', di Amartya Sen, in Giornale di diritto del lavoro e di relazioni industriali,* 2013, pp. 206 et seq.
11. A.K. Sen, *L'idea di giustizia,* I° ed., Milano, Mondadori, 2010, p. 357.

economic activity. So, it is income that must be primarily protected. As a distinct value, work cannot be assumed to be superior to any other attribution of meaning.

Perhaps one of the reasons why, from this perspective, workers' protection should shift from the employment relationship to the labour market is precisely the concept of work as an object of the law, mainly as the source of income. By contrast, the legal system must remain, in principle, extraneous to work understood as self-realisation or in its personal and existential dimension. What inspires this position is thus neither the rejection of Marxian alienated labour nor the movement towards a non-labour, post-salarial society, but, once again, a vision of freedom as non-interference in the individual life.

A neo-republican stance is also taken by Adalberto Perulli,[12] who speaks of a '*civic justification*' for labour law: '*the civic world expresses the value of the human persons not so much in their singularity but above all in their being part of a collectivity*,' and this collectivity is the labour collectivity (which gives rise to a form of '*cooperative inclusion in the social division of labor*') but, above all, the democratic collectivity.[13]

This author also maintains that the main value of labour law is freedom. However, as he writes with co-author Speziale, '*we need to understand the meaning of the term freedom: it is certainly not the negative freedom of the liberal matrix, but the social freedom that unites-with a common thread – the Kantian imperative of respect, the Hegelian principle of intersubjective recognition and the neo-republican idea of "non domination"*'. The fulfilment of this form of social freedom – which takes Honneth's theory on recognition as its main point of reference – presupposes a freedom not only of the individual but of all the '*ethical institutions provided for in positive law*'.[14]

According to this approach, the recognition of work as the founding value of a democratic society by the Italian Constitution is a project for the unification of society through work and work itself as one of the basic capacities of the human being. As a consequence, even the legal limits on dismissal are described as a reflex of the '*moral-social dimension*' of work.

Turning now to the other main point of reference of labour law, i.e., the market, Bruno Caruso has suggested that one of the virtues of the capability approach is its capacity to overcome one of the main failures of traditional labour law: namely, the view of the market as an irreparably hostile environment for subordinate workers.[15] In this view, the only way to serve workers' interests is to protect them from the market through a static, paternalistic type of regulation. This concept of the market has been incapable of resisting the progress of market liberalism, condemning labour law to ineffectiveness and failing, at the same time, to promote the autonomy and responsibility of the worker. The capability approach, on the contrary, is able to distinguish

12. A. Perulli, *Il diritto del lavoro tra libertà, riconoscimento e non-dominio* in AA.VV., *Valori e tecniche nel diritto del lavoro, supra* n. 1, pp. 101 et seq. and A. Perulli & V. Speziale, *Dieci tesi sul diritto del lavoro,* Bologna, Il Mulino, 2022.
13. *See* A. Perulli & V. Speziale, *Dieci tesi, supra* n. 12, pp. 22-23.
14. *Ivi*, pp. 49 and 62.
15. *See* his groundbreaking article *Occupabilità, formazione e 'capability' nei modelli giuridici di regolazione del rapporto di lavoro*, in *Giornale di diritto del lavoro e di relazioni industriali*, 2007, pp. 1 et seq.

between a *good* market and a *bad* market, between a socially responsible market and pure and unleashed market liberalism.

A different view of the worker and the market is accompanied by a different view of the aims and role of the enterprise. The enterprise as an economic institution with a social vocation becomes a full-fledged subject of labour law: '*The enterprise and the innovative entrepreneur (in flesh and blood) also become subjects who bring about change and social innovation, transforming and humanising the workplace; they therefore fully fall within the epistemological, but also value-based perimeter of labor law.*'[16]

The reflection on the Nature of the enterprise and its new role has revived interest in the topic of industrial democracy and brought some authors to conceive new forms of democratic corporate governance. Curiously, however, according to Perulli and Speziale, the 'struggle for recognition' by the workers is directed towards the enterprise as personified by the employer, not towards the enterprise as a social institution.

Finally, in recent years, another value has forcefully entered the framework that I have outlined so far: the value of sustainability. This has occurred not on the basis of some kind of 'elective affinities' towards a certain system of values but rather as an acknowledgement of the inescapable character of the issue and driven by the regulatory push coming from supranational institutions. In many cases, sustainability seems to have become the new surrogate value of labour law after the drying up of its precursors – labour and enterprise – capable of legitimising the system without ever questioning the oxymoronic character of the term 'sustainable growth'.

Even in these cases, however, the legal discourse did not take place only on a pragmatic level but soon veered towards a theoretical dispute over the very concept of sustainability[17] and, in a perhaps less pronounced but no less relevant way, over the grand issue of the relationship between Nature and the human person.

3 A CRITICAL APPRAISAL OF THE CURRENT VALUE-BASED THEORIES

I would like to offer some reflections on the positions I described above; I hope faithfully. There is no doubt that the anti-paternalistic approach of the capability theory constitutes one of its major conceptual gains and that it reflects deep changes in the market position and the self-perception of many workers. The capability approach aims to promote and value the human capital of the worker, their knowledge, personal growth, and self-fulfillment, which are also to be considered a crucial competitive resource by the enterprise. However, anti-paternalism can only apply, as even its own advocates recognise workers who are already strong in the labour market or in the productive sphere. If we consider the weak, precarious, blackmailable workers who fill

16. B. Caruso, *Massimo D'Antona e l'idea di soggetto nel diritto del lavoro*, in *Biblioteca '20 Maggio'*, No. 1, 2023, p. 23.
17. B. Caruso, R. Del Punta & T. Treu, *Manifesto per un diritto del lavoro sostenibile*, 2020, in https://csdle.lex.unict.it/sites/default/files/Documenti/OurUsers/Manifesto_Ca-ruso_Del_Punta_Treu.pdf; A. Perulli & V. Speziale, *Dieci tesi sul diritto del lavoro*, *supra* n. 12.

many sectors of the workforce, we must admit (as also these authors do) that classic labour law protections continue to be necessary. On the basis of this premise, it is argued that the non-domination principle can offer a rationale for the reduction of the employer's freedom.

It seems to me, however, that the discourse of non-domination is quite different from the classical labour law narrative of rebalancing the inequality of power underlying the employment relationship. The neo-republican understanding of non-domination, defined as freedom from dependence and from the arbitrary will of another, does not capture old and new forms of domination characterised by systemic types of control and subordination.[18]

This doesn't happen by chance. As it has been observed,[19] this strand of neo-republican theory rejects structuralism and conceives of domination in terms of interpersonal relationships. From a structuralist perspective, domination is a matter of the ways social structures are able to secure hierarchical power relations while at the same time making them legitimate in the minds of their members. In this view, domination has to do with specific *systems* of power, not just with unequal, individual relationships and arbitrary power. Accordingly, labour law specifically deals with institutionalised structures of domination within the production domain, which the contract, the law, and workers' collective action partly legitimise and partly counteract in an exercise of shifting balance.

The other problem which arises from the adoption of the non-domination principle is that labour law tends not only to reduce arbitrariness but also to redistribute social power and opportunities in life. This reflection leads me to talk of the apparent eclipse of the value of equality with respect to a re-established primacy of the value of freedom.[20]

4 THE (APPARENT) ECLIPSE OF THE VALUE OF EQUALITY

I would suggest that this is partially due to the idea of justice that is implied in most of the capability and neo-republican approaches. According to the liberal tradition, there is a distinction between the sphere of freedom and the sphere of equality. The problems of justice are above all problems of commutative justice, to be solved according to rules of equity, by which everyone is given his or her own share, namely a compensation for higher talents and skills, according to stabilised and fair expectations. The vision of inequality that derives from this approach is, to some extent, reassuring: inequalities

18. Riccardo Del Punta himself acknowledges that the concept of freedom from domination implies an essentially negative type of regulation. This is why he proposes to enrich it by referring to a series of already existing labour law norms and institutions (R. Del Punta, *Is the Capability Theory an Adequate Normative Theory for Labour Law?*, *supra* n. 10). He seems aware, however, that this is a circular and basically tautological reasoning.
19. J. Atkinson, *Human Rights as Foundation for Labour Law*, in H. Collins, G Lester & V. Mantouvalou, *Philosophical Foundations of Labour Law*, *supra* n. 2, p. 113.
20. This eclipse is perhaps most evident, even explicitly declared, in some of the positions that I am analysing (I am thinking of not only Riccardo Del Punta, especially, but also to some extent of Bruno Caruso); but it is also present in those positions which although insisting on the concept of 'social freedom' rarely mention equality (Perulli).

are linked to individual skills and qualities. In the egalitarian tradition, on the contrary, it is not possible to distinguish between the two spheres because freedoms are affected whenever there are substantial inequalities. Equal distribution of wealth is therefore a constituent part of freedom, and ensuring freedoms implies redistributive choices that must be democratically justified.

Actually, the principle of equitable distribution responds in reality to a problem of justification of the economic distribution of the wealth produced, but it does so in accordance with the perspective that what is at stake is the justice of individual exchanges. From this perspective, it is a question of justifying why person A receives 100 and person B 50, but the justification for the share of person A remains independent from the justification for the share of person B. If we are satisfied with this justification, we must give up asking ourselves why there is inequality in the first place: why individuals receive a certain share of wealth and not another. In this latter case, in fact, what interests us is not only why A receives 100 and B receives 50 but also what the 'global properties' of the distribution are, the general scheme that ensures that what A receives influences what B receives.[21]

The fact is that, as Alan Bogg has pointed out, Sen's work is mainly aimed at developing a comparative measure of human development that is alternative to that provided by the Gross Domestic Product index or by the distribution of primary goods.[22] This means that Sen is not interested in elaborating a comprehensive theory of justice capable of telling us something about the fairness and correctness of the distribution processes and about the citizen's right to demand a fair share of wealth. His is a 'minimalist theory of justice,' a discussion of what basic skills we should ensure for everyone, which says little about the criteria that should guide the distribution above this basic threshold.

I doubt that this liberal perspective, which in essence abandons the attempt to explain the reasons for social inequality, can really be taken up *as it is* by the labour law culture, which is used to deal with redistribution problems. This happens both in the vertical dimension of the employment relationship due to the disparity of economic power that characterises the relations not only between the parties but also in the horizontal dimension, the ways in which income, opportunities, and advantages are distributed among workers.

But it is also difficult to imagine that this theory can act as a normative paradigm of reference for a sector of law that is strongly and constitutionally anchored in equality. In constitutional systems, the problem of equality is inextricably linked to the problem of power and its justification: to the problem of public power but, increasingly, also the problem of private power. To resist power as interference, indeed, freedom is enough. But what can lead to the demand for a *just* exercise of power if not the idea of equality that requires a justification of any similar or different treatment?

21. *See* M. Barbera, *L'eguaglianza come scudo e l'eguaglianza come spada*, in *Rivista giuridica del lavoro e della previdenza sociale*, 2002, pp. 805 et seq.
22. S.A. Bogg, *Labour Law and Trade Unions: Autonomy and Betrayal*, in A. Bogg et al. (eds), *The Autonomy of Labour Law*, Oxford and Portland, Hart Publishing, 2015, p. 87.

Even if we want to restore a view of workers as individuals, is *freedom* alone really capable of capturing the differences among individuals? Or is it not, perhaps *equality,* with its relational character, that leads us to see the singularity of one person in relation to another while, at the same time, grasping the deep ties that bind us to different communities?[23]

This last remark leads to the issue of what subject to look at when we talk about values – the individual as such or the individual as part of a collective entity.

5 THE COMMUNITARIAN CRITICISM TO LIBERALISM. WHICH IDEA OF COMMUNITY?

Like all liberal theories, the capability approach suffers from communitarian criticism. After all, it is no wonder, as Walzer wrote, that *'liberalism is a doctrine that self-subverts, for this reason it requires periodic communitarian corrections'*.[24] The problem is that liberalism has defective foundations: in order to give absolute priority to the abstract principles of justice, we cannot admit that our personal identities are largely defined by our community ties. According to liberals, the self is, in large part, a pre-social self, which confronts society in a solitary and sometimes heroic way and is formed, although incompletely, before the confrontation with others begins.

This idea of the self is somehow also expressed in the paper in which Riccardo Del Punta is in dialogue with Perulli and Speziale, where he recalls the primacy, in his personal scale of preferences, of the *'sovereignty of the person, with his or her background of singular instances and desires*,' endowed with his or her own choices.[25]

Whereas the earlier critics of liberalism were inspired by Marx, more recent critics are inspired by Aristotle and Hegel. The Aristotelian idea that justice is rooted in a community whose primary bond is a shared understanding of both the good for man and the good of that community explicitly informs Alasdair Maclntyre's criticism of John Rawls. The Hegelian conception of man as a historically conditioned being implicitly permeates both Roberto Unger's and Michael Sandel's rejection of the liberal view of man as a free and rational being.[26]

Today, Charles Taylor and, as we have seen, Axel Honneth are the two most influential theorists of Hegelian 'recognition', understood as an ideal and reciprocal relationship between subjects in which one sees the other as his equal and at the same time as other than himself.

---

23. As also Maria Vittoria Ballestrero highlighted when reviewing the book of Perulli and Speziale; *see* M.V. Ballestrero, *Spigolando tra dieci tesi sul diritto del lavoro*, in *Lavoro Diritti Europa*, No. 3, 2022, p. 13.
24. M. Walzer, *The Communitarian Critique of Liberalism*, in *Political Theory*, 1990, pp. 6 et seq.
25. R. Del Punta, *Recensione*, in *Rivista italiana di diritto del lavoro*, 2022, p. 118.
26. *See* A. Gutmann, *Communitarian Critics of Liberalism*, in *Philosophy and Public Affairs*, 1985, pp. 308 et seq. She notes that the political implications of these communitarian criticisms were correspondingly more conservative. Whereas the good society of the old critics was one of collective property ownership and equal political power, the good society of the new critics was one of settled traditions and established identities (p. 309).

Is there really a need to go back to Aristotle and Hegel to keep an escape route from the primacy of the individual open? What I can say is that the problematic relationships between individualism and liberty, on the one hand, and equality and community, on the other, are already recognisable at the level of history before the level of metaphysics.[27] Having construed the relationships between these two couples of values in terms of conflict has harmed both.

It seems to me that this conflict can be discussed today in more fruitful terms by discussing how it can be possible to refocus labour law on the person who works without abandoning the broad theme of a fair distribution of resources and wealth. For this reason, I would like to close this paper by reflecting on other approaches that might avoid monism and propose a dualism of perspectives.

6 A DUALIST PERSPECTIVE

I am referring, in particular, to the positions of an author like Nancy Fraser who brings forward a dualist conception of justice, a conception that binds together demands for recognition and demands for redistribution.

In the book *Redistribution or Recognition?*[28] Fraser engages in a passionate debate with Axel Honneth about the prevalence to be given to one category or the other. The first category – redistribution – refers to a term widely used in moral philosophy but also in the social struggles of the Fordist era. It indicates an egalitarian paradigm of distributive justice which seemed particularly suitable for describing both the social demands of workers and other subordinate classes and the conflicts over the distribution of economic resources that the Welfare State was called upon to resolve. Issues relating to different identities of gender, race, ethnicity, religion, and personal status in general were considered mere distribution epiphenomena.

In the Post-Fordist era, on the contrary, the category of recognition seems to be at the centre of the civil society's battles. In the recognition paradigm, the remedy for injustice does not consist so much in structural transformations of economic relations but rather in the re-evaluation of disrespected or even despised personal identities. For this reason, group differences should not be eliminated but exalted, or – according to a second, less conservative version of the recognition paradigm – deconstructed and reconstructed in different terms from those in which differences are generally elaborated.

Nancy Fraser proposes a dualistic perspective that holds together the two categories – redistribution and recognition – and integrates them without reducing one to the other. Only in this way – she argues – is it possible to grasp the connection between class inequalities and status hierarchies in contemporary societies, but also to take seriously 'the fact of pluralism', that is, the existence of different points of view regarding the meaning of justice. Fraser claims that any political culture that separates distribution and recognition, judging them to be incompatible with each other, is

27. A. Schiavone, *Eguaglianza. Una nuova visione sul filo della storia*, Torino, Einaudi, 2019, p. 290.
28. N. Fraser & A. Honneth, *Redistribuzione o riconoscimento? Lotte di genere e diseguaglianze economiche*, Milano, Meltemi editore, 2020.

doomed to failure and employs gender inequalities as the epitome of status hierarchies that cannot be localised in a single sphere. But she also maintains that it is necessary to distinguish redistribution and recognition because they correspond to different, even if overlapping, social dynamics.

Honneth replies that the recognition turn does not aim to defend, on a theoretical level, the 'politics of difference'; rather, it represents the attempt to ground a moral pre-understanding of the sources of social discontent. Honneth identifies this pre-political element with the impulse to achieve a recognition of one's own identity, which would be the foundation of the recognition of one's needs in the intimate sphere and the recognition of the value of the cultural and economic contribution of the individual – also in terms of work – in the public and social sphere. In this way, the problem of the redistribution of income and wealth is subsumed under the struggle for recognition.

In her reply to Honneth, Nancy Fraser argues that this monism is incapable of understanding the systemic dynamics of contemporary capitalism, in which inequalities are rooted in both economic structure and status hierarchy. This two-dimensional character of inequalities requires thus both redistribution and recognition policies.

The discussion between the two authors is too complex to be summarised here. Personally, I believe Fraser's dualist theory is more convincing and promising because it also takes into consideration the social conditions that are necessary for the realisation of the value of equality. What I want to highlight, however, is that, in the dialogue of the two authors, monist conceptions and dualist conceptions, foundationalist approaches – in which one element explains everything – and polycentric and multicentric approaches – in which each element of a theory is sensitive to the other – are discussed with a view to a common goal. This goal is to build a critical theory of justice that can bear the weight of a world in which struggles for status proliferate under conditions of growing economic inequalities. Only by deploying concepts capable of structurally understanding contemporary society – the two authors claim – does the 'grand theory' retain its validity and effectiveness.

Part III Labour Law and Its Interlocutors: Economy, Enterprise, State, Market

CHAPTER 13

Labour Law and the Economic Sphere

Valerio Speziale

1 INTRODUCTION

The issue I have to speak about is a topic which has characterized Labour law for the last 25 years. I expressed my opinion that the economy has literally 'invaded' Labour law with a real process of 'colonization'. The objectives, techniques and even the typical functions of this social science have become the main characteristics of this legal subject matter.

I'll try to explain why this process has happened. I will also try to illustrate whether and to what extent this process, which seems to be now weaker and less intensive, can be countered or at least limited in its effects.

2 THE ECONOMIC DIMENSION OF THE LABOUR CONTRACT

The intrinsic economic nature of the labour contract is evident.

The employee has always had the role of a factor of production, which, together with others (machines, tools, raw materials, invested capital, etc.), is organized by the entrepreneur to produce goods. And, as a consequence of a characteristic of the productive structure, the employer tends to use this factor as he would any other, within a pure calculation of efficiency and cost. In relation to this last aspect, the salary has an impact on the economic competitiveness of the producer, influencing the amount of profits, which are the fundamental purpose of the new capitalist enterprise.

In addition, the development of the social protection system, financed by mandatory contributions from the employers, increased the cost of labour. And it is universally known that the cost of labour, in addition to affecting profits, is reflected (along with other costs) in the prices of goods and services put on the market and is one of the factors that most affect the competitiveness of the enterprise. It is no coincidence that globalization, with the creation of a single world market and the participation of producers who combine high-quality products with extremely low labour costs, has had particularly negative effects on Western companies, with consequences that, as we will see, also explain the process of reducing workers' rights that has been underway for some time.

The cost of labour is also influenced by legal regulations that have an impact on the management of the workforce. This economic influence can be direct, such as in the case of reducing or extending working hours, which affect productivity and the overall organization of the company. It can also be indirect, as the growth or reduction of rights (related to skills, constraints on employee transfers or dismissals) can indirectly lead to an increase or decrease in the company's costs.

While having indisputable economic significance at the individual company level in multiple aspects (production costs, work organization, productivity, etc.), work plays an even greater role in the macro dimension, whether it be within a specific industry or the national economy itself.

In this context, collective bargaining plays a crucial role in regulating wages and workers' rights. This regulation has the potential to increase both direct and indirect costs for companies. However, collective agreements have always served the purpose of limiting competition between companies and workers. Moreover, through the predetermination of wages, collective agreements have an impact on important macroeconomic functions, such as income redistribution, impact on aggregate demand for goods, supply of products (thus affecting quantity and quality of production), price levels, inflation trends, state tax revenues, and employment and unemployment rates.

In a more general sense, it can also be said that, as a result of the recent increased economic integration of the European Union, Labour law has become a tool of economic policy, influencing key factors such as employment, GDP growth, inflation rate, and system productivity. It is important to emphasize how the economic dimension of this branch of law, which has been present since its origins, has further expanded, with effects that have radically had an impact on its own function. This profound interplay is justified by the fact that labour law can be considered a 'right of production' of goods or services, directly or indirectly impacting the economic dimension at both micro and macro levels.

3 THE EVOLUTION OF LABOUR LAW

The development of Labour law can be analysed from various perspectives that highlight the historical reasons for its evolution. Undoubtedly, one of the key interpretations that justifies this dynamic is the elimination or drastic reduction of the economic dimension of the employment relationship. This process is linked to the fact that the worker is a person, and it is impossible to separate work, understood as a commodity (the energies used), from their human essence. Furthermore, subordinate work entails legal subjection (subordination to the directives of the other party to the contract), organizational subjection (because the worker is part of the structure of a company that is alien to them from an ownership standpoint and is organized by others), and economic subjection (as the employee derives his sole income from the performance of work, in a market characterized by an imbalance between labour supply and demand and structural unemployment).

These characteristics have determined – as a result of a plurality of factors (the growth and spread of trade unions; the birth and development of pro-labour political movements and their influence on the governance of nation-states; the constitutionalization of labour law; the diffusion of the welfare state, etc.) – a juridification of the employment relationship in its individual and collective profile, which gradually produces the effect of 'immunizing' (totally or partially) the worker from their dimension as a factor of production.

The economic dimension of the employment contract is not eliminated. However, it is strongly conditioned by individual and collective rights and trade union action. The result is the growth of workers' rights and the prevalence of non-market 'values' linked to the dignity of the worker.

4 THE 'REVENGE' OF THE ECONOMY

If Labour law is a 'law of production,' it is evident that it cannot be indifferent to the changes that have occurred in the productive context in which the employment relationship operates.

The epochal changes that have characterized the late 20th century and the first two decades of the current century are of such magnitude that a summary analysis cannot even begin to capture their scope. It is sufficient to say that companies have changed (in terms of organizational models and technologies employed), and markets have become globalized and characterized by various producer/consumer dynamics, along with a significant growth in the financial dimension. These changes have also affected the labour market (with the spread of precarious jobs or poor working conditions, and even in relation to stable contracts, with reduced wage growth), the characteristics of production systems (through the development of the tertiary sector and the spread of digital techniques), political systems (with the end of 'real socialism' and China's adoption of a market economy), economic policies (moving away from Keynes economic theories and adopting ordoliberal models based on the social market economy or more comprehensive forms of liberalism), industrial relations, and so on.

All these changes, when considered individually and collectively, outline a transformation that assumes the systemic and paradigmatic characteristics described by Polanyi in the process known as the 'great transformation.' They necessarily had to influence labour law, which, as we have seen, is sensitive to all these innovations.

The response of legal systems (not only in Italy) has been one of flexibility. The fundamental assumption is that the protective framework introduced by law and collective agreements would make the employment relationship too 'rigid' leading to negative economic effects. To solve these problems, the path to follow had to involve reforms that made the employment relationship more flexible, modifying its content. The consequence is that these reforms, without being clearly stated by public regulators (national and European legal systems) and opinion-makers (including major international economic institutions), require a reduction in workers' rights. In the Italian legal system, the techniques employed to achieve the goal of flexibility in the employment relationship have involved devolving derogatory powers from legal regulations to collective bargaining and introducing legislative reforms that modify the pre-existing regulatory framework, returning to companies a significant portion of the managerial prerogatives that have been questioned over decades of labour law development.

I have already expressed my criticism of these regulatory policies, considering the social and economic effects they have produced, which are certainly not consistent with the 'promises' of improving living and working conditions upon which they were based.

Apart from these considerations, it is important to note that one of the most significant consequences of these economic, social, and legal innovations is the radical transformation of labour law, which can be summarized in its complete 'functionalization' to achieve economic targets.

This process, driven by the factors I have described above (economic globalization, technological innovations, the end of the welfare state, etc.), is also the product of neoliberalism and its economic variant (neoclassical theory) and economic-legal variant (Law and economics). The influence of these theories, which began in the 1980s, became significantly stronger in the following decade.

Within this framework, the legal regulation of labour, both in terms of the individual contract discipline and that defined by a collective agreement, has been considered a factor which has a direct impact on macroeconomic variables (employment level, inflation rate) and on the productive efficiency of individual companies. This approach, adopted by all major international economic institutions (the OECD, the International Monetary Fund (IMF), the European Central Bank, etc.), has also been accepted by the European Commission. In particular, the Commission has based its European labour strategies on flexibility (in contracts, regulations on job employment protection, wages, etc.), issuing increasingly stringent recommendations to member countries to introduce reforms considered crucial for development and competitiveness. In this context, labour law has become a tool of economic policy.

The interconnection between labour law and economics is undeniable. It has been previously mentioned that labour discipline has an impact on macroeconomic variables and at the level of single companies. However, it is important to note that, contrary to the historical development of this field, which aimed to prioritize legal protection for individuals over those related to the productive dimension of labour, there has been a true 'twist' in labour law over the past 40 years, with a particular emphasis since the 1990s, towards an economic perspective.

This shift has affected virtually all areas of labour law. Dismissals, flexible employment contracts, wages, worker expertise, and working hours have been primarily considered from the standpoint of their economic efficiency. Collective bargaining, whose historical role is to limit competition between companies and workers by extending rights, is now expected to tailor legal frameworks to individual business realities, even impacting rights derived from mandatory legal norms and individual protections. It is no coincidence that recently, it has been explicitly stated that collective bargaining (particularly at the company level) should be 'at the service of the competitiveness of companies.'

It is obvious that this new dimension of labour law has had an impact on legislation in the field. Economic objectives have become the main focus of legislative interventions, and the legal system expects collective bargaining to pursue the aforementioned goals. Non-economic targets are often mentioned in laws regarding 'job quality and stability,' 'social inclusion,' and 'worker dignity.' However, these objectives primarily have a rhetorical value, as they do not constitute the fundamental structure of the new regulations. Both the content of the regulations, which are strongly oriented towards economic targets and the evaluation of their impact are approached from a strictly non-legal perspective (influence on employment/unemployment levels, reduction of precarious work in favour of stable employment to increase income and consumer spending, etc.).

5 SOME CRITICAL CONSIDERATIONS ON THE DYNAMICS OF LABOUR LAW

The predominantly economic approach to labour law raises several critical considerations.

First, economic literature and empirical data have highlighted the lack of evidence for the presumed correlation between regulatory flexibility and employment levels or between reducing legislative rigidity and greater dynamism in the labour market, resulting in increased social welfare. It is significant that one of the most important global economic organizations, the IMF, which had advocated greater flexibility as a tool to modernize labour law and facilitate economic growth, later stated that 'reforms that make it easier to dismiss permanent workers do not have statistically significant average effects on employment and other macroeconomic variables' (IMF – World Economic Outlook April 2016, p. 115).

The OECD has arrived at similar conclusions, suggesting that 'most empirical studies analysing the medium- to long-term effects of labour flexibilization reforms suggest that they have a null or marginally positive impact on employment levels in the long run' (OECD – Employment Outlook 2016).

Therefore, the reduction of labour protection has not been able to achieve the promised results in terms of increasing competitiveness of businesses or improving the quality and quantity of work.

Furthermore, all reforms that have prioritized the economic dimension of the employment relationship conflict with the principles of Italian and European sources of labour law. The Constitution, with its value framework, aims to limit the economic aspects of work and make them compatible with the protection of the fundamental rights of individuals. This is achieved through a significant body of regulations that establish the theorization of a true 'labour principle,' which positions work as a constitutionally necessary and privileged tool for the emancipation and socialization of citizens, making it irreducible to its mere economic dimension. This approach is confirmed by the jurisprudence of the Constitutional Court, even in relation to the principles of labour protection established by international and European law. Labour law is qualified as a fundamental right of the human person, for which the State must provide specific safeguards because the Constitution assigns work for the purpose of achieving the full development of the individual's personality. These judgments, all related to individual dismissals, have emphasized how the regulations in this area pursue objectives that are incompatible with an economic interpretation of dismissals.

European legal sources, to some extent, differ. They are more sensitive to values such as competition and the market compared to the Italian Constitution. However, even though some judgments of the European Court of Justice are based on an idea of freedom of enterprise that tends to limit the relevance of labour protection, both the provisions of the Treaties and the Charters of Rights highlight that work is a fundamental social right requiring special protections that limits the freedom of enterprise. Therefore, an interpretation of labour law primarily from an economic perspective is not justified even under European law and represents an evident 'twist' of the existing legal framework.

6 THE 'GENETIC MUTATION' OF LABOUR LAW

The considerations made highlight the limits and contradictions of the dynamics that have characterized labour law in the last 25 years.

The prevalence of the economic dimension of the employment relationship, which had largely been 'immunized,' especially throughout the 20th century, has also had effects on the scientific level, altering the epistemological status of the field. This phenomenon has constituted a true change in the scientific paradigm of labour law, with an approach entirely based on Law & Economics.

This new paradigm has first and foremost modified the reference values of the field. These values, contained in constitutional norms, European sources, laws, and collective bargaining agreements, are manifold (dignity, safety, freedom, right to work, formal and substantive equality, job stability, social inclusion, fundamental rights in the execution of the employment contract, etc.) and outline a program of protection and emancipation for workers. Conversely, the predominantly economic interpretation of labour law has resulted in the absolute prevalence of efficiency and its associated objectives, creating a veritable 'tyranny of economic values' (Carl Schmitt), which has progressively eroded the axiological order enshrined in the constitutional charter. All the legislative reforms that have characterized the major European countries in recent years, also as a result of strong pressures exerted by the European Union, are all oriented towards achieving economic objectives (which, as we have seen, have not been achieved). They have completely marginalized the non-economic values that constitute, as mentioned before, the fundamental core and the very reason for the existence of labour law.

In this context, labour law has been called upon to ensure the competitiveness of businesses and economic systems, leading to a complete reversal of perspective and a situation in which the needs for worker protection, although still existing, are entirely subordinate to other purposes.

The change in paradigm also influences methodologies, which characterize the structure of any science, including law. In particular, within the field of interpretative techniques – which undoubtedly constitute one of the main 'toolkits' available to legal scholars to develop their conceptualizations – there is a clear prevalence of consequence-oriented interpretation. The legal norm is evaluated in terms of the positive or negative effects produced in relation to the efficiency of the system and the increase in well-being. This rule of interpretation, in the Italian legal system, can be deduced from Article 12 of the preliminary provisions, 'as it can be attributed to the logical systematic argument or the teleological one'. However, it certainly cannot become the sole or predominant criterion of interpretation, as this would obscure other fundamental criteria, such as literal interpretation or the 'legislator's intent,' which should be understood as 'the purpose, the rational result that the norm can objectively pursue when applied.' This characteristic certainly does not coincide with the economic effects that the provision may concretely produce but rather with the objectives it intended to pursue (regardless of the concrete consequences it may entail).

Some years ago, it was argued that a labour law not aimed at protecting the personality of the worker could lead to an 'irreversible genetic mutation' in the field. It seems to me that this process has indeed occurred, altering its objectives (from the protection of workers to a tool for ensuring the competitiveness of businesses and economic systems), reference values, and scientific developments (in terms of content and applied methodologies).

7 THE LATEST DEVELOPMENTS IN LABOUR LAW

In an essay I wrote a few years ago, I argued that Labour law had been 'colonized' by the economy and that the hegemony of economic thinking over juridical thinking was unlikely to end. However, my prediction has been partly contradicted. In the last years of the second decade of this century, the situation has changed, partly due to the shifting cultural and political context in which the productive system operates.

As a result of the intensification of climate change and its increasingly serious effects on the environment, the concepts of 'sustainable company,' 'sustainable development,' and 'just ecological transition,' which have long been present in the international political debate, have gained further momentum, with significant repercussions also in the national and international legal frameworks.

These phenomena are so vast and complex that they cannot even be briefly mentioned here. The underlying assumption is that a company is not solely focused on generating profits but also has environmental and social objectives, including the protection of stakeholders (which also include workers). Sustainable development and the process aimed at achieving a 'just ecological transition' deeply affect the goals of the economic system and require significant changes in the relationship between production, the environment, production cycles, and consumption patterns.

These innovations entail a different approach to work and Labour law, based on the principle that '*violations of decent work and fundamental principles and rights at work cannot be part of the competition*' (Declaration of Ministers of Labor at the 2017

G20 Summit). The pursuit of this new production model is realized with new legal rules that aim to condition the 'if' and 'how' of production, affecting the core of managerial prerogatives (enterprise governance, control over global value chains) and extending their effects to the employment relationship as well.

In this regard, the debate on international minimum standards that guarantee workers' fundamental rights, as well as the proposed European directives on minimum wage, platform work, and global value chains, despite all their limitations and contradictions, express a new paradigm based on a different type of enterprise and a different conception of human labour and the legal norms that govern it.

The disruptive effects of the COVID-19 pandemic, which have had an impact on the perception of individual and collective life, along with the decisive choice in favour of sustainable development and the rejection of 'hyper-globalization' and unbridled, ungoverned capitalism, have accelerated the decline of neoliberal thinking. Consequently, even the predominantly economic dimension of the employment contract, which was a direct consequence of neoliberalism, is currently experiencing a downturn.

Work seems to have returned to being seen as a means of personal fulfilment and the realization of fundamental rights rather than a mere factor of production governed by cost-benefit logic and the principle of efficiency. It is a return to those values that, as we have seen, are integral parts of the Italian Constitution, fundamental charters of rights, and the European Treaties.

8 LABOUR LAW AND ECONOMICS

The decline of the economic approach to Labour law does not exclude the need to question relationships with the economy. This issue is in the 'genetic code' of the subject, both in the micro and macro dimensions, affecting the company and the economic system. For this reason, it is impossible to think that Labour law can be completely separated from economic rationality.

First of all, Labour law must be open to the methods and results of Economics. The analysis of the economic effects of a norm could be useful in understanding the consequences that it could have on the functioning of the company, on its costs, on its competitiveness, etc. However, this dialogue must be realized with all the economic theories and not only with the economic mainstream. Some of these theories have adopted targets like equity and individual welfare which are not necessarily linked to income and even happiness, sharing common values with Labour law. In addition, Labour law scholars must be able to highlight limits and contradictions of economic theories, challenging them on the field of the empirical evidence of the targets obtained. And this method, for instance, can be applied to the unproved link between the reduction in Labour law protection of the workers and the increase in the level of employment, to relationships between job employment protection and the level of foreign investments and, in a more general sense, to the influence of Labour law reforms on economic variables and so on.

This critical approach to the economy is not simple because the scholar is obliged to face language, methods, and contents very differently from those he knows, which can determine mistaken evaluations and incomprehension.

The defence of the autonomy of juridical thought must be carried out even with methodologies. In this context, it must be reaffirmed that the economic targets, even though they have been included in Labour law norms, must face 'interpretations constraints' deriving from the text of the law and the juridical system in which the norm is included.

However, theories like remedies based on specific performance of the right or on compensation, as well as between objective liability and fault liability, have a specific technical meaning which cannot be expressed in terms of 'aggregate well-being' or the analysis of 'cost/benefits'.

The labour scholars, then, must defend the axiological dimension of their field. This is the most difficult task but certainly constitutes their main 'mission.' The reference values have already been indicated. It is important to highlight that these values do not constitute a subjective choice of the scholars – which thus reaffirms their identity and justifies their existence – but are a constraint of positive law based on fundamental Charters of Rights, European Treaties, our Constitution, and many ordinary laws, as well as collective agreements which implement them. When the economy demands that Labour law ensures the competitiveness of the company and economic systems, it is not only distorting the 'history' of the subject but also violating a fundamental body of regulations that effectively assigns to this branch of law the task of protecting, elevating, and ensuring equality for workers.

In this context, defending the values and objectives of labour law involves a close confrontation with the goals of economic science. There is no doubt, for example, that employment is a value pursued by both economics and Labour law. However, the two sciences approach it differently. Indeed, at least according to mainstream economic thought, the quantitative increase in employment achieved through temporary contracts is undoubtedly seen as a positive objective. This explains why, always within a framework dominated by economic rationality, fixed-term contracts have increased enormously in European legal systems over the past 25 years. However, for Labour law, the quality of employment and the protection of fundamental rights such as dignity, equality, fairness, the social value of wages, and guaranteeing security are fundamental values. It is no coincidence that, at national and European levels, stable contracts are qualified as the 'common form' of employment relationship, with a clear position that inhibits the generalization of temporary contracts. The latter, which in a purely quantitative logic of increasing employment could be perfectly in line with economic objectives, do not reflect a 'value choice' made by the legal system in favour of employment stability. Therefore, they should condition the different objectives pursued by the economy.

There are economic studies that claim the inefficiency of anti-discrimination protection, which would result in various types of diseconomies. Even if these conclusions were verifiable and therefore possessed their own truth, there is no doubt that the legal rationale behind such protection – preventing personal conditions related to fundamental attributes of human beings from being the basis for differentiated legal treatments – must prevail, considering the supremacy of non-economic values as stipulated in European Treaties and the Italian Constitution.

The axiological specificity of Labour law can serve as a barrier against a 'totalizing' logic that interprets employment contracts solely in terms of efficiency and costs. There is no doubt that it does not make sense to horizontally oppose Labour law to the economy since Labour law is also composed of economics and other justifications, without being absorbed by any one of them. However, law in general (including Labour law in particular) must necessarily be conceived as a system of values that complements economic and commercial ones.

Therefore, it is undeniable that labour scholars must continue their work of reaffirming the constitutive characteristics of the field in terms of its subject matter, methodologies, objectives, and pursued values. Only in this way can the epistemological autonomy of this branch of law be reaffirmed and, at the same time, prevent economic rationality from becoming the sole evaluation parameter for the effects of norms and the basis for proposals to introduce reforms.

It has already been mentioned that the dominance of economic rationality over Labour law has diminished in recent years. This new trend suggests less pessimistic evaluations regarding the ability of this branch of law to defend its epistemological status and its value framework. However, the danger of economic dominance is always present and requires a significant conceptual effort from labour scholars. Many years ago, a great legal philosopher, while positively evaluating the openness and attention to other legal disciplines, emphasized the risk that 'jurists, when they have abandoned their island' – understood as a science based on autonomous epistemological assumptions – 'have drowned in the vast ocean of an indeterminate science of society' (Bobbio 1971). Therefore, labour scholars must not only prevent the development of Labour law from occurring exclusively or predominantly in light of economic needs and objectives but also defend the scientific autonomy of this field, which is seriously challenged by economic science and its tendency to be the overwhelmingly dominant form of rationality.

CHAPTER 14

Labour Law, the Market and Industrial Relations

Orsola Razzolini

1 INCOME INEQUALITIES AND LABOUR MONOPSONIES IN THE USA: ANTITRUST LAW AS 'A RESIDUAL LABOUR MARKET REGULATOR'

The traditional labour law approach has always stressed the importance of both labour laws and unions in counteracting the unbalance of bargaining powers inherent within the employer/employee relationship in the market.[1] Recently, growing income inequalities, which affect both employees and self-employed workers, and increasing concentration of labour market powers (labour monopsonies) have led scholars to stress the need to find new forms of legal regulation for a more equitable distribution of powers in the labour market. Typically, such forms of legal regulation lie in the fields of individual and collective labour law. However, in recent times, alternative approaches have been investigated in the realms of competition law and tax law. The latter perspective is gaining importance in the United States (US) legal system, while the former remains the preferred approach in European Union (EU) legal systems.

The concept of labour monopsonies has been explored by American labour economists and antitrust lawyers.[2] By 'labour market power', economists refer to the

1. *See* Paul Davies & Mark Freedland (eds), *Kahn Freund's Labour and the Law* (London, Stevens, 1983); Simon Deakin & Frank Wilkinson, *The Law of the Labour Market. Industrialization, Employment and Legal Evolution* (Oxford University Press, 2004).
2. *See* Suresh Naidu, Eric A. Posner & E. Glenn Weyl, *Antitrust Remedies and Labor Market Power*, 132 Harvard L. R. (2018) 537 ff. https://doi.org/10.2139/ssrn.3129221; Eric A. Posner, *How Antitrust Failed Workers?* (Oxford University Press, 2021). In Italian *see* Lorenzo Luisetto & Luca Nogler (eds), *Una nuova agenda statunitense di contrasto al monopsonio nei mercati del lavoro* (Quaderni della Fondazione Giacomo Brodolini, 2022); Lorenzo Luisetto, *La regolazione (residuale) antitrust dei mercati del lavoro statunitensi* (Mercato concorrenza e regole, 2022) 585 ff.

ability of employers to set wages below workers' marginal revenue product. American economic studies suggest that 'many labour markets around the country are not competitive but instead exhibit considerable market power enjoyed by employers, who use their market power to suppress wages'.[3] The rise of labour monopsonies is one of the reasons for increasing inequalities, wage stagnation and poor working conditions. Additional factors contributing to this trend may be attributed to the growing fragmentation of employers and the fissuring of the workplace.[4] Large buyers, situated outside of the traditional employer-employee dynamic, are increasingly able to exert strict control over and decrease the wages paid to workers by their suppliers (as seen in cases like Walmart and McDonald's).[5] Furthermore, the overall decline in unions and union membership should be taken into account.

One question is whether we should combat inequalities by relying on tools provided by antitrust law or, rather, we should continue to rely on labour laws and unions. American labour economists suggest that antitrust law tools, traditionally focused more on product market power than on labour market power and on labour monopsonies, should be taken into account as a residual labour market regulator.[6]

This significant recommendation was endorsed by President Joe Biden, who, on 9 July 2021, issued an executive order aimed at promoting competition in the American economy. This order expanded the scope of competition law to include the promotion of the welfare of workers, farmers, small businesses, startups, and consumers.[7] The Executive Order acknowledged competition as a cornerstone of the American economy and recognized that 'for workers, a competitive marketplace creates more high-quality jobs and the economic freedom to switch jobs or negotiate a higher wage'.[8] The order adopts a 'whole-of-government approach' – which seems to recall the 'joined-up government approach' of Tony Blair – whereby all Administrations must pursue competitive challenges with the aim of promoting consumer, workers, farmers, and businesses welfare. Administrations and agencies (like firms in Europe) are charged with sustainable goals and responsibilities, and they are called to promote and pursue environmental justice, economic justice, and racial equity by coordinating their efforts. More precisely, the order affirms: 'it is the policy of my Administration to enforce the antitrust laws to combat the excessive concentration of industry, the abuses of market power, and the harmful effects of monopoly and monopsony – especially as these

3. *See* Posner, *supra* n. 2, 1 ff.
4. *See* David Weil, *The Fissured Workplace. Why Work Became So Bad for So Many and What Can Be Done to Improve It* (Harvard University Press, 2014). This topic has been explored in Italy (and in Europe in general) since the 1990s. *See* Pietro Ichino, *Il diritto del lavoro e i confini dell'impresa* Giorn. Dir. Lav. Rel. Ind.(1999) 251 ff.
5. *See* Nathan Wilmers, *Wage Stagnation and Buyer Powers: How Buyer-Supplier Relations Affect US Workers' Wages, 1978 to 2014*, 83 American Soc. Rev. (2018) 213 https://doi.org/10.1177/0003122418762441.
6. The idea that antitrust should pay more attention to labour market power, 'which is ubiquitous and costly to society, it is bad for economic growth and fuels political conflict', than to product market power, is stressed by Naidu, Posner & Weyl, *supra* n. 2, at 1 and 7 ff.
7. *See* the Executive Order on Promoting Competition in the American Economy (9 July 2021), at https://www.whitehouse.gov/briefing-room/presidential-actions/2021/07/09/executive-order-on-promoting-competition-in-the-american-economy/.
8. *Ibid.*

issues arise in labor markets, agricultural markets, Internet platform industries, healthcare markets (including insurance, hospital, and prescription drug markets), repair markets, and United States markets directly affected by foreign cartel activity'.

Economists and lawyers have shown a growing interest in no-poaching and non-solicit agreements, commonly found in franchise contracts such as McDonald's. These agreements are viewed as tools by which both the franchisor and franchisees exploit their market power and engage in collusive actions that result in the suppression of employee wages and the restriction of competition in labour markets.[9] The well-known 'Fight for $15' movement originated from strikes and collective protests organized by McDonald's franchisee employees against the franchisor, since they were experiencing significantly reduced pay levels. This protest highlighted the need to reconsider the American prohibition on secondary actions, which pertains to strikes conducted against entities other than the formal employer.[10]

From a different perspective, non-compete agreements, which in the US cover all workers, even low-skilled workers or workers with low levels of education, have started to be regarded as one cause of the growth of earning inequalities.[11] On 5 January 2023, the Federal Trade Commission (FTC) proposed for the first time a rule, exercising a rule-making power, that would ban employers from imposing non-compete agreements on their workers, regarded as a widespread and often exploiting practice. This decision was supposed to increase wages by 300 billion per year and employment opportunities for about 30 million Americans.

In 2022, a Memorandum of Understanding between the FTC and the National Labour Relations Board was signed. In the agreement, it is underlined: 'The FTC and the NLRB (each individually a "Party" and collectively, "the Parties") recognize that continued and enhanced coordination and cooperation concerning issues of common regulatory interest will help to protect workers against unfair methods of competition, unfair or deceptive acts or practices, and unfair labour practices. Issues of common regulatory interest include labour market developments relating to the "gig economy" and other alternative work arrangements; claims and disclosures about earnings and costs associated with gig and other work; the imposition of one-sided and restrictive contract provisions, such as noncompete and nondisclosure provisions; the extent and impact of labour market concentration; the impact of algorithmic decision- making on workers; the ability of workers to act collectively; and the classification and treatment of workers.' The two authorities basically agree to share information and cooperate, though they cannot create legally binding obligations.

Last, on 18 December 2023, the Department of Justice and the FTC jointly released the 2023 Merger Guidelines, which are non-binding statements describing factors and frameworks the Agencies often utilize when reviewing mergers and

9. Alan B. Krueger & Orley Ashenfelter, *Theory and Evidence on the Employer Collusion in the Franchise Sector*, J. Human Resources (2021) 324 ff. https://doi.org/10.3386/w24831.
10. Ruben A. Garcia, *Modern Accountability for a Modern Workplace: Reevaluating the National Labor Relations Board's Joint Employer Standard*, 84 George Washington L. Rev. (2016) 741.
11. *See* Tito Boeri, Andrea Garnero & Lorenzo Luisetto, *Non-compete Agreements in a Rigid Labour Market: the Case of Italy* (IZA Institute of Labour Economics, 2023, No. 1602).

acquisitions.[12] This is also part of the 'whole of government approach'. According to Guideline 10, when the merger involves competing buyers, the Agencies should examine whether it may substantially lessen competition for workers, just as they do when analysing competition in the market for products and services. Notably, the ability of firms to freeze wages and/or slow wage growth after the merger will be particularly taken into account.[13] One interesting example was provided by the US District Court for the District of Columbia that, on 31 October 2022, ruled in favour of the Justice Department in its civil antitrust lawsuit to block book publisher Penguin Random House's proposal of USD 2.2 billion acquisition of Simon & Schuster as the effect of the proposed merger would have been substantially to lessen the competition in the market for the US publishing rights, thereby decreasing authors' compensations.[14]

This interesting line of thought suggests antitrust law might serve as a 'residual labour market regulator'.[15] Additionally, it points towards a growing trend of 'administrativization of labor law'. In the era of sustainability, government administrations and agencies are increasingly tasked with traditional labour law goals, such as promoting a more equitable distribution of power in the market.

2 OTHER REASONS FOR INCREASING EMPLOYER POWERS IN THE LABOUR MARKET AND LEGAL RESPONSES

The concept of antitrust law serving as a (residual) labour market regulator, along with the increasing involvement of administrations and agencies in the promotion of sustainable social goals, appears to be highly promising and warrants attention in Europe. In the recent Draghi Report, titled 'The Future of European Competitiveness, Part B' (2024), which the European Commission regards as highly significant for its future policies, it is clearly said that 'Competition policy should also address practices that limit labour mobility between companies like the non-compete and no-poach agreements' (p. 255). At the same time, the Italian Competition Authority has recently required undertakings that are involved in concentrations to communicate information about the consequences that these economic operations have on workers.[16]

However, employing an antitrust approach does not necessarily lead to the abandoning of other traditional labour law tools, such as legal intervention and collective labour rights. Eric Posner himself, in his book, emphasizes that, in the light of the limits of antitrust law, other traditional legal tools should be used to tackle labour monopsonies. These tools include minimum wage laws, tax and transfer policies, mandatory protections (such as health and safety and dismissal laws), workers' participation and

12. Merger Guidelines. U.S. Department of Justice and the Federal Trade Commission (18 December 2023).
13. *Ibid.*, at 26-27.
14. *See* https://www.justice.gov/opa/pr/justice-department-obtains-permanent-injunction-blocking-penguin-random-house-s-proposed. *See also* the description by Luisetto, *supra* n. 2.
15. *See* Luisetto, *supra* n. 2.
16. *See Comunicazione sulle modalità per la comunicazione di un'operazione di concentrazione*, 27 February 2024, at 24.

unions' support.[17] Unions, in particular, stand out as a crucial tool for reducing employers' market power, counteracting their ability to set wages and other working conditions.[18]

Further, labour monopsonies cannot be considered the sole reason for increasing relative employer power in the labour markets. Another possible explanation is represented by 'the collapse of policies and institutions that have buttressed workers' leverage and market power'.[19] Among these 'assaults', American scholars identify the following ones. First, the advent of right-to-work laws led to the elimination of closed shops and union shops agreements. This has consequently deprived unions of one of their most crucial sources of income.[20] In *Janus,*[21] the US Supreme Court ruled that union fees in the public sector violate the First Amendment right to free speech, overturning the 1977 decision in *Abood*[22] that had previously allowed such fees. In *Abood,* the Supreme Court placed significant emphasis on the role of unions as key components of industrial peace and stable management-labour relations. It highlighted that the risk of free-rider effects and the importance of maintaining labour peace are essential public interest goals (compelling state interests). Conversely, in *Janus*, reflecting a different composition of the Court, the Supreme Court criticized this perspective, asserting that 'it is now undeniable that labor peace can be achieved through means that are much less restrictive of associational freedoms than the imposition of agency fees'. The individual freedoms of speech and the right to work without being a union member should take precedence.

According to Kate Andrias,[23] the *Epic System* judgment is also very significant.[24] An individual had signed pre-dispute contracts agreeing to individualized arbitration of future employment disputes about wage and hours, thereby waiving collective litigation rights under the FLSA. Collective litigation has always been a source of concern for employers, leading them to include clauses in contracts that waive collective and class action rights, binding employees to individual arbitration agreements. On 21 May 2018, with a 5-4 decision, the Supreme Court ruled that the Federal Arbitration Act makes this individual arbitration agreement enforceable. In the dissenting opinion, Ruth Bader Ginsburg (RBG) highlighted the imbalances between employers and employees. Collective action waivers are similar to 'yellow dog agreements' whereby the employee promises not to participate in any union activities. Article 7 of the NLRA protects the

17. *See* Posner, *supra* n. 2, at 122 ff.
18. *Ibid.*, at 132.
19. *See* Josh Bivens, Lawrence Mishel & John Schmitt, *It's Not Just Monopoly and Monopsony. How Market Power Has Affected American Wages,* at https://www.epi.org/publication/its-not-just-monopoly-and-monopsony-how-market-power-has-affected-american-wages/ (2018).
20. *See* Raymond L. Hogler, *The End of American Labor Unions: The Right-to-Work Movement and the Erosion of Collective Bargaining* (Praeger, 2015); Charles Szymanski, *Scalia's Shadow: The Friedrichs Case and the Fate of American Labor Movement*, Giorn. Dir. Lav. Rel. Ind. (2016) 761 ff.
21. *Janus v. American Federation of State,* County, and Municipal Employees, Council 31, No. 16-1466, 585 U.S. (2018).
22. *Abood v. Detroit Board of Education,* 431 U.S. 209 (1977).
23. Kate Andrias, *An American Approach to Social Democracy: The Forgotten Promise of the Fair Labor Standards Act,* 128 The Yale L. J. (2019) 616 ff.
24. *Epic Systems Corp. v. Lewis,* 584 U.S. (2018).

right to engage in other concerted activities for the purpose of collective bargaining mutual aid or protection. According to RBG, 'There can be no serious doubt that collective litigation is one way workers may associate with one another to improve their lot.' Suits to enforce workplace rights collectively fit comfortably under the umbrella of concerted activities. By joining hands in litigation, workers can spread the cost of litigation and reduce the risk of employer retaliation. On the contrary, the majority opinion led by Justice Neil Gorsuch (appointed by the Trump Administration) concluded that section 7 NLRA does not confer a right to collective litigation.

As mentioned earlier, another important factor to consider is the increasing fragmentation of employers in the fissured workplace. In complex business structures, such as franchise agreements, supply chains, and corporate groups, it has become evident that wages and working conditions are heavily influenced and controlled not by the formal employer but by the leading firm or controlling company. For example, franchisors like McDonald's and main contractors in supply chains like Amazon exert a significant amount of control over franchisees and subcontractors, a control that has only intensified with technological advancements. It is worth emphasizing that the employer's reliance on larger buyers leads to lower wages for employees and contributes to wage stagnation.[25]

As a consequence, in recent years, the National Labor Relations Board (NLRB) has tried to broaden the joint-employer standard for the scope of the National Labor Relations Act. By taking into account the effect of large buyers' control on conditions of employment, the NLRB suggests the need to bring them to the bargaining table in order to facilitate a meaningful bargaining.[26] In *Browning Ferris Ind. of California* (2015), the NLRB acknowledged that the former joint employer standard, in the light of technological evolution, was too strict; nowadays, it is necessary to consider joint employer for the scope of NLRA, those entities who share control over terms and conditions of employment.[27] According to the unions' opinion, an entity that is not the formal employer should be regarded as joint employer whenever it 'possesses sufficient authority over the employees or their employer such that its participation is a requisite to a meaningful collective bargaining'. The new joint employer standard should be used to include the joint employer in the collective bargaining table and consider it eventually responsible for unfair labour practices; it should also permit strikes and secondary actions against the joint employer even if it is not the formal employer (*see* the McDonald franchisee's workers fight for USD 15).

To implement these suggestions, the Pro Right to Organize Act of 2021 has proposed codifying the new joint employer standard for the scope of the NLRA. The Bill suggests amending section 2(2) of the NLRA concerning the joint employer, as it follows: 'Two or more persons shall be employers with respect to an employee if each

25. *See* Wilmers, *supra* n. 5.
26. As to franchise contracts, *see* Thomas J. Walsh III, *Supersizing the Definition of Employer for the National Labor Relations Act: Broadening the Joint Employer Standard to Include Franchisor and Franchisee*, 47 University of Toledo Law Review (2016) 589.
27. *See* Walsh III, *supra* n. 26; Garcia, *supra* n. 10.

such person codetermines or shares control over the employee's essential terms and conditions of employment. In determining whether such control exists, the Board or a court of competent jurisdiction shall consider as relevant direct control and indirect control over such terms and conditions, reserved authority to control such terms and conditions, and control over such terms and conditions exercised by a person in fact.' The Bill also enshrines the new ABC test for determining the status of employees/ workers within the scope of the NLRA. This measure aims to include gig workers (such as Uber drivers and food delivery riders) in the labour exemption from antitrust laws, granting them collective rights such as collective bargaining and the right to strike.[28]

3 EUROPEAN LEGAL RESPONSES: THE NEW GUIDELINES ON COLLECTIVE BARGAINING OF SELF-EMPLOYED WORKERS AND THE EU DIRECTIVE ON ADEQUATE MINIMUM WAGES

Thus far, the European debate has not focused much on the role antitrust law could play as a 'residual labour market regulator'. As said above, the exception is represented by the 2024 Draghi Report that mentions the importance of competition law to increase and support workers' freedom of movement. Broadly speaking, Europe continues to view labour laws and unions as the primary response to growing inequalities in the labour market. Additionally, Europe has embraced a robust sustainability approach, exemplified by the recent Directive on corporate sustainability due diligence (CS3D). This Directive aims to hold firms accountable for sustainable goals, particularly in terms of respecting labour rights and the environment, rather than placing the responsibility on administrations or agencies.[29]

A first European legal response to inequalities and monopsonies might be found in the enlargement of the boundaries of the labour exemption from antitrust law in order to recognize that self-employed workers, under certain circumstances, should also be entitled to collective bargaining. The new Guidelines of the European Commission on collective bargaining by solo self-employed people of 9 December 2021[30] are part of a package including a Commission's proposal for a directive improving

28. According to s. 101 of the Bill: 'an individual performing any service is an employee and not an independent contractor unless (1) the individual is free from the employer's control in connection with the performance of the service, both under the contract for the performance of service and in fact; (2) the service is performed outside the usual course of the business of the employer; and (3) the individual is customarily engaged in an independently established trade, occupation, profession, or business of the same nature as that involved in the service performed'.
29. *See* Directive (EU) 2024/1760 of the European Parliament and of the Council of 13 June 2024 on Corporate Sustainability Due Diligence and amending Directive (EU) 2019/1937.
30. *See* Brussels, 9 December 2021 C(2021)8838 final. The draft follows the consultation launched by the European Commission on 30 June 2020 for addressing the issue of collective bargaining for the self-employed in order 'to ensure that the EU competition rules do not stand in the way of collective bargaining for those who need it [...] and to ensure that working conditions can be improved through collective agreements not only for employees, but also for those self-employed who need protection'.

conditions on platform work[31] and represent a step forward towards the recognition of right of self-employed workers to engage in collective bargaining.[32]

The Guidelines provide for the first time a definition of self-employed workers who are clearly distinguished from business undertakings: solo self-employed workers are 'persons who do not have an employment contract or who are not in an employment relationship and who rely primarily on their own personal labor for the provision of the services concerned'.[33] For the first time, the obligation of personal service is acknowledged as the line drawn between a self-employed worker and a business undertaking. The labour exemption should operate on a case-by-case assessment. According to the European Commission, inequality of powers and economic dependency should justify the labour exemption and emerge in at least four cases.

First, a condition of economic dependency affects self-employed workers when they cannot independently determine their conduct in the market and are largely dependent on the counterparty 'forming an integral part of business'. This is the so-called economic integration test or single entity test which has traditionally been used by the Court of Justice in order to exempt labour agreements from competition law.[34] In the light of the integration test or the single entity test, gig workers should easily qualify for the labour exemption, even in the absence of the new Guidelines.[35] Second, self-employed workers are economically dependent and should be given collective rights when they earn at least 50% of the total annual income from a single counterparty. Third, collective bargaining should be immune from competition law if self-employed workers who work 'side by side' with employees who perform same or similar tasks. In this case, the labour exemption appears to work as a tool to fight workers' misclassification and to reduce the risk that self-employed workers are engaged for social dumping purposes. Fourth, the counterparty (or the counterparties) represents the whole sector or industry and is at least a small or medium-sized enterprise (with the exclusion of micro-enterprises).[36]

31. *See* Brussels, 9 December 2021 COM (2021) 762 final.
32. *See*, in general, among others, Ioannis Lianos et al., *Re-Thinking the Competition Law/Labour Law Interaction: Promoting a Fairer Labour Market*, 10 Eur. Lab. L. J., 291 (2019) 325 https://doi.org/10.1177/2031952519872322; Eva Grosheide & Mark Barenberg, *Minimum Fees for the Self-Employed: A European Response to the 'Uberized' Economy?*, 22 Colum. J. Eur. L. (2016) 193; Viktoria Daskalova, *The Competition Law Framework and Collective Bargaining Agreements for the Self-Employed: Analysing Restrictions and Mapping Exemptions*, in Bernd Waas et al. eds, *Collective Bargaining for Self-Employed Workers in Europe* (Kluwer, 2021) 40 ff; Adalberto Perulli, *Oltre la subordinazione. La nuova tendenza espansiva del diritto del lavoro* (Giappichelli, 2021); Orsola Razzolini, *Self-employed Workers and Collective Action: A Necessary Response in Front of Increasing Income Inequality*, Comp. L.L. & Pol'y J. (2021) 293 ff. https://doi.org/10.2139/ssrn.4244169; Massimo Pallini, *Libertà di contrattazione collettiva dei lavoratori autonomi e tutela della concorrenza: apologia della giurisprudenza della Corte di giustizia dell'Ue*, in *Scritti in onore di Massimo Roccella* (Giappichelli, 2021) 857.
33. *See* Brussels, 9 December 2021 C(2021)8838 final, at 7.
34. *See FNV Kunsten Informatie en Media v. Staat der Nederlanden*, ECLI:EU:C:2014:2411 (4 December 2014).
35. *See* Pallini, *supra* n. 32.
36. For the definition of micro and SMEs, *see* the Commission Recommendation of 6 May 2003 concerning the definition of micro, small and medium-sized enterprises (Text with EEA relevance) (notified under document number C (2003) 1422).

The last definition of economic dependency derives from antitrust law and is more focused on the existence of labour monopsonies within certain markets and sectors which make it impossible to conduct arm's length transactions. The European Commission also introduces two categories of self-employed workers who are presumed to be placed into a condition of economic dependency and whose collective agreements won't fall under its scrutiny: self-employed workers working through digital platforms and authors and performers who conclude collective agreements with their counterparties in pursuance to the scope of the Copyright Directive 2019/790 of 17 April 2019 and, notably, of Article 18 providing for the principle of appropriate and proportionate remuneration.

A second legal response to growing inequalities was provided by the Directive (EU) 2022/2041 of the European Parliament and of the Council of 19 October 2022 on adequate minimum wages.[37] The Directive responds to the European Commission's commitment to ensure that every worker in the Union has a fair minimum wage that allows for a decent living while stressing the importance of social dialogue and the need to combat in-work poverty.[38] The Directive implements Article 6 of the European Social Pillar on fair minimum wages, providing guidelines for setting adequate minimum wages, strengthening the role of unions and the coverage of collective bargaining at the sector level.[39] At the same time, the Directive promotes a fair regulatory competition between Member States, taking for the first time a clear position against wage and social dumping within the internal market.[40]

In this framework, collective bargaining at the sector level is regarded as the appropriate source for wage setting in the labour markets and the essential element for adequate wage dynamics,[41] while Member States with statutory minimum wages are strongly recommended to involve unions and social partners in the institutional mechanisms for wages setting (bottom-up approach).

As regards the enforcement of the right to an adequate minimum wage, Article 12 can be criticized for not including a system of collective litigation, as seen in the American case. Instead, it relies on a system of individual litigation (right to individual redress), and it allows for the so-called 'Nordic' or 'Danish' exception. Pursuing legal recourses against employers remains difficult for individual workers, particularly if they are low-wage workers. Allowing unions or other organizations and entities with a legitimate interest to engage, either on behalf or in support of the complainant, in any

37. *See* Luca Ratti, Elisabeth Brameshuber & Vincenzo Pietrogiovanni (eds), *The EU Directive on Adequate Minimum Wages. Context, Commentaries and Trajectories* (Hart Publishing, 2024).
38. *See* Luca Ratti, *The Directive on Adequate Minimum Wages and the Revival of European Social Union*, in Ratti, Brameshuber & Pietrogiovanni (eds), *supra* n. 37, 105 ff.
39. *See* Claudia Schubert, *The impact of AMW Directive on EU Labour law*, in Ratti, Brameshuber & Pietrogiovanni (eds), *supra* n. 37, at 39 ff.
40. *See* Recital 7 of Directive 2022/2041: 'Competition in the internal market should be based on high social standards, including a high level of worker protection and the creation of quality jobs, as well as on innovation and improvements in productivity, while ensuring a level playing field.'
41. *See* Vincenzo Bavaro, *The Legal Institutions of Industrial Relations on Wage Settings*, in Ratti, Brameshuber & Pietrogiovanni (eds), *supra* n. 37, at 53 ff.

judicial and/or administrative procedure, as seen in the anti-discriminatory directives, would improve effectiveness of the right to adequate minimum wage.[42]

In conclusion, while it is not feasible to go into the details of the Directive here, it is evident that the European Commission has opted to address income inequalities and promote fair wages by enhancing sector-level collective bargaining and the role of unions and industrial relations.

4 RECONSIDERING THE BOUNDARIES OF COLLECTIVE RELATIONS AND THE CORPORATE SUSTAINABILITY DUE DILIGENCE DEBATE

As seen above, employer fragmentation has placed considerable stress on the ordinary way the boundaries of collective relations and collective industrial conflict are shaped. In systems such as the US legal system, which prohibits secondary industrial actions, the 'capital boundary problem'[43] also has profound social effects on the legality of strikes and industrial action. More generally, employer fragmentation results in unions lacking a real and effective counterpart - an economic entity with the ability to significantly impact working conditions and wages. As a consequence, collective bargaining is not meaningful and effective. Further, the lead company can easily carry out unfair labour practices while enjoying the benefits of legal immunity and irresponsibility as it is not a formal employer.

In the US, the Pro Right to Organize Act has suggested broadening the joint-employer standard to include entities that, while not the formal employer, codetermine or share control over the employees' essential terms and conditions of employment. In Spain, the *Tribunal Constitucional* has established a significant principle: outsourcing cannot be used to undermine workers' fundamental rights, including the right to strike.[44] In *Samoa*, a case involving a main contractor terminating a contract with a supplier due to employee strikes, the *Tribunal Constitucional* emphasized that if the employment contract's continuation relies on the supplier partnership, both the formal employer and the main contractor may violate workers' fundamental rights. Therefore, it is unjustifiable to exempt the main contractor from employment responsibilities, as its actions can hinder and penalize the supplier's employees' lawful right to strike, even indirectly.[45]

42. *See* Sylvaine Laulom, *Right to Redress and Protection Against Adverse Treatment and Consequences*, in Ratti, Brameshuber & Pietrogiovanni (eds), *supra* n. 37, at 289 ff.
43. *See* Hugh Collins, *Ascription of Legal Responsibility to Groups in Complex Patterns of Economic Integration*, 6 Mod. L. Rev. (1990) 731 ff. https://doi.org/10.1111/j.1468-2230.1990.tb01838.x. According to Hugh Collins, 'because the firms determines its own size, it also chooses the limits of its legal responsibilities which in turn provides an open invitation for the evasion of mandatory legal duties' (p. 737).
44. STC, No. 75/2010, 19 October 2010. Wilfredo Sanguineti Raymond, *La tutela sustancial del derecho de huelga en las estructuras empresariales complejas*, Revista de derecho social (2016) 12; Juan Bautista Vivero Serrano, *Redes empresariales y derecho de huelga: nue-vos escenarios para la tutela y la limitación*, in Wilfredo Sanguineti Raymond, Juan Bautista Vivero Serrano (Dirs.), *Impacto laboral de las retes empresariales* (Granada: Editorial Comares, 2018) 277.
45. STC, No. 75/2010, 19 October 2010.

A notable example is the Italian national strike within Amazon's supply chain on 22 March 2021, which quickly gained global attention. Workers and unions organized the strike not against the formal employers and Amazon's suppliers but against Amazon directly. They soon realized that the reason for wage stagnation was Amazon's strong control over its suppliers, coupled with its refusal to engage with unions. The supply chain strike ('sciopero di filiera') aimed to establish a new model of industrial relations and prevent large multinational buyers from using separate legal entities and organized irresponsibilities to evade interactions with unions and shirk employer responsibilities.

Fragmented responsibility in enterprise networks and supply chains has been addressed by beginning to consider the lead company as bound by a duty of care and sharing responsibility for any harm caused to employees of controlled companies or suppliers.[46] Since the Rana Plaza disaster, the idea that parent companies and large buyers are no longer considered irresponsible, solely due to their separate legal personalities, for harms and human rights violations that occurred throughout global enterprise groups and global supply chains has gained considerable attention at both the international and EU levels.[47]

At the EU level, the debate has recently led to the EU Corporate Sustainability Due Diligence Directive (CS3D) of 13 June 2024 (Dir. 2024/1760). The Directive is part of a broader effort which started with the European Commission's Sustainable Finance Action Plan.[48] In the beginning, the idea was that corporate governance could significantly contribute to a more sustainable economy. In this respect, according to the Action Plan, the Commission should carry out 'analytical and consultative work with relevant stakeholders to assess: (i) the possible need to require corporate boards to develop and disclose a sustainability strategy, including appropriate due diligence throughout the supply chain, and measurable sustainability targets; and (ii) the possible need to clarify the rules according to which directors are expected to act in the company's long-term interest'.[49]

This approach was exemplified in Article 25 of the Directive Proposal, whereby 'when fulfilling their duty to act in the best interest of the companies, Directors [...] take into account the consequences of their decisions for sustainability matters, including, where applicable, human rights, climate change and environmental consequences, including in the short, medium and long term'. Had this article been approved, the nature of the firm and its scopes would have undergone a significant transformation akin to a Copernican revolution. This shift has already taken place in

46. *See* Sheldon Leader, *Enterprise-Network and Enterprise-Groups: Trends and National/International Experiences. The Duty of Care*, in Adalberto Perulli & Tiziano Treu (eds), *Enterprise and Social Rights* (Wolters Kluwer, 2017) 121 ff.

47. *See* Vania Brino, *Diritto del lavoro e catene globali del valore* (Giappichelli, 2020); Michele Murgo, *Global value chains e diritto del lavoro. Problemi e prospettive* (Cedam, 2021); Wilfredo Sanguineti Raymond, *Teoría del Derecho Transnacional del Trabaho* (Aranzadi, 2022); Federico Micheli, *Il lavoro nelle catene globali del valore* (Giappichelli, 2023).

48. European Commission, Action Plan: Financing Sustainable Growth, Brussels, 8 March 2018 COM(2018) 97 final.

49. *Ibid.*, at 11.

France following the 2018 Notat-Senard Report[50] and the amendment of Article 1833 of the French Civil Code. Specifically, companies' interests are no longer aligned solely with those of shareholders. Instead, companies are now seen as '*objet d'intérêt collectif*,' with their interests expanded to encompass stakeholder interests and sustainability concerns.[51]

However, Article 25 has disappeared from the final text of the CS3D. The final text appears to be less focused on corporate governance and more in coherence with the EU Action Plan on Human Rights and Democracy 2020-2024, which 'defines as a priority to strengthen the Union's engagement to actively promote the global implementation of the United Nations Guiding Principles on Business and Human Rights and other relevant international guidelines such as the OECD'.[52] Companies formed in accordance with the legislation of a Member State should be subject to due diligence requirements when they meet certain conditions, including turnover and employee thresholds. More precisely, companies should take appropriate steps to set up and carry out due diligence measures with respect to their own operations, those of their subsidiaries, as well as their direct and indirect business partners throughout their chains of activities in accordance with the provisions of this Directive. These measures aim at identifying, preventing, and mitigating actual and potential negative human rights impacts in their operations, supply chains and other business relationships. Human rights listed in the Annex include collective labour rights such as the right to form and join a Trade Union, the right to collective bargaining and the right to strike.

The Directive is highly complex. It suffices to emphasize that due diligence requirements represent the vehicle by which the EU has initiated efforts to address the issue of 'capital boundary problem'[53] and 'firms' organized irresponsibility'. Companies based in the EU but also companies formed in accordance with the legislation of a third country that generate in EU a relevant turnover are required to take care of and respect fundamental human rights, including collective labour rights, throughout the global chain of activities; they are also bound to closely monitor the behaviour of their global suppliers when they are acting as employers.

In conclusion, Europe seems to tackle the increasing inequalities in labour markets by relying on minimum wage laws, strengthening trade unions' rights and collective bargaining, and implementing sustainable policies through European private corporations that are more and more entrusted with greater responsibilities.[54] Conversely, the

50. Nicole Notat & Jean-Dominique Senard, *L'entreprise, objet d'intérêt collectif* (9 March 2018).
51. According to Art. 1833 of the French Civil Code: 'La société est gérée dans son intérêt social, en prenant en considération les enjeux sociaux et environnementaux de son activité'. For a critical assessment of these legal changes, regarded as a new 'French Revolution', *see* Pierre-Henri Conac, *Le nouvel article 1833 du Code civil français et l'intégration de l'intérêt social et de la responsabilité sociale d'entreprise: constat ou révolution?*, Rivista Orizzonti del Diritto commerciale (2019) 497.
52. Dir. 2024/1760, Recital 14.
53. Collins, *Ascription of Legal Responsibility to Groups in Complex Patterns of Economic Integration*, *supra* n. 43.
54. For this perspective, *see* broadly Jean-Philippe Robé, Antoine Lyon-Caen & Stéphane Vernac (eds.), *Multinationals and the Constitutionalization of the World Power System* (Routledge, 2016).

US has placed significant emphasis on antitrust laws as a 'residual labour market regulator' as well as on sustainable policies implemented through agencies (such as the FTC) and administrations while still maintaining other general labour law remedies.

CHAPTER 15

International Organizations and Labour Law

Giuseppe Casale

Labour law acts mainly at the national level, but it is subject to the respect of international labour standards. Labour law takes on a variety of forms and operates in highly diverse national and regional contexts. When discussing international organizations' (IO's) positions vis-à-vis labour law, it is helpful to rely on some key benchmarks as developed by the International Labour Organization (ILO) through the creation of international labour standards. Labour law reflects the multi-dimensional concept that is made up of a variety of elements such as 'hiring and firing regulations', laws that prohibit forced labour and child labour, right to unemployment benefits, maternity protection, freedom of association and the right to collective bargaining, working and employment conditions, and so on.

Yet, when looking at the definitions of the various labour laws, they are aligned with two main competing views: the 'neo-liberal' and the 'social' perspectives. According to the neoliberal perspective, labour laws are problematic because they undermine the 'free' operation of the market, hampering the generation of profit. Labour laws are only beneficial when they are geared towards productivity and compliance. Labour laws are seen critically, and a limited set of rights, such as the core labour standards (CLS), is favoured. The social approach, however, includes a strong commitment to a set of far-reaching labour rights, even though there is disagreement in regard to insider/outsider division within such an approach.

Interestingly, for both approaches, freedom of association and the right to collective bargaining are considered universal rights, even though they have some distinction. If, for the majority, the creation of a trade union, good faith collective bargaining, and withholding one's labour to improve terms and conditions of employment are considered enabling rights to mitigate the inherent power imbalance in the employment relationship, for others, freedom of association and the right to collective bargaining affect how markets are regulated and the way society is organized. Since freedom of association and the right to collective bargaining touch upon fundamental social power relations, they are likely to be contested and are in fact threatened in a good number of countries. In this regard, it would be interesting to examine freedom of association and the right to collective bargaining as a benchmark to assess how IOs have approached labour laws at the international level.

Let's take a look at three major IOs towards labour law. First, the ILO is the most influential standard-setting IO in the field of labour law. Other organizations rely on the authority of the ILO to define benchmarks in their respective fields of operation. In this regard, let's also look at those IOs that are not 'responsible' for labour laws in the narrower sense. One is the World Trade Organization (WTO), which could potentially provide effective enforcement instruments but has refrained for years from taking an active position on labour laws. The other is the World Bank which has moved from a rigid position to a more cooperative approach with the ILO.

At the same time, it should be noted that IOs are not the only influential actors in the field of global and national labour laws; multi-stakeholder initiatives, multinational corporations, international trade unions, NGOs and grassroots movements have become important actors, particularly when it comes to implementation, control and enforcement of labour laws. For example, the United Nations (UN) Global Compact is of special relevance. Though initiated and overseen by the UN, it is a voluntary association of businesses that aims to ensure adherence to a set of social and environmental laws.[1]

1 THE INTERNATIONAL LABOUR ORGANIZATION AND LABOUR LAW

In 2019, the ILO celebrated its centenary anniversary. It is the oldest IO and the only tripartite UN agency, having representatives of governments, employers and workers in its decision-making process. To date, the ILO has adopted 191 Conventions (including eleven fundamental Conventions), 6 Protocols and 208 Recommendations. Needless to say, freedom of association and the right to collective bargaining represent the backbone of the existence and operation of the ILO. Furthermore, promoting these fundamental rights has been one of the ILO's objectives from the very beginning of its existence. The Declaration of Philadelphia of 10 May 1944 mentions both 'freedom of expression and of association' and 'the effective recognition of the right of collective bargaining'. The two relevant conventions, Convention No. 87 – Freedom of Association and Protection of the Right to Organise Convention and Convention No. 98 – Right to Organise and Collective Bargaining Convention, date from 1948 and 1949, respectively. In this regard, it should be noted that the social discourse pursued by the ILO has gone well beyond freedom of association and the right to collective bargaining. In fact, ILO conventions and recommendations deal with a wide variety of different aspects covered by national labour laws, dealing not only with protection for those at work but

1. *See* G. Casale, *The Fundamentals of International Labour Law*, 4th ed., Giappichelli, Turin, 2024.

also protection for those unable to work (unemployment, old age, sickness and disability insurance). This shows the increasing influence of international labour laws, as adopted by the ILO, on the national labour legislation of its Member States.

It has been argued that the social approach pursued by the ILO was relatively strong in a world system characterized by two competing political ideologies. The collapse of the Soviet Union removed the threat of communism as a credible alternative to market capitalism and consequently weakened the ILO. During the 1990s, the organization started to focus on the promotion of a narrower set of international labour standards. In 1998, the 'CLS' were introduced. In June 2022, the Occupational Health and Safety Conventions were added to the core list of international labour standards. Today, eleven fundamental principles and rights Conventions cover five core areas: abolition of forced labour, abolition of the worst forms of child labour, non-discrimination in occupation and employment, freedom of association and the right to collective bargaining, and a safe and healthy working environment. The CLS apply to all ILO Member States regardless of whether they have ratified them. This constituted an important shift in the social approach. CLS were framed as truly global, a set of rights which does not need national government approval and which have an important impact on the drafting of the national labour laws.[2]

In other words, the introduction of the CLS in June 1998 marks a watershed in the ILO's action in the field of labour law.

At a closer look, the CLS were an adequate response to the increasing dominance of trade liberalization and neoliberalism in national and IOs. For example, after the introduction of the CLS, ratification of the core conventions has increased considerably. Despite some criticism, the CLS continue to be considered the most influential source of defining minimum standards, with freedom of association and the right to collective bargaining remaining at the heart of the ILO's mandate.

Furthermore, the CLS do not stand alone but are accompanied by the Decent Work Agenda (DWA), which includes a more encompassing conceptualization of international labour laws and, hence, of national labour legislation. The DWA encompasses the CLS with a view to implementing at the country's level the main areas covered by the fundamental principles and rights at work. Through the CLS and the DWA, the ILO continues to define benchmarks for international labour law that include and go beyond such fundamental principles and rights at work.

In recent years, however, the ILO's significance has been challenged in two ways. First, the ILO has had to consider its relations with other actors that have newly emerged or gained importance. The role of international trade unions has continued to expand in scope in recent years, with unions developing into effective actors in international labour relations. For example, international unions directly negotiate with multinational companies and sign International Framework Agreements that ensure the company-wide respect of labour laws across regions and countries. Similarly, grassroots and civil society organizations are channelling consumers' awareness of working conditions in the global production chain. This has resulted in influential

2. *See* G. Arrigo, G. Casale & M. Fasani, *Dictionary of International and European Labour Law*, Giappichelli, Turin, 2023.

public campaigns that have led to responses from multinational corporations. Among those responses, there has been an increase in the use of corporate codes of conduct since the 1990s. The ILO's role has been one of support through capacity building, technical assistance and provision of legitimacy, but actual control over these actors is still limited. In this regard, more recently, policy entrepreneurs within the ILO have promoted the idea that a new form of governance is needed that can target transnational actors, notably multinational enterprises.

A second challenge arises from the fact that the ILO has traditionally tended to represent formal workers and neglected the situation of marginalized workers, such as informal workers or migrant workers that represent a large part of the global workforce. The ILO's legitimacy as the IO most knowledgeable about any issue in the field of work has thus started to incorporate and support these groups more and more in their policies and programmes of technical assistance. Moreover, interest groups representing informal workers are emerging across the globe. The response of the ILO has been to suggest unionizing the informal workforce. Today, the ILO continues to hold a pro-social-oriented discourse on labour laws and to normatively define labour law within the global discourse through a systematic comparative approach.

2 THE WTO AND LABOUR LAW

The WTO is the largest international economic organization in the world. In contrast to the ILO's tripartite structure, the WTO gathers only governmental and business representatives at the negotiating table of trade treaties and is operated by consensus. The bargaining power of workers or domestic politics in labour law promotion is often limited during the process. The WTO has persistently pursued a neoliberal discourse, which challenges labour-related laws and regulations as factors of market distortion. According to this point of view, there is no obligation for the WTO to contribute to ensuring adherence to international labour law, for instance.

From the 1980s onwards, the debate on 'social clauses' raised the question as to whether there should be a formal link established between global trade and international labour law. Interestingly, it was not primarily the ILO that initiated this discussion. In fact, among ILO officials, there was some reluctance to adopt sanctioning mechanisms in order to achieve compliance with labour law. At that point, the then International Confederation of Free Trade Unions (ICFTU), now the International Trade Union Confederation (ITUC), took the initiative. The main argument of the ITUC was that there was a risk of a 'race to the bottom' in the global trade and production network. Their argument was that in a globalized economy, weak labour laws give a competitive advantage. Low labour standards in one country may therefore trigger a deterioration in labour standards in other countries which face competitive pressures to weaken or refrain from strengthening their own labour legislation. A social clause would have allowed importing countries to make use of trade sanctions against exporting countries that did not respect a previously defined set of labour standards.

The proposition to include a social clause was met with fierce opposition by developing countries in the Global South. They believed that this clause would be used for protectionist purposes. Workers' representatives were also divided on the issue. Those from countries with solid labour laws supported the clause, whereas workers from countries with lower labour standards faced a dilemma, as raising labour standards posed a threat to competitiveness and the creation of new jobs. The last major effort to link labour standards to global trade through concerted efforts of the ILO and the WTO took place at the WTO Ministerial Meeting in Singapore in 1996. At the conference, all WTO member governments agreed to commit to CLS but emphasized that the WTO should not be the body responsible for enforcing them. Instead, the WTO asked the ILO to do it, being the international competent body responsible for setting and monitoring the implementation of international labour standards in Member States. The WTO talks held in Seattle in 1999 ultimately resulted in a failure to make any progress on the contents of the next round of global trade negotiations. One of the main causes of dissent among the participants was again the issue of including labour standards in international trade agreements. Given the shortcomings of multilateral trade negotiations, the number of bilateral trade agreements outside the ambit of the WTO has since exploded. A number of these include CLS. In the global discourse, however, the WTO ultimately retained the position that labour laws are neither its competency nor responsibility. Even though the secretariats of the ILO and WTO work together on technical issues under the banner of 'coherence' in global economic policy-making, there is evidence that labour standards are not only not promoted by the WTO but that they are framed as impeding WTO objectives. Analysing World Trade Reports of the last decade, one could find that the WTO Secretariat continues to frame deregulatory reforms as the most desirable.[3]

3 THE WORLD BANK AND LABOUR LAW

The International Financial Institutions (IFIs), that is, the World Bank, the International Monetary Fund (IMF) and the regional development banks, have often put labour laws into question and, for the sake of development projects, demand more labour flexibility over labour protection. Empirical studies have shown that IFIs have actually undermined labour rights in the countries in which they were active. For instance, some studies find that policy reforms recommended by IFIs undermined collective labour organization and the adoption of protective laws.

However, the World Bank is an example of how ideas and discourse may evolve within IOs. Having followed a neoliberal agenda from the 1980s, demanding structural adjustments in return for much of its lending, the World Bank refused to promote labour laws for a long time. From the late 1990s onwards, the organization entered into dialogue with the ILO, trade unions and civil society organizations. It is important to note that freedom of association and the right to collective bargaining were only promoted once it had been proven that they would not threaten the main objective of the neoliberal approach, that is to say, economic growth. In response to comparative

3. *See* G. Casale, *The Fundamentals of International Labour Law*, *supra* n. 1, chapter on Decent work and international trade.

research that proved there were no negative impacts of freedom of association and the right to collective bargaining on economic growth, the World Bank's executive board agreed to support the promotion of good practices related to CLS.

The World Bank also changed the methodology of its influential Doing Business report to no longer penalize countries with strong labour regulations in its 'ease of doing business' index. Labour standards also figure in the World Bank's Environmental and Social Framework, in the second set of standards. The Environmental and Social Standards (ESS) 'Labour and Working Conditions' has the following objectives with regard to World Bank projects: health and safety at work, fair treatment, non-discrimination and equal opportunity, protection of vulnerable workers, including migrants, prevention of forced and child labour, the support of principles of freedom of association and collective bargaining of project workers in a manner consistent with national law and the creation of labour disputes mechanisms. In other words, since the late 1990s, the World Bank has moved from a position of contestation of ideas brought forward by the ILO to a more cooperative approach.

4 ORGANIZATIONS AT THE REGIONAL LEVEL AND LABOUR LAW

In examining IOs at the regional level towards labour laws and, specifically, freedom of association and the right to collective bargaining, one could find that labour laws are highly contextual, and the sets of rights which are considered both desirable and feasible are likely to differ between countries and regions. As it is well known, regional differences have, in some instances, led to deadlock at the international level, notably within the WTO. Regional organizations, as intermediary levels of agency between the nation-state and global institutions, may be better equipped to avoid such deadlocks. The groups of countries coming together in regional organizations tend to be more similar to each other than those involved in global multilateral negotiations, and hence, decision-making processes are less protracted.

Both the Association of Southeast Asian Nations (ASEAN) and Mercosur have Member States that were opposed to the social clause within the WTO. The two organizations differ, however, in regard to how much their countries rely on labour-intensive production, and the share of exports as a percentage of GDP is higher among ASEAN countries, making them more dependent on cheap labour.

Another difference stems from the fact that while freedom of association and the right to collective bargaining remain limited in most ASEAN countries, Mercosur's approach to freedom of association and the right to collective bargaining is shaped by the strong involvement of trade unions at the country level. This is mirrored in the ratification of the relevant ILO Convention. Whereas only four and six of the ten ASEAN countries have ratified ILO Conventions No. 87 and No. 98 respectively, all Mercosur countries have done so.

More recently, ASEAN has started promoting freedom of association and the right to collective bargaining, but this has been piecemeal and has had a limited impact on Member States. Mercosur's approach to freedom of association and the right to collective bargaining, however, is more participatory, as evidenced both by the strong involvement of trade unions in the elaboration of labour laws and in the emphasis put on these rights in the various declarations.

5 THE ASSOCIATION OF SOUTHEAST ASIAN NATIONS

ASEAN countries have a mixed track record when it comes to engagement with global labour governance.[4] Before the early 2000s, ASEAN did not explicitly include human rights in its agenda and did not adopt a social approach to labour standards either. Questions of sound labour laws were peripheral, even though sectoral issues like work environment, the elimination of child labour, and occupational health and safety were discussed. ASEAN was even hostile towards the promotion of labour rights in international forums. In fact, the organization's Economic Ministers' Meeting in April 1996 announced their refusal to accept social clauses in the WTO.

From the early 2000s, ASEAN adopted a discourse that was more amenable to workers' rights, and the concept of 'people-centered ASEAN' became a leitmotif in many of the organization's documents. This shift resulted, among other things, in the 2012 ASEAN Human Rights Declaration (AHRD). While it should be stressed that this Declaration is non-binding, it includes many workers' rights, including the right to social security and freedom from forced labour.

In regard to freedom of association and the right to collective bargaining, however, the Declaration contains the limitation that these rights must be 'in accordance with national laws and regulations'. In the following years, ASEAN also issued some Guidelines on Industrial Relations and called for freedom of association and the effective recognition of the right to collective bargaining. Furthermore, there is some evidence that ASEAN is responding to the ILO's authority with regard to the DWA. In fact, the DWA appears in documents such as the 'ASEAN Socio-Cultural Community Blueprint 2025' and the 'Vientiane Declaration on Transition from Informal Employment to Formal Employment towards Decent Work Promotion in ASEAN.' The objectives set out for labour laws in the Blueprint are aimed at reaching the implicit goal of harmonizing labour laws and industrial relations.

Regional free trade agreements also tend not to include labour provisions. For instance, the proposed Regional Comprehensive Economic Partnership between ASEAN countries, China, Japan, South Korea, Australia and New Zealand, has never reached such an objective. Regional frameworks on labour standards are also rare. An exception is the ASEAN Convention against Trafficking in Persons, signed in 2015, which builds on global initiatives and requires ASEAN countries to transpose it into their national legislations. ASEAN has thus taken up global discourses seeking to harmonize labour standards across countries, but these attempts have been met with little success. Both the notion of 'organizational field' and the intrinsic features of ASEAN may explain some of these difficulties. First, with regard to the former, there are different value systems underlying national labour laws. For instance, labour

4. Out of the ten ASEAN Member States, only Cambodia, Indonesia and the Philippines have ratified all Core ILO Conventions.

market regulation in Malaysia focuses on employers' interests in providing an inexpensive workforce, whereas worker protections take centre stage to a larger extent in the Philippines, indicating that harmonization of their labour laws will continue to be difficult. But lack of progress in regional harmonization of labour laws can also be traced back to intrinsic features of the organization itself. ASEAN has in fact promoted its soft approach as well as prevailing norms of non-interference and consensus decision-making, so much so as to call this the 'ASEAN way' to approach regionalism. Consequently, many of the above-mentioned regional legal instruments remain non-binding and thus have questionable impact.[5]

6 SOUTHERN COMMON MARKET (MERCOSUR)

In the years, Mercosur has created a relatively coherent legal framework for the protection of workers' rights, starting with freedom of association and the right to collective bargaining. It is interesting to note that the organization promotes the participation of social partners in tripartite social dialogue. In doing so, the organization references and promotes CLS.

When Mercosur was created, it focused on free trade without any provision on labour rights. However, early treaties on Mercosur's institutional set-up created a Working Sub-Group No. 10 on labour issues, employment and social security, as well as the Economic and Social Advisory Forum. It is worth noting that a regional association of trade unions that participates in Mercosur, the Coordinadora de Centrales Sindicales del Cono Sur, established in 1986, has a seat in both of these groups and has played a critical role in promoting workers' rights in Mercosur in the 1990s.

Mercosur countries signed the Multilateral Social Security Agreement in 1997 and the Mercosur Socio-Labour Declaration in the following year. The Declaration referenced a number of human rights treaties. In addition, it made explicit reference to the ILO Declaration on Fundamental Principles and Rights at Work, which was adopted in the same year. It contained a number of individual worker rights, including freedom of association and the right to collective bargaining. It referenced explicitly the exercise of the right to strike. In addition, the parties to the Declaration committed to promote social dialogue at all levels. The Declaration was non-binding, and Mercosur treaties needed to be incorporated into the national laws of the respective Member States for being mandatory.

In terms of enforcement bodies, the Declaration created a Regional Socio-Labour Commission, though with purely promotional tasks and without any system of sanctions. It should be noted that as the Socio-Labour Declaration was not directly linked to the founding documents of Mercosur, violations of the law could also not be dealt with within the Mercosur dispute settlement mechanisms. There has been quite some debate on whether it might be directly applicable, and this depends on the legal systems of the Mercosur countries. Only the Argentinian constitution follows the

5. *See* G. Casale & A. Sivananthiram, *Labour Inspection and Child Labour in Selected Countries*, Giappichelli, Turin, 2018.

principle of monism, that is, direct applicability of international treaties. In any case, the Declaration contained many rights that were granted with reference to national legislation. However, despite the country's differences in transposition of Mercosur treaties, labour tribunals in all Mercosur countries have made reference to the Declaration when ruling.

The Declaration was updated in 2015 after a tripartite process and aimed to reaffirm and deepen labour rights. The 2015 Declaration reiterates its support for the ILO Declaration on Fundamental Principles and Rights at Work. It also takes up more recent international discourse on labour laws, putting the ILO DWA at the centre of Mercosur's action. This entails the inclusion of a number of labour standards for individual workers, like maximum working hours, remuneration, paid holidays, etc. In this regard, signatory countries commit to actively strengthen workers' and employers' representation as well as collective bargaining mechanisms, the latter now also open to public sector employees. This Declaration also substantiates the competencies of the Socio-Labour Commission which can now make recommendations to Mercosur countries in terms of labour law.

In addition to the number of legal framework agreements on the protection of workers' rights, Mercosur has also promoted technical cooperation in this area. For example, the Mercosur Labour Market Observatory was established in 1998 with a view to monitoring labour market developments. In how far Mercosur advocates labour rights in its relations with other countries is less clear. As a matter of fact, Mercosur has concluded international trade agreements with various countries in the Middle East, North Africa, Latin America and South Asia without including workers' (human) rights provisions.

In a nutshell, Mercosur can be seen as a broadcaster of ideas regarding sound labour laws at their own country level but less influencing on the international scene.[6]

7 CONCLUDING REMARKS

We have examined how three international (ILO, WTO, World Bank) and two regional organizations (ASEAN and MERCOSUR) approach the global governance of sound labour laws. We have seen that two main approaches have been pursued in international and national debates: a social one and a neoliberal one. We find that IOs whose intrinsic features allow for an institutionalized representation of workers' interests pursue variations of the social approach, whereas those that do not stay closer to the protection of workers' rights pursue a neoliberal approach. This is true at the international, regional and national level.

The coexistence of these two approaches has led to a change in approach of an IO such as the World Bank that over the years has moved from an antagonist approach to labour law to a more cooperative approach, especially in its relation with the ILO.

6. *See* M. Pucheta, *The Mercosur Socio-Labour Declaration: The Development of a Common Regional Framework in the Global South*, International Journal of Comparative Labour Law and Industrial Relations 37, No. 4 (2021), pp. 325-354, Kluwer Law International, the Netherlands https://doi.org/10.54648/ijcl2021016.

However, it seems that the main challenge ahead is given by the lack of enforcement of labour laws due mainly to labour inspection capacity constraints. In how far this gap will be closed depends on the ability of the ILO and powerful Member States, such as the United States (US) and the European Union (EU) countries, to incentivize the efficiency of pro-labour reforms, when signing international trade agreements, with the strengthening of national labour inspection systems. Moreover, the rapid technological transformation across industries and manufacturing sites results in a wide range of changes in terms of the nature of formal work contracts, industrial relations at the workplace and how the global production network was, and still is, organized across countries.

This new wave of technology will alter the traditional understanding of actual bargaining power of low-skilled workers at firms and factories in both developed and developing countries. The coming leap forward in technology challenges the existing global labour governance regime to catch up with industry practices and market forces as well as to come up with new governance strategies in order to limit the effect of negative externalities or social disruption on the poor, low-skilled working class. In how far these developments will weaken or strengthen the relative power of the social approach remains to be seen. This is the reason why the role of labour law should be modernized with a view to better responding to future challenges.

CHAPTER 16

Labour Law and the State: Towards a Renewed Social Contract for the 21st Century

Anna Zilli

1 UNDERSTANDING THE SOCIAL CONTRACT

By investigating the relationship between Labour law and the State, many different paths can be taken. In the first place, it can be considered that the issue concerns only the legislation on labour and the Welfare State. In this way, however, it is taken for granted that the State has the competence to influence the market, rebalancing the forces operating in the market itself to the benefit of the workers. However, neither the influence of the State in the market nor in the labour market is so obvious. In the labour market, the State can influence by regulating who can work and what the minimum protections and guarantees related to the job position are.

The relationship between Labour law and the State is therefore rooted in the social contract, the hypothetical pact through which individuals belonging to the same society decree the rules that underlie its foundation. Political philosophy has been dealing with this issue since the classical age, and although in 1600, we were already in the presence of an evolved doctrine, starting from T. Hobbes, the theory of the social contract takes on modern connotations. Very superficially and succinctly, in his most famous text, Leviathan (1651), Hobbes tries to show how the State could arise as an escape from the State of nature in which individuals, driven by selfishness, move incessantly in incessant war to exploit common resources.

To escape such a situation, people agree to give power to the sovereign, who will ensure peace by governing the use of the resources. However, this is an unacceptable absolutism, so Locke (1690) wants to see in the State of Nature the self-preservation of people, which is based on mutual respect for property, freedom, and life. It follows that in the State of nature, individuals are free, equal, reasonable, and rational persons.

The State that arises from the pact between these individuals is not, as in Hobbes, the depository of individual natural rights but rather becomes their guarantor, indicating forms and terms of a just exercise of power. If the State is a free choice of the citizens, they will want their union to bring about peace and well-being.

Hence, the most famous reading of Rousseau, who bases the State on the guarantee of respect for the equality of citizens, would have belonged to the State of nature. From there, the well-known revolutionary motto invokes Liberty, Equality, and Fraternity for all. It was with Rawls, in the early 1970s, that the theory of the social contract was reread.

The State of nature has a 'veil of ignorance', which means that individuals are unaware of 4 elements: (1) The status (position) of everyone at present and in the new society that emerges after the social contract, (2) The division of psycho-physical capacities and attitudes among individuals, (3) The preferences and attitudes towards risk, (4) The fourth element comes from the other fundamental variables (e.g., age, wealth, political situation, etc.).

With these premises, Rawls argues that individuals, both free and equal, determine the norms of a just society.

Individuals will unanimously agree on a system in which 'every person has an equal right to the widest total system of equal fundamental freedoms, consistent with such a system of liberty for all' and in which 'economic and social inequalities shall be: (a) for the greatest benefit of the least advantaged ... and (b) linked to open offices and positions under conditions of equal equality of opportunity' (Rawls 1971).

Among the different States of the world, that is, among all possible solutions, the one that maximizes the well-being of the individual who is at the lowest level of utility will be socially preferable. The Nobel Prize winner J. Stiglitz, at the end of the 1980s, demonstrated that the Rawlsian social welfare function could prefer less egalitarian situations to more egalitarian situations if the former favours the most disadvantaged person at all.

2 TIMES, THEY ARE A-CHANGIN': FROM THE 800 SOCIAL CONTRACT TO THE CAPITALISM OF SHAREHOLDERS

The social contract therefore defines the fundamental rules for realizing the prospect of a prosperous society of well-being for all. These objectives must be placed in the epochal changes we are experiencing, which require an update of the social contract as we have known it until now.

We need to update the social contract first because people's needs are changing in response to a quickly evolving context. In addition to the multitude of ways in which digitalization and the internet have impacted the way we live our daily lives, there are new expectations about more mobile lifestyles and things like remote working arrangements.

People also want more responsive action to address the effects of climate change, the renewed threat of nuclear war, and - more recently - a global cost of living crisis.

Second, people may change their minds over time. The rise of more right-wing governments in Sweden and Italy suggests, for example, that the public may have more restrictive views than before about issues like immigration, especially as longstanding economic grievances remain unaddressed.

Third, social contracts require renegotiation when governments fail to deliver as promised.

During the s.c. Engels' pause (Allen, 2009),[1] people moved from villages to cities, from farms to factories. In the period from 1790 to 1840 British working-class wages stagnated and per-capita gross domestic product (GDP) expanded rapidly during a technological upheaval. In that period the ancient social contract was rewritten, by introducing the Welfare State (pensions, schools, minimum wage). It was updated in the XIX Century, too, from a Labour law point of view, by supporting unionism, prohibiting child labour, and enlarging social protection (sick, ill, injured workers and their families ...). From a general point of view, the State provided antitrust law and income tax law.

However, the system failed when the Capitalism of stakeholders into the Capitalism of shareholders (Friedman, 1962).[2] In the Capitalism of stakeholders, the interests of all stakeholders in the economy and society are taken on board, companies optimize for more than just short-term profits, and governments are the guardians of equality of opportunity, a level playing field in competition, and a fair contribution of and distribution to all stakeholders with regards to the sustainability and inclusivity of the system. Capitalism of shareholders is the form of capitalism in which the interests of one stakeholder, the shareholder, dominate over all others. Companies operate with the sole purpose of maximizing profits and returning the highest possible dividends to shareholders.

It happened when companies increasingly became global, the power of unions evaporated, and the ability of national governments to act as arbiters declined. It led to a situation where shareholders became not just preeminent nationally but dominant globally, and many other stakeholders - employees, communities, suppliers, governments, and the environment - lost out consequently.

3 WELCOME TO THE RAGING 2020S: THE TRANSFORMING WORLD OF WORK AND ITS IMPLICATIONS FOR THE SOCIAL CONTRACT

Twenty-first-century technological upheaval and wage stagnation have led economists and academics to draw parallels between the Industrial Revolution and nowadays,

1. Allen, R.C. (2009). *Engels' Pause: Technical Change, Capital Accumulation, and Inequality in the British Industrial Revolution*. Explorations in Economic History, 46(4), 418-435 https://doi.org/10.1016/j.eeh.2009.04.004.
2. Friedman, M. (1962). *Capitalism and Freedom*.

referring to a new Engels' Pause (A. Ross, 2021).[3] Companies care about little other than shareholder profit; governments have become weak and ineffective as global companies have grown stronger.

One of the major challenges to the social contract in the 21st century is the high and often growing level of inequality and income insecurity in many parts of the world, despite some progress made in reducing poverty and significant advances in human development, including lower maternal and child mortality, as well as a rise in education levels (UNDP, 2015).[4]

Yet, people living in the most extreme forms of poverty are still left behind (Ravallion, 2014),[5] and social exclusion, particularly of disadvantaged groups, is still a major concern (UN DESA, 2016).[6]

Workers and their families across the globe are facing a range of challenges, including low and unpredictable incomes, inadequate working conditions, and inadequate social protection, leading many to remain poor despite hard work. In many countries, the dreams of educated and skilled people seeking decent work have been dashed due to high unemployment rates, lack of employment opportunities, and informal work.

Social mobility has not lived up to previous expectations. Younger generations no longer have the same opportunities as their parents to rise above the poverty line in many regions. Some have expressed concern that the recession and lack of employment possibilities may cause today's kids to become a 'lost generation' (ILO 2012). In addition, disparities in access to jobs, education, healthcare, and skills obstruct social mobility as well as economic and social advancement. Numerous variables, including migration, differences between rural and urban areas, gender, and disabilities, contribute to these inequities (ILO, 2016a).[7]

Concerns about downward social mobility (including among the middle class) are fuelled by stagnant real wages and weak income security, weighing heavily on the perception of equity and social justice. These changes necessitated significant challenges to the social compact. Different countries have very different ideas of what constitutes a fair allocation of resources, but some elements are shared across all of them. One such element is equal opportunity, which deals with how to give people the opportunity to thrive regardless of their background, how to reward excellence, and to what degree those with more resources should share it with others in the interests of progress. The fact that inequality has recently become the focus of global discussion may be connected to the recognition that inequality has reached such a level that it is eroding the fundamental principles of the social compact.

Social and economic exclusion not only fuels dissatisfaction and political instability, but it is also seen as a permanent impediment to development by leaving a large

3. Ross, A. (2021). *The Raging 2020s: Companies, Countries, People: And the Fight for Our Future.*
4. UN (2015). *Human Development Report 'Work for Human Development'.*
5. Ravallion, M. (2014). *Income Inequality in the Developing World, Science,* 344 (New York, N.Y.), 851-855 https://doi.org/10.1126/science.1251875.
6. UN DESA (2016). *Leaving No One Behind: The Imperative of Inclusive Development.*
7. ILO (2016a). *Non-Standard Forms of Employment: Understanding Challenges, Shaping Prospects,* Geneva.

portion of the world's population behind. The world of work is constantly changing, and the relationship between the Market, the State, and citizens is constantly changing. When the work world changes profoundly, tensions grow and threaten to disrupt the social contract, which is based on a shared vision of how power and resources should be allocated to create social justice.

4 PLATFORM WORK WITH NO SOCIAL RESPONSIBILITY

It should not come as a surprise that, as ways of achieving fair globalization, the World Commission for the Social Dimension of Globalization (2004, p. 65)[8] has called for a 'new social contract' that includes:

(a) commitment to social dialogue in the formulation of economic and social policies;
(b) recognition that the desire for greater efficiency and higher productivity must be balanced against the right of workers to security and equal opportunities; and
(c) commitment to take the 'high road' of business-labour collaboration to achieve efficiency gains and avoid the 'low road' of cost-cutting and downsizing.

The Commission's call has gained traction in recent years, especially in the wake of the global economic downturn and the fast-changing world of work. Employment is a fundamental component of the social contract and shapes the rights and obligations of workers, employers, labour, and capital.

When we look at technology and new ways of working, we can see that technological advances, such as automation and digitization, can have a radical and transformative effect on the way we work. Some argue that this will lead to a race against the machine or a 'jobless future' (Rifkin, 1994).[9]

However, there is a growing sense of polarization in tomorrow's societies, with a sharp rise in the number of workers and households living in precariousness, a decline in the middle class, and a further rise of a small group of ever-richer people at the highest levels of income.

Of course, automation and digitalization also make better economic prospects and more flexibility feasible. For example, mobile phone services enable farmers in remote areas to check crop prices and enhance their capacity to negotiate the sale of their produce.

Thanks to telework, crowdsourcing, and other remote work practices, people who are caring for family members (or they have limited mobility, or they are parents of young children) now have more options when it comes to working remotely.

8. World Commission for the Social Dimension of Globalization (2004). *A Fair Globalization: Creating Opportunities for All.*
9. Rifkin, J. (1994). *The End of Work: The Decline of the Global Labour Force and the Dawn of the Post-Market Era.*

Anyway, whether or not digitalization and automation help worker groups, they could be the cause of increasing inequality.

While the industrial relations system is built on the idea that employers have a responsibility for the well-being of their workforce, in the 'on-demand' or 'gig' economy, such responsibility is not willingly assumed by either the 'buyers' of labour (those requesting the services) or the 'organizers' (platforms). States are currently battling to define the status of these workers and put adequate protection in place, owing to the blurring of the lines between Labour law and business law.

Even if these 'new' kinds of employment today affect a small percentage of overall employment, many analysts believe they will rise shortly. The rise in inequality and economic insecurity has been linked to changes in job and earnings patterns, as well as persistent unemployment and underemployment (ILO, 2016b).[10]

Especially for small and medium-sized businesses, migrants, and workers in non-standard forms of employment, countries that supported inclusive collective bargaining through a variety of policy measures were able to increase collective bargaining coverage during the recent global economic crisis (ILO, 2015).[11]

5 CLOSING REMARKS: REPRESENTATION AND PARTICIPATION IN REWRITING THE SOCIAL CONTRACT

All of the trends discussed above result in rising inequality and greater income insecurity, challenge societal values about fairness and equity and, ultimately, the social contract itself.

Social cohesion is in jeopardy if the wealthiest people reap the benefits of economic prosperity while most of the society does not. More people are now aware of the fact that excessive levels of inequality limit the possibility of future economic development and impede sustainable economic progress (Ostry et al. 2014; OECD, 2012; ILO, 2014a; ILO, 2008).[12]

At the start of the 21st century, increased inequality, insecurity, instability, and informality have severely damaged the social compact. These issues are already being debated in various ways: how can countries develop a new 'social compromise which benefits employers and workers alike' (Government of Germany, 2015); 'a new social settlement that can meet the challenges of the twenty-first century' (New Economics Foundation, 2015); a 'social compact 2.0' (Aspen Institute, 2015).[13]

10. ILO (2016b). *Social Contract and the Future of Work: Inequality, Income Security, Labour Relations and Social Dialogue*. The Future of Work Centenary Initiative Issue Note Series 4, Geneva.
11. ILO (2015). *Rationalizing Social Protection Expenditure in Ghana (Consolidated Report)*, Geneva.
12. Ostry J.D. et al. (2014). *Redistribution, Inequality, and Growth*, IMF; OECD (2012) *Closing the Gender Gap: Act Now*, OECD Publishing, Paris, https://doi.org/10.1787/9789264179370-en; ILO (2014). *World Social Protection Report 2014/15: Building Economic Recovery, Inclusive Development and Social Justice*, Geneva: International Labour Office.
13. Aspen Institute (2016). *Social Compact 2.0. In Turbulence & Transition: Winning the Clean Energy Race*, 24-26. Aspen Institute. http://www.jstor.org/stable/resrep42625.10.

Each of these formulations shows an important focus on a renewed social contract. The rising question is about the instruments to face this challenge that must ensure the representation of different groups in the decision process.

On the workers' side, enlarging representation includes the challenge of organizing the collective voice of informal workers, as well as those outside of established employment relationships, and the need to build broad-based coalitions with organizations that have similar interests, such as cooperatives, user groups, traders' associations, and other civil society membership-based organizations.

On the employers' side, this includes the challenge of effectively representing the interests of small and medium-sized enterprises (SMEs) and strengthening the relationship between MNEs (multinational corporations) and national employer organizations.

Achieving such representation and participation is necessary for social discussion to be effective. In this regard, the State's role in encouraging businesses to positively contribute to society for inclusive growth and sustainable development is receiving more and more attention.

Expanding upon current conversations, the discourse can be further advanced by examining ways to guarantee that the social compact incorporates the most marginalized segments of society and involves all parties. State, citizens, enterprises, and workers: they all have the common interest in fighting (social, economic, climatic) inequalities for a more peaceful and safe world.

STUDIES IN EMPLOYMENT AND SOCIAL POLICY

1. W. Beck, L. van der Maesen & A. Walker (eds), *The Social Quality of Europe*, 1997 (ISBN 90-411-0456-9).
2. R. Blanpain, M. Colucci, C. Engels, F. Hendrickx, L. Salas & E. De Smyter, *Institutional Changes and European Social Policies after the Treaty of Amsterdam*, 1998 (ISBN 90-411-1018-6).
3. V. Lo: *Law and Industrial Relations: China and Japan after World War II*, 1998 (ISBN 90-411-1075-5).
4. A. Den Exter & H. Hermans (eds), *The Right to Health Care in Several European Countries*, 1998 (ISBN 90-411-1087-9).
5. M. Biagi (ed.), *Job Creation and Labour Law from Protection towards Pro- Action*, 2000 (ISBN 90-411-1432-7).
6. W. Beck, L. van der Maesen, F. Thomése & A. Walker (eds), *Social Quality: A Vision for Europe*, 2000 (ISBN 90-411-1523-4).
7. F. Pennings, *Introduction to European Social Law*, 3rd ed., 2001 (ISBN 90-411-1628-1).
8. J. Murray, *Transnational Labour Regulation: The ILO and EC Compared*, 2001 (ISBN 90-411-1583-8).
9. R. Blanpain & C. Engels (eds), *The ILO and Social Challenges of the 21st Century*, 2001 (ISBN 90-411-1572-2).
10. M. Biagi (ed.), *Towards a European Model of Industrial Relations? Building on the First Report of the European Commission*, 2001 (ISBN 90-411-1653-2).
11. J. Clasen (ed.), *What Future for Social Security? Debates and Reforms in National and Cross-National Perspective*, 2001 (ISBN 90-411-1671-0).
12. A. Numhauser-Henning (ed.), *Legal Perspectives on Equal Treatment and Non-Discrimination*, 2001 (ISBN 90-411-1665-6).
13. R. Blanpain (ed.), *Labour Law, Human Rights and Social Justice* 2001 (ISBN 90-411-1697-4).
14. M.-C. Kuo, H.F. Zacher & H.-S. Chan (eds), *Reform and Perspectives on Social Insurance: Lessons from the East and West*, 2002 (ISBN 90-411-1819-5).
15. P. Foubert, *The Legal Protection of the Pregnant Worker in the European Community*, 2002 (ISBN 90-411-1842-X).
16. M. Biagi (ed.), *Quality of Work and Employee Involvement in Europe*, 2002 (ISBN 90-411-1885-3).
17. F. Pennings, *Dutch Social Security Law in an International Context*, 2002 (ISBN 90-411-1887-X).

18. T. Carney & G. Ramia, *From Rights to Management: Contract, New Public Management and Employment Services*, 2002 (ISBN 90-411-1889-6).
19. R. Blanpain & M. Colucci, *European Labour and Social Security Law, Glossary*, 2002 (ISBN 90-411-1905-1).
20. I.U. Zeytinoglu (ed.), *Flexible Work Arrangements: Conceptualizations and International Experiences*, 2002 (ISBN 90-411-1947-7).
21. J. Berghman, A. Nagelkerke, M. Boos, R. Doeschot & G. Vonk (eds), *Social Security in Transition*, 2002 (ISBN 90-411-1969-8).
22. R. Blanpain, *The Legal Status of Sportsmen and Sportswomen under International, European and Belgian National and Regional Law*, 2003 (ISBN 90-411-1980-9).
23. R. Blanpain & M. Weiss (eds), *Changing Industrial Relations & Modernisation of Labour Law, Liber Amicorum in Honour of Professor Marco Biagi*, 2003 (ISBN 90-411-2008-4).
24. J. Malmberg (ed.), *Effective Enforcement of EC Labour Law*, 2003 (ISBN 90-411-2160-9).
25. M. De Vos (ed.), *A Decade Beyond Maastricht: The European Social Dialogue Revisited*, 2003 (ISBN 90-411-2163-3).
26. M. Sewerynski (ed.), *Collective Agreements and Individual Contracts of Employment*, 2003 (ISBN 90-411-2190-0).
27. R. Blanpain & M. Van Gestel, *Use and Monitoring of E-Mail, Intranet and Internet Facilities at Work: Law and Practice*, 2004 (ISBN 90-411-22-66-4).
28. A. C. Neal (ed.), *The Changing Face of European Labour Law and Social Policy*, 2004 (ISBN 90-411-2312-1).
29. E. Sol & M. Westerveld (eds), *Contractualism in Employment Services: A New Form of Welfare State Governance*, 2005 (ISBN 90-411-2405-5).
30. F. Pennings (ed.), *Between Soft and Hard Law – The Impact of International Social Security Standards on National Social Security Law*, 2006 (ISBN 978-90-411-2491-3).
31. L. Dickens & A. C. Neal (eds), *The Changing Institutional Face of British Employment Relations*, 2006 (ISBN 978-90-411-2541-5).
32. G. Sebardt, *Redundancy and the Swedish Model in an International Context*, 2006 (ISBN 978-90-411-2503-3).
33. A.M. Swiatkowski, *Charter of Social Rights of the Council of Europe*, 2007 (ISBN 978-90-411-2608-5).
34. M. Sargeant (ed.), *The Law on Age Discrimination in the EU*, 2008 (ISBN 978-90-411-2522-4).
35. G. Di Domenico & S. Spattini (eds), *New European Approaches to Long- Term Unemployment: What Role for Public Employment Services and What Market for Private Stakeholders?*, 2008 (ISBN 978-90-411-2614-6.)
36. C. Welz, *The European Social Dialogue under Articles 138 and 139 of the EC Treaty: Actors, Processes, Outcomes*, 2008 (ISBN 978-90-411-2744-0).
37. M. Rönnmar (ed.), *EU Industrial Relations v. National Industrial Relations: Comparative and Interdisciplinary Perspectives*, 2008 (ISBN 978-90-411- 2770-9).

38. F. Pennings, Y. Konijn & A. Veldman (eds), *Social Responsibility in Labour Relations: European and Comparative Perspectives*, 2008 (ISBN 978-90- 411-2783-9).
39. F. Pennings & C. Bosse (eds), *The Protection of Working Relationships: A Comparative Study*, 2011 (ISBN 978-90-411-3289-5).
40. S. Devetzi & S. Stendahl (eds), *Too Sick to Work?: Social Security Reference in Europe for Persons with Reduced Earnings Capacity*, 2011 (ISBN 978-90- 411-3426-4).
41. Ulrich Becker, Frans Pennings & Tineke Dijkhoff (eds), *International Standard Setting and Innovations in Social Security*, 2013 (ISBN 978-90-411-3233-8).
42. E. Ales (ed.), *Health and Safety at Work: European and Comparative Perspective*, 2013 (ISBN 978-90-411-4661-8).
43. F. Pennings, T. Erhag & S. Stendahl (eds), *Non-public Actors in Social Security Administration: A Comparative Study*, 2013 (ISBN 978-90-411-4917-6).
44. A. Neal (ed.), *Cross-Currents in Modern Chinese Labour Law*, 2014 (ISBN 978-90-411-4763-9).
45. B. Waas (ed.), *The Right to Strike: A Comparative View*, 2014 (ISBN 978-90-411-5007-3).
46. A. Ojeda-Avilés, *Transnational Labour Law*, 2015 (ISBN 978-90-411-5858-1).
47. A. Numhauser-Henning & M. Rönnmar, *Age Discrimination and Labour-Law: Comparative and Conceptual Perspectives in the EU and Beyond*, 2015 (ISBN 978-90-411-4979-4).
48. A. Perulli & T. Treu (eds), *Enterprise and Social Rights*, 2017 (ISBN 978-90-411-8234-0).
49. Dr F.C.A. van Haasteren, *Decent Flexibility: The Impact of ILO Convention 181 and the Regulation on Temporary Agency Work*, 2017 (ISBN 978-90-411-9236-3).
50. T. Dijkhoff & L.G. Mpedi (eds), *Recommendation on Social Protection Floors: Basic Principles for Innovative Solutions*, 2018 (ISBN 978-90-411-8623-2).
51. A. Perulli & T. Treu (eds), *Sustainable Development, Global Trade and Social Rights*, 2018 (ISBN 978-90-411-9235-6).
52. M. Mironi & M. Schlachter (eds), *Regulating Strikes in Essential Services: A Comparative 'Law in Action' Perspective*, 2019 (ISBN 978-90-411-8997-4).
53. A. Perulli & T. Treu (eds), *The Role of the State and Industrial Relations*, 2019 (ISBN 978-94-035-0661-6).
54. T. Gyulavári & E. Menegatti (eds), *The Sources of Labour Law*, 2020 (ISBN 978-94-035-0284-7).
55. V. Cagnin, *Labour Law and Sustainable Development*, 2020 (ISBN 978-94-035-2074-2).
56. A. Perulli & T. Treu (eds), *The Future of Work: Labour Law and Labour Market Regulation in the Digital Era*, 2021 (ISBN 978-94-035-2853-3).
57. A. Perulli & T. Treu (eds), *Labour Law and Climate Change: Towards a Just Transition*, 2023 (ISBN 978-94-035-0877-1).
58. A. Perulli & T. Treu (eds), *Labour Law in the Mirror: Categories, Values, Interlocutors*, 2025 (ISBN 978-94-035-2798-7).

www.ingramcontent.com/pod-product-compliance
Lightning Source LLC
Chambersburg PA
CBHW071331230926
51849CB00002B/369
9789403527987